THE BIRTH PROJECT

BY JUDY CHICAGO

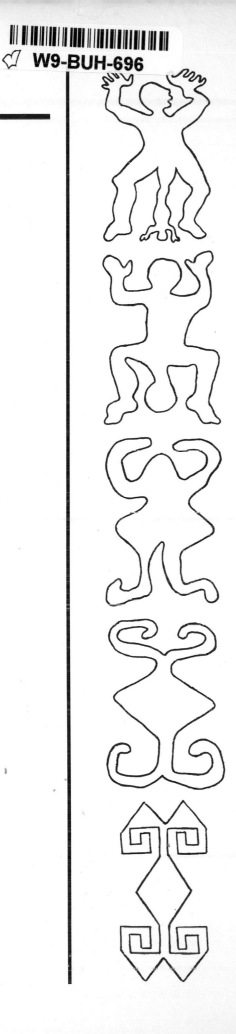

Doubleday & Company, Inc.
Garden City, New York   1985

**Design:
Stephen Hamilton,
San Francisco**

**Primary photography:
Michele Maier**

Editorial coordination:
Kate Amend

Copy editing:
Peggy Kimball

Graphic production:
Webb Design Studio, Taos

Darkroom production:
Deborah Lohrke

Typography:
Avalanche, Taos

Library of Congress Cataloging in
   Publication Data.

Chicago, Judy, 1939-
The Birth Project.

1. Chicago, Judy, 1939-.
2. Needlework-United States.
3. Group work in art-United States.
I. Title
N6537.C48A4   1985
   746'.092'4   84-18783

Hardcover edition
   ISBN: 0-385-18709-2
Paperback edition
   ISBN: 0-385-18710-6
Library of Congress
   Catalog Card Number
   84-18783
Copyright
   © 1985 Judy Chicago
Printed in the
   United States of America
First editions

Table of Contents

Introduction

I began work on *The Birth Project* in 1980. By the time it is finished, it will have taken five years. I have approached the subject of birth with awe, terror, and fascination and have tried to present different aspects of this universal experience—the mythical, the celebratory, and the painful.

The Birth Project evolved out of a number of discoveries that I made during and shortly after *The Dinner Party.** The first was my realization that I had a natural ability to design for—and an intense interest in—needlework. The second was an awareness that, after years of exploring female subject matter, I still had more to say as an artist about the nature of women's lives and experiences. The third discovery had to do with the huge audience response to *The Dinner Party* (as well as some of my earlier work) and to the possibility of participating in my ongoing art-making process.

I had never been interested in needlework when I was growing up. I did not learn to sew at my mother's knee. My experience with needlework was nil. Even now—after years of involvement with the needle arts—if a button falls off or a seam rips, I either take the piece of clothing to the nearest cleaners for repair or throw it away.

And, of course, needlework was not considered art at any of the art schools I attended. In fact, in the sixties, working in fibers virtually guaranteed that you would not be considered a "serious artist." As I described in my first book, *Through the Flower: My Struggle as a Woman Artist* (Anchor/Doubleday), I was determined to be taken seriously as an artist, and therefore all my decisions were based on producing that result.

Needlework in all its forms was "women's work," and as long as I was compelled to deny my identity as a woman in my life and in my work, I never considered it as a medium for art-making. It would have been humiliating to me if a male artist or dealer discovered me sewing a button on my artist husband's shirt or sitting at an embroidery machine or a loom. It would have confirmed the already taken-for-granted idea that my place in life was either supporting my husband's aspirations or working in the "minor arts."

It is no accident that at the mighty Bauhaus, where the tenets of modern art were formed, Josef Albers taught painting—while Anni Albers, like most of the women there, was an instructor in weaving. Earlier, at the great Royal School of Needlework, where the theories and ideas of William Morris and the other visionaries of the Arts and Crafts Movement were translated into fabulous stitchery, the men did the designing and the women did the needlework. What men did was "art," while what women did was, at best, "craft."

This is not to suggest that I believe the value judgments assigned to "art" versus "craft" are right or just, but rather to define the background of esthetic assumptions against which I developed as an artist. If hiding my womanly feelings and eschewing all womanly skills would guarantee my participation in the art community, then that is what I would do.

The Dinner Party is a multi-media work of art which is discussed in detail in two books I wrote, *The Dinner Party: A Symbol of Our Heritage* and *Embroidering Our Heritage: The Dinner Party Needlework* (Anchor Press/Doubleday, 1979 and 1980, respectively). Both books chronicle the participatory nature of the studio process involved in executing this work, and the latter book provides considerable historical information on needlework.

However, from the time I finished graduate school, I began to explore techniques that were outside the traditional framework of art. Shortly after I received my master's degree, I began to learn the "craft" of painting, something I felt my classical art training had not provided. This led me to study spray-painting at an auto body school; investigate the world of plastics; work with boat-builders in the construction of fiberglass pieces; and apprentice myself to a fireworks company in order to do a series of "atmospheres" with the same materials used in Fourth of July displays.

All of these techniques had something in common; they were on the "fringe" of traditional art media. This meant that they did not have the historical associations that, say, oil painting does, and thus they allowed me a freer visual vocabulary. As I began to develop my own, more personal imagery, I continued to be drawn to "fringe" techniques. But at first, all the techniques I explored were in the "masculine" domain.

In all these situations, I was a woman in a man's environment, a fact that I was constantly reminded of. At auto body school, I was forced to wear a long smock so that my body would not "distract" the male students; at the boatworks, I was consistently stared at and razzed; and during my sojourn with the fireworks company, my boss made sexual advances toward me. However, learning these traditionally masculine working techniques brought me respect from some men in the art world, largely because of my sense of purpose, my long work hours, and my refusal to have my options limited in any way because I was a woman. As Jan Butterfield, an art critic and long-time friend, wrote recently in a catalog essay for a ten-year retrospective of my work: "...Begrudgingly or not, she is now, at last, fully recognized as 'one of the boys.'... And however sexist that may be, in the macho arena of Los Angeles art (which is where she developed as an artist) it is, backhandedly, a supreme compliment...Judy Chicago has earned her stripes with the 'white, western, male mainstream...; that is a hard-won victory." [1]

I include Jan's comments because my struggle during the 1960s, when I "earned my stripes," provided the impetus for my achievements in the 1970s. Her essay also illuminates my interest in "fringe" techniques and my approach to those techniques, which were honed by years of working with men. Despite the sexism I encountered, both in the art world and in the world of male technology, I learned the value of craft, a commitment to visual rigor, the necessity for risk-taking, the need for courage in confronting the unknown, and, most of all, the ability to withstand rejection.

When I left the world of male-dominated skills and entered the relatively unknown world of female-dominated skills—china-painting and needlework—I did so with the enthusiasm for unexplored techniques that had led me to auto body school.

However, even though the "female arts" of china-painting and needlework were "fringe" techniques and thus allowed potentially greater esthetic freedom, they suffered from a different kind of historical association. They were (and are), of course, identified with the "feminine" world from which I tried so hard to escape during the sixties. By the end of that decade, I had come to realize that there was no way I could escape from such an identification. Everywhere I turned, I was confronted by the social and political implications of my gender. I subsequently stopped denying my femaleness and began, instead, to confront and explore it.

This process eventually led me to women's history (and, out of my investigation of that history, to the creation of *The Dinner Party*) and to an examination of the reality of women's lives. This in turn brought me to the fundamental difference between women and men—the fact that women give birth—and to the decision to make a series of images of birth in various needlework techniques.

During *The Dinner Party*, when I decided to place china-painted plates representing different women in history onto a table set with cloths, I was, whether I knew it or not, moving quite naturally into needlework. From the time my first design was translated into fabric and thread, I realized that I had a talent for visualizing what needlework techniques could do. By the time *The Dinner Party* was completed, I had designed almost fifty works in various textile media. Although I was done with *The Dinner Party*, I knew that I was not finished exploring the visual properties of the needle and textile arts.

In many ways, it was a great relief to enter, first, the world of the china-painter and, later, that of the needleworker. I enjoyed the warmth of women's conversations, the open sharing of feelings, and, because most women know how to cook, the frequent sharing of food. I liked the fact that women cooperate much more readily than men, that I didn't feel alienated because of my gender, and that my sex was not something to be thrust into my consciousness every day.

I was involved in a "women's world" not only because of my interest in china-painting and needlework, but also because it was primarily women who came to work with me when I opened my studio during *The Dinner Party.* Even though it was wonderful to be in an environment where I could forget my gender and concentrate on my art, there were many aspects of working with women which I did not like.

Some of the women I studied and worked with were professionals, but most were not. My thoroughgoing professionalism was often seen by them as "not being nice." Moreover, most of the women were terrified of rejection, afraid of criticism, too eager to please, and therefore too quick to dissemble; their dishonesty frequently caused problems both in our interactions and in the work itself. Most of them knew very little about how the world really operates and even less about the nature of power. For example, I spent many frustrating hours trying to explain to both china-painters and needleworkers why china-painting and embroidery are not considered art. Their inability to understand my explanations grew out of a total failure to comprehend that it is power, not justice, which determines the nature of the world and, therefore, the definition of art.

My grounding in feminism enabled me to understand that many of these problems grow out of the oppression of women, but it was one thing to understand that intellectually and quite another to have to deal with it in relation to my art. However, during *The Dinner Party* I was not engaged with the women I worked with in the way I would be when I began to make art on the subject of birth.

My first ideas in developing imagery for *The Birth Project* involved using the birth process as a metaphor for creation. Long before I finished *The Dinner Party,* I became interested in creation myths. In 1975, while I was having an exhibition at The College of St. Catherine, in St. Paul, Minnesota, I met a radical nun who collaborated with me in writing a reinterpretation of the myth of Genesis from a female point of view. As soon as I could, I began trying to build a visual analog to this myth—one that would affirm the fact that it was women who created life. When I approached this subject matter again in preparation for *The Birth Project,* I went to the library to see what images of birth I could find. I was struck dumb when my research turned up almost none. It was obvious that birth was a universal human experience and one that is central to women's lives. Why were there no images? Attracted to the void, I plunged into the subject.

Since there were so few images, I decided that I would have to go directly to women, ask them to tell me about their birth experiences, and then use that raw material in the development of images. It is very unusual for an artist to work out of direct experience rather than out of the history of art. It requires building a form language almost "from scratch." In addition, gathering testimony about birth meant asking women to let me be involved with them on a very basic level. Many of the women I talked to had never spoken to anyone about their birth experiences. As I listened and studied and read, I realized that it was not only birth I was learning about, but also the very nature of these women's lives, and that both of these subjects were shrouded in myth, mystery, and stereotype. I knew that I wanted to dispel at least some of this secrecy.

I had approached the subject of birth twice before. As a graduate student, I had done a series of paintings including one entitled *Birth.* Years later, I included a birth scene in *The Dinner Party:* the back of the runner for Mary Wollstonecraft, the feminist author and theoretician, portrays her death as a result of childbed fever. Both of these images had made me uncomfortable when I was creating them. However, I had transformed my rather graphic drawing for the runner through a series of needlework techniques. I decided to soften the powerful and unfamiliar subject matter of birth by designing everything in such a way as to be translated into and embellished by needlework.

By this time, *The Dinner Party* had begun its long, rather tortured journey in and out of view. After its initial, enormously successful showing at the San Francisco Museum of Modern Art in 1979, the rest of its museum tour collapsed, and it went into crates in a warehouse. In 1980, it was exhibited in Houston as the culmination of a grass-roots organizing drive which raised the money for its showing. This pattern was repeated in city after city in the United States and Canada and was completely unprecedented in the art world.

People all over the country, incensed that museums would not bring *The Dinner Party* to its obviously wide potential audience, got together, raised money, pressured museums, or set up alternative spaces to exhibit the work. In the process, many women and men were educated about the caprices of the art establishment and about the power of art. I received hundreds of letters from people telling me how affected they were by seeing my work and how much they would like the opportunity to work with me if I ever undertook another participatory art-making project. Many of these letters were from needleworkers.

By this time, I was pretty well convinced that I was not going to receive support from the art establishment. I had no galleries, was selling very little work, and was encountering continued museum resistance despite all the evidence of audience interest. My only chance, I thought, was to draw upon the network that had arisen as a result of *The Dinner Party*. I started to think about developing birth images for needlework which could be executed and distributed through this network.

I did not conceive *The Birth Project* all at once, but rather, like *The Dinner Party*, it evolved. This book chronicles its evolution and the problems I encountered in the process. Unlike *The Dinner Party*, *The Birth Project* is not one single work of art, but is, instead, a large series of works intended to be exhibited in small groupings. All the images are mine, and all of them are executed in or embellished with needle or textile techniques. All the art is accompanied by written and photographic documentation, which includes information about and personal testimony from the needleworkers involved or explains the techniques used, the sources of my imagery, the process and development of the piece, or the meaning of my forms.

The *Birth Project* needlework was done in the homes of women all over the United States, as well as in Canada and New Zealand. Except for the small, paid core staff which administered the project, everyone worked as a volunteer, including me. All the work is owned by Through the Flower, the nonprofit corporation formed during the making of *The Dinner Party*, under the auspices of which it is exhibited and maintained. Through the Flower is solely responsible for the ongoing care and circulation of the *Birth Project* textile collection, which consists of eighty exhibition units (a work or works of art plus accompanying documentation).

Each exhibition unit is packed and crated for easy shipping—and for easy storage, as needlework must be taken out of circulation regularly and allowed to rest. We have developed systems for the installation of *Birth Project* work which allow even the most inexperienced people to mount a show.

The Birth Project extends the democratization of art begun by *The Dinner Party*. It is meant to travel for years, to be inexpensive to exhibit and to ship, to be accessible to many different types of organizations and spaces, and to introduce images of birth and information about the reality of women's lives to a wide audience of viewers.

I began work on *The Birth Project* in 1980. By the time it is finished, it will have taken five years. I have approached the subject of birth with awe, terror, and fascination and have tried to present different aspects of this universal experience—the mythical, the celebratory, and the painful.

Judy Chicago

7

A Vocabulary of *Birth Project* Terms

These are terms we used in *The Birth Project* and what they meant to us:

acrylic   A type of water-soluble, polymer-based paint which I've used on canvas and, for *The Birth Project*, on fabric.

appliqué   An ancient technique of sewing one piece of fabric onto a larger piece to form a design.

batik   An Indonesian method of hand-printing textiles by coating parts of the fabric with wax to resist dye, boiling off the wax, and repeating the process for each color used.

beading   The use of beads to create an outline, texture, or solid surface. Often done on a loom.

birth garment   A term I coined to describe a series of *Birth Project* pieces which resemble both a garment and the body of a pregnant woman.

blending   The term we used to describe the mixing of threads to produce a gradual change of color.

brad   A type of large-headed tack or nail we used to secure the laminated panels accompanying *Birth Project* art to the wall.

cartoon   The term used for the full-scale drawing from which a tapestry is woven.

childbed fever   A disease that sometimes follows childbirth. Usually caused by infection of the uterus during or after delivery, because of a lack of hygiene.

china-painting   An overglaze technique in which china-paints are applied and fired onto already fired ceramic ware, most commonly on porcelain.

closure packet   A packet of materials sent to needleworkers who successfully completed a *Birth Project* work. Included slides and photographs of the finished piece, copies of the documentation accompanying the work, a *Birth Project* T-shirt, a letter from me, and a lifetime membership in Through the Flower.

clitoridectomy   See *female circumcision.*

color fade   The changing or blending of colors that is typical of my work.

consciousness-raising   A communication process central to the women's movement, in which discussions are held in an egalitarian manner. Particularly effective in small groups, this process allows group members to become "conscious" that many of their personal experiences can be seen in a larger political framework.

couching   A method of securing a strand or strands of thread (or cord) with another, usually finer, thread.

crowning   That phase in the second stage of labor when a large segment of the fetal scalp is visible. *The Crowning* also refers to one of the series of *Birth Project* images.

decentralized art making   The process I used to create *Birth Project* art, which was executed in homes all over America rather than in a single place or center.

dhai   The term for midwife in India. Customarily from the lower classes.

DMC   The company name on a line of embroidery floss, perle cotton, and other threads.

embellish   To enrich the surface of a painting or a piece of fabric with embroidery or decorative motifs or objects.

embroidery   The art or process of ornamenting or embellishing with needlework.

execute   To implement and enrich, through needlework, an image I designed.

exhibition unit   Our term for a work or works of *Birth Project* art with accompanying documentation, consisting of text and photographs which provide a context for the art.

episiotomy   The cutting or surgical incision into the perineum and vagina during childbirth.

fabricate   To assemble the parts of a textile work into a whole.

female circumcision   (Or *clitoridectomy*) The practice of removing the clitoris, usually done on young girls.

feminism   A theory or philosophy which advocates those legal and social changes that will establish political, economic, and social equality between women and men.

feminist   A person who believes in and practices the theory and philosophy of feminism.

filet crochet   A needlework technique involving the making of both the solid and open patterns in one step. The word *filet* is French and means "slender thread."

floss   A soft, lustrous thread used primarily for embroidery, made from short, fine fiber, carded and spun, but of strands not twisted together.

Gore-Tex   The trademarked name for a waterproof, breathable laminated fabric normally used for sports clothes. In *The Birth Project*, we made bags out of Gore-Tex to protect the needlework during shipping and storage.

hymo   A hair canvas woven of goat hair and wool, known for its stability.

illuminate   To develop a visual counterpart to a text so that the words are heightened in their meaning, as in medieval illuminated manuscripts. I "illuminated" some of the text panels which accompany *Birth Project* art.

image   A visual representation or presentation which is drawn, painted, sculptured, or otherwise made perceptible to the sight.

infibulation The practice of fastening the prepuce or labia majora (of the vagina) with clasps or stitches, usually accompanied by clitoridectomy.

laminated panel The text and/or photographs which accompany *Birth Project* art after they have been coated with plastic to protect them.

love packet Materials sent to *Birth Project* participants, including newspaper and magazine articles on the project, updates on exhibitions, and/or letters from me.

macramé The technique of tying threads into knots to form designs.

Medici Brand name for a fine wool yarn used primarily for needlepoint and weaving.

mesh The number of vertical threads in each inch of needlepoint canvas and petit-point canvas or silk.

midwife A woman skilled in the practice of assisting in childbirth.

mock-up A preliminary model or prototype.

mola A type of panel worked in reverse appliqué by women of the San Blas Islands, Central America.

multiples A series or edition of similar works of art.

needlepoint Embroidery worked over or on canvas, usually in simple, even stitches across counted threads.

participant A term we used for anyone who made a significant contribution to *The Birth Project* as a needleworker, photographer, researcher, staff member, or graphics and/or design worker.

parturient A woman in labor.

Paternayan The brand name for a wool yarn used primarily for needlepoint and weaving.

pellon A material used to reinforce fabric.

pending needleworker A term used for people whose needlework sample had been accepted and who were either completing the application procedure or waiting to be given a work of art to execute.

perle cotton Twisted embroidery thread.

petit point Needlepoint done in the tent stitch on extremely fine mesh.

photostat or stat The result of a process of reproduction in which a copy is made directly onto the surface of prepared paper. Most of the panels in the *Birth Project* documentation are laminated stats.

potluck A gathering where everyone brings a "pot" of food, which is then shared by the group.

prismacolor A type of colored pencil which I frequently use.

purdah The system of secluding and veiling women, practiced primarily by the Muslims but also introduced by them into non-Muslim cultures.

quilting The process of sewing layers of fabric together with running stitches.

reverse appliqué Cutting through and sewing back the edges of successive layers of fabric to reveal the fabric below.

reverse stitching A euphemistic phrase used in *The Birth Project* to describe the often arduous process of removing stitches.

reviews The time when the stitchers met with Sally Babson (the technical supervisor of *The Birth Project*) and me for an evaluation of their work and a discussion of the next section of work to be done.

sample A needleworked version of a pattern I designed, submitted to demonstrate the skill level of someone who wanted to execute a piece of *Birth Project* art.

smocking A historical technique normally used for clothing, which involves the pleating and embellishing of fabric.

spray-painting The process of applying paint with an airbrush or spray gun—something I've done frequently in my work and on many different types of materials.

stripping thread The process of separating strands of thread in preparation for blending.

stumpwork A style of raised embroidery which was very popular in England in the seventeenth century.

swaddling The process of tightly wrapping babies in yards of fabric bands in the misguided notion that it was good for them.

tapestry A type of weaving used to create flat, pictorial images.

Through the Flower The name of a painting I did in 1973; the title of my autobiography, published by Anchor/Doubleday in 1975; and the name of the nonprofit corporation set up in 1979 to maintain and circulate *The Dinner Party*, under the auspices of which *The Birth Project* was done.

suttee A Hindu rite in which widows were forced to immolate themselves on the funeral pyres of their husbands.

translation sample A sample submitted to Sally Babson and me, demonstrating how a needleworker intended to work a section of my design.

translate In *The Birth Project*, this meant working from my design and interpreting it in a needlework or textile technique—i.e., "translating" my drawing into fabric or thread.

Velcro A trademarked material used for fastening or adhering objects together or onto a surface—consisting of two parts, one the "hook," and the other the "loop." Used to hang *Birth Project* art.

Versatex A paint made specifically for fabrics, which is heat-set after it is applied.

Zwicky silk A type of thread used for fine embroidery.

From *The Dinner Party* to *The Birth Project*

The *Birth Project* actually began before I was finished with *The Dinner Party,* inasmuch as one of the things I became interested in while I was working on *The Dinner Party* was the whole notion of creation myths and how they reflect the values of the culture. The Mary Wollstonecraft image for the back of the *Dinner Party* runner prefigured my interest in the subject of birth and creation. It was an image that frightened me when I did it because it was so raw and graphic. Its transformation through the needlework process showed me how this subject matter could be dealt with. I suppose that's part of what led me to the notion of developing images of birth in various needlework techniques. In the spring of 1980, I began to develop creation imagery.

The Dinner Party, ©Judy Chicago, 1979. A multimedia installation; ceramics, china-painting, textiles, needlework, aluminum, and wood, 48' x 48' x 48'.

©MICHAEL ALEXANDER

The Dinner Party consists of an open, triangular table, 46 feet, 6 inches on each side. The table, which is covered with white linen cloths edged in gold, contains thirty-nine place settings. Individually sculpted and china-painted plates represent women in Western civilization from prehistory to the present. Needlework runners employ historic textile techniques to symbolize the circumstances of each woman's life. The name of the woman represented, embellished with an illuminated capital letter, is embroidered on the front of the runner.

The *Dinner Party* table rests on a large, triangular floor comprising 2,300 handcast porcelain tiles. These are inscribed in gold luster with the names of 999 women of achievement grouped around the women represented at the table.

BETH THEILEN

Back of runner for *Mary Wollstonecraft,* from *The Dinner Party.* Stumpwork, needlepoint, petit point, embroidery, and appliqué. Overall size: 13'' x 30''.

In this scene, the great feminist writer and theoretician Mary Wollstonecraft is dying of childbed fever after having given birth to a daughter (who would one day become famous for writing *Frankenstein,* under the name Mary Shelley). On the left is Mary's older daughter, by the painter Gordon Imlay, and on the right, holding his newborn daughter in his arms, is the grieving father, William Godwin, a publisher and staunch advocate of women's rights.

This is the first image of birth I ever created. My drawing was, I feel, overly graphic, but its transformation through needlework suggested that textiles might be the appropriate medium for this subject matter. The figures and the bed were done in "stumpwork" and appliquéd onto the runner, as were the needlepoint chest of drawers, the petit-point rug, the crocheted runner, and the china-painted ceramic jug and bowl. The London scene was embroidered directly on the runner back.

These myths are typical of ancient, long-held beliefs based on the idea that the origin of life lies with a female creator. Unless otherwise noted, all myths quoted were compiled by Barbara Sproul in her book *Primal Myths* (2).

Babylon

...Thou art the mother womb
The one who creates mankind...

Nigeria

Woyengi (the Mother) molded humans from the Earth while seated with *her* feet resting on the Creation Stone. (Emphasis added.)

North America (Huron)

In the beginning, there was nothing but water, populated by various water animals. A woman fell from the upper world. The toad brought *her* mud from the bottom of the sea. She took it and placed it carefully around the edge of the tortoise's shell. It became the beginning of dry land and of the life upon it. (3)

(Emphasis added.)

The next myths include dual creators. In some cases, male and female beings were born simultaneously or are presented as having created the world together.

Japan

Heaven was formed first and Earth established subsequently. Thereafter, eight Divine Beings were produced between them. Being formed by the mutual action of the Heavenly and Earthly principles, the last two were made female and male.

Hawaii

The intense darkness, the deep darkness,
Darkness of the sun, darkness of the night
Nothing but night.
The night gave birth
Born was Kumulipo in the night, a male
Born was Po'ele in the night, a female.

This beautiful Mesopotamian poem describes the commingling of the male and female creative forces. A later myth altered this description in favor of one in which Tiamat is destroyed and the world created from her body.

Mesopotamia

When on high the heaven had not been named,
Firm ground below had not been called by name,
Naught but primordial Apsu, their begetter,
Mummu-Tiamat, *she* who bore them all,
Their waters commingling as a single body. (4) (Emphasis added.)

The Babylonian epic poem, the *Enuma Elish*, outlines how Tiamat was slaughtered and her body dismembered and used to create the world.

Babylon

The lord shot *his* net to entangle Tiamat . . . And now *he* shot the arrow that split the belly, that pierced the gut and cut the womb . . .
Now that the lord had conquered Tiamat *he* ended *her* life... Tiamat was dead.
. . . *he* straddled the legs and smashed her skull . . . *he* severed *her* arteries and the blood streamed down . . . *he* gazed at the huge body, pondering how to use it, what to create from the dead carcass. (Emphasis added.)

This last myth asserts the idea that the world was created as a result of the death of an original female deity. The development of these myths closely parallels the end of matriarchal cultures; most later myths, like Genesis, reverse reality altogether and depict the male as the giver of life. Even the embryo and egg cease to be associated with the female.

Australia (Bushman)

Cajn was the first being; *he* gave orders and caused all things to appear, and to be made, the sun, the moon, stars, wind, mountains, and animals. (Emphasis added.)

The first thing I did was to study creation myths from around the world. I divided them into different categories: myths that feature a female divinity or divinities creating the Universe; myths presenting the act of creation as the work of both female and male gods; myths that depict the creation of the world as arising from the destruction of a female god by a male divinity; and myths representing the creation of life as the act of a male god alone. It was interesting to me to see that all these myths followed the same kind of historical chronology symbolized by *The Dinner Party*—i.e., the gradual changeover from matriarchal societies (reflected in myths featuring the female as the source of life) to patriarchal civilizations like the Judeo-Christian one we've inherited (mirrored in myths about "God the Father" creating "Man").

The Creation of Adam, by Michelangelo, from the ceiling of the Sistine Chapel, The Vatican, Rome, Italy (5). Even though this is a beautiful painting, it does nothing to make women feel like an essential part of the human race.

...the Lord God formed man of dust from the ground, and breathed into his nostrils the breath of life; and man became a living being....the Lord God caused a deep sleep to fall upon the man, and while he slept took one of his ribs...and the rib which the Lord God had taken from the man he made into woman.... (6)

Tuesday, May 27, 1980

I spent today studying and struggling with creation myths, trying to figure out what I want to do with them. I thought about trying to combine different creation myths— Judeo-Christian (in the rewritten form I had come up with), Afro-American, Native American, perhaps even some Eastern myths— and trying to create cross-cultural images. But in studying a lot of these, it became clear to me that Western culture has not been fundamentally shaped by African myths, but rather by Judeo-Christian myths which depict men creating life. These are then reflected in "great" art and music like Michelangelo's Sistine Chapel and frescoes and Handel's Messiah. Though I revere these works, they are built on a distortion of the truth, one that negates women.

However, I don't just want to revise male myths or history. I already did that in The Dinner Party. I'd like to take a step beyond that. The whole issue of myths and their function in culture is what I'm struggling with. Do I want to confront them, reverse them, challenge them, substitute better ones? If so, how? I had planned to spend this week studying myths and images, but I'm already restless to start the struggle on paper. I always assumed I'd use words, too, but they present such visual problems. I don't have answers yet, that's for sure. I need to give myself permission to explore and try and fail and try again for the next few weeks. That's difficult for me, however.

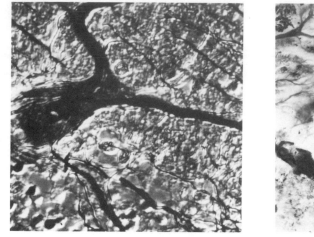
A nerve cell (8).

The Chialing River (7).

It was fascinating to see the visual similarity between a human nerve cell and the patterns of a river.

Detail from rough sketch for *Creation of the World*, ©Judy Chicago, 1980. Ink and crayon on paper.

In this section of an early scroll/drawing, I began trying to incorporate the forms of the body and of the earth into an image that could represent the process of labor.

Creation Drawing #2, ©Judy Chicago, 1980. Prismacolor on rag paper, 24" x 33½".

In this drawing, I was trying to take the cries and screams of a laboring woman and create a visual wail.

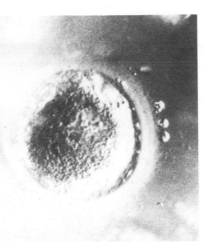

An ovum entering a fallopian tube (8).

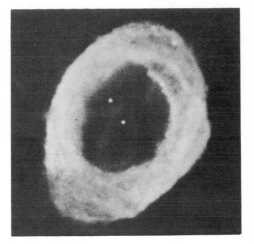

A ring nebula (9).

In these pictures, one can see microcosm and macrocosm merge as the shapes of the body are repeated in the universe.

Detail from rough sketch for *Creation of the World*, ©Judy Chicago, 1980.

This detail from my rough sketch illustrates the way I took the natural forms of ovum and supernova and began to integrate them into a birth and creation image.

Creation Drawing #1, ©Judy Chicago, 1980. Prismacolor and ink on rag paper.

In this drawing, I was trying to make the "ovum of life" visually radiate outward into a series of rhythmic forms reminiscent of the rhythm of labor.

I spent Friday and Saturday doing a rough sketch for the Creation of the Universe tapestry I'm designing. Now I want to do a full-scale black and white drawing. The sketch is rough, but the ideas are there, though they need to be developed and worked out. I'm looking forward to working steadily on the imagery for the next few weeks and on the color mock-up after that.

After spending a week reading creation myths, I began to study pictures of the reproductive system, the birth process, and the solar system, looking for parallels in iconography. Needless to say, they were there—macrocosmic and microcosmic reflections of the creation and life process, just as I suspected. A nova looks just like an ovum, and the oceans on the earth's surface make patterns like nerve cells.

I was looking for a way to use the physical process of giving birth as a metaphor for the birth of the universe and of life itself. Now I have to make each form become itself, a human or female form, and a universal form. I want to make forms that resonate to our substance, are recognizable at a cellular level, and, of course, I want to make the creation of the universe an intimately feminine act.

Creation of the World

It's 7 p.m. I've been working like a maniac all week, and I'm feeling very lonely. I've been working so hard in the studio that I've had no energy left at the end of the day and have had to just come home and rest. I've been struggling to figure out how to make the creation imagery work: simultaneously trying to find a pictorial language that would be consistent with tapestry technique and also to delineate the forms more clearly than in my small sketches. I've been working full scale, which means 42 inches high and 12 to 16 feet long, depending upon how the imagery works out. I did the first section over and over, as I felt that it was not working at all. Finally, I began to know what I really wanted, though it took me several days to muster up the courage to do it. I really struggled intensely and finally broke through today. Now I feel anxious and upset and excited all at once.

Friday, July 11

I'm sitting in my apartment drinking coffee and listening to the record player. It's 9:15 a.m. I've been up since 5:30 and had breakfast after spending almost 3 hours walking, running, and exercising. I fell asleep last night by 7:30, slept 10 hours, which is very unlike me, but I didn't feel real well. I did a design for a quilt for Sally Babson, a woman who has been making clothes for me. I had had her make a little sewn book for a lover of mine,

Creation of the Universe, ©Judy Chicago, 1984. Woven by Audrey Cowan. Wool and silk, 42'' x 14'.

Although this tapestry is not part of *The Birth Project*, the imagery is certainly related. This was the first textile piece I started when I began working on birth and creation imagery. Audrey Cowan, the weaver, worked with me on *The Dinner Party*, weaving the top of the *Eleanor of Aquitaine* runner. I designed this work specifically for her to ex-

Detail from *Creation of the Universe* tapestry.

and when I saw it, I sud-
denly wondered if she
might like to work with
me. Well, one thing led to
another, and on Friday we
picked fabric colors for a
quilt. I had done a full-
scale black and white
drawing incorporating
some of the imagery I had
been developing for the
tapestry. At the fabric
store, we laid it out on the
floor. I nearly had a heart
attack when women kept
coming over and asking
"What's that?" We ex-
plained as best we could,
but I couldn't help feeling
uncomfortable at having
everyone staring at my
"unfinished" work in an
atmosphere of needlework
kits featuring mushrooms
and teddy bears.

ecute. Working from a full-scale color sketch and a detailed black and white cartoon, she began preparing her loom in the summer of 1980 and completed the tapestry in the spring of 1984.

At work in my Benicia, California, studio.

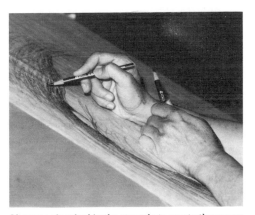

I became absorbed in the struggle to create these new images.

I must admit, I was scared that after all the *Dinner Party* related work was over I wouldn't be able to face the void again, to plunge back into the nothingness and create from scratch again. But after about a day and a half of being in the studio alone, I was completely absorbed. It was as if *The Dinner Party* had never happened, and I was doing what I had done since I was a child—struggling alone to give form to the feelings that well up inside me.

I feel that I have accomplished what I set out to do at the beginning of the seventies, to expand my language to include the content I want to express and to elucidate it more clearly without sacrificing the quality and formal structure that I developed in the sixties. Now, with two decades of art-making behind me, I feel in control of my forms and in touch with my power and ready to go forward and produce all the work I can.

Sally Babson fabricated and quilted this lovely little book containing some small erotic images I had done a few years earlier.

Thursday, August 21

I've been working on a series of quilt designs; I've begun to work on ideas for making it possible for people to work on my images in their own houses as well as here in California. I get so many letters from people around the country, particularly needle-workers, who have seen The Dinner Party *and who want to work with me.*

Saturday, September 13, 1980

I'm going to set up the quilt Sally is working on at the publication party for the Dinner Party *needlework book next week and see if it generates any interest. I'm preparing some fliers explaining that I'm developing images of birth in different needlwork techniques that people can work on at home. We'll take the fliers and if some people want to work with me, I'll have a meeting to show them the images and let them select those that match their skills and interests. I have a contract for them to sign, and I'm asking people to show me samples of their needlework. But it scares me to death when I realize I'm spending $700 on fabrics and patterns, which I'm planning to give out to people I barely know. I'm going to go ahead with the plan, but I'd better not give this too much thought or I'll begin to question my sanity.*

Sunday, September 21

The publication party went very well; a lot of people watched Sally quilting, said they'd be interested in working with me, and took fliers. Yesterday we had a meeting and about thirty women showed up. Sally and I put up the patterns of each of the images I had been working on all summer.

The women's responses to the images were very positive, and most of the pieces were taken by the end of the day. Everyone who took an image signed a contract and had her picture taken, and we carefully recorded her address and phone number. But it still felt scary.

JULIET MYERS

Sally Babson with the first *Birth Project* work, *Creation of the World Q 1,* at the publication party for *Embroidering Our Heritage: The Dinner Party Needlework* at the San Francisco Museum of Modern Art, September 1980.

This quote from the poet Susan Griffin perfectly expresses the feelings that were aroused by my investigation of the birth experience.

Everywhere motherhood is mystified. Pregnancy, the body of it, menstruation, the blood of it, the lining of the uterus that would have nourished an embryo, concealed . . . In childbirth, one experiences all the natural power of a woman's body, and in the practice of institutionalized childbirth one experiences all the faces of woman's oppression.

—Susan Griffin (10)

"I remember that shortly after the first meeting, Judy asked me to make some follow-up phone calls to the needleworkers. This involved calling to see how the person was doing; asking whether they were working; if they weren't, finding out why not; and generally making contact. The trouble was that I *hated* using the telephone. And I also hated to write; I misspelled so many words in the early letters I wrote out of sheer resistance to having to do all those things I didn't want to do—talking on the phone, writing letters, speaking in front of groups, and, later, supervising people's work.

"I don't know how I thought the work was going to get done—I guess I thought Judy would just 'wave a magic wand.' I had no idea what was involved in doing 'professional' work. Changing that has been an enormous struggle, and I resisted all the way. I think my struggle mirrors what a lot of our needleworkers went through."

Technical Supervisor
The Birth Project
Sally Babson
Benicia, California

Giving Birth to a New Art Work
by Mildred Hamilton

What is new with Judy Chicago? To ask that question, it was necessary to find her. The happy surprise was the discovery that she has been in the Bay Area, quietly working at her regular driven pace in another art project promising to be disturbing, controversial and enlightening.

"There are no birth images in the history of art," said the artist, whose intense feelings shone in the dark eyes behind her amethyst-tinted glasses. "No paintings of women giving birth. When have you seen this subject in a museum or gallery?" The birth process seems to have been a taboo. *The Birth Project* will change that. (11)

The above *Examiner-Chronicle* article appeared in fall 1980; I was inundated with letters from people who were interested in working with me. I am often asked where I "get" all the people who work with me; I try to explain that I don't recruit anyone—that people write to me and express a desire to participate in my projects. The letter included here gives some idea of why that happens.

Dear Judy,

I hope this note reaches you directly, as I recently had a very rewarding experience. On Yom Kippur, I attended synagogue, the second time in perhaps ten or fifteen years. The sermon concerned the oppression of women throughout history, with emphasis on the Jewish woman. The rabbi concluded with *your poem* from *The Dinner Party* . . . "and then all that has divided us will merge. . . ." I felt restored and renewed to know that your work is considered of such value as to be read on the most "holy" of days in the Jewish calendar.

For four years, I have been a great admirer of your work. In such a troubled and alienating world, it is a joy to know that there are people like you dedicated to aesthetic/social concerns. If you are interested in stitchers, I would like to receive the application forms.

Sincerely,
Jan M. Leone
Ft. Lauderdale, Florida

Mary Ross Taylor.

"In 1979, I decided to try to bring *The Dinner Party* to Houston. At the time I owned an eclectic feminist bookstore—everything from art to medieval texts. Evelyn Hubbard, my Doubleday book sales representative, suggested bringing *The Dinner Party* to Houston even before it opened for the first time at the San Francisco Museum of Modern Art. I started in January of 1979, and in March 1980 *The Dinner Party* opened at the University of Houston/Clear Lake City.

"The response to the exhibition astonished me. So many people, of diverse ages and backgrounds, were moved by it—far more people than my bookstore could ever reach. Judy's art bridged many communities, and I wanted to keep working on that scale, with women's culture as the subject. I was often alone with the art before and after hours; it was endlessly fascinating to me. And I got to see Judy work with people during the installation. She was very demanding, but attentive to their needs and feelings as well. I watched her tell the group that hung the documentation panels that the whole job had to be done over. The panels were too high, which meant filling and painting the first holes. Then she went to each person, asking 'Have you had lunch? How long have you been here today? Are you tired?' I remember thinking at that point that I would like to work with her; that I could learn a lot."

Executive Director
Through the Flower
Mary Ross Taylor
Houston, Texas

We went around the table, with everyone introducing herself and saying something about what she did and why she had come. Then I explained what I had in mind and answered questions. There was some discussion around my insistence on retaining esthetic control, but then almost everyone supported that, especially after we talked about how I planned to use the same work process that had produced The Dinner Party; *they all agreed that that process had worked, so why not continue with it?*

I have no idea whether this decentralized process will work, but everyone took "her" piece home. On November 8, we will have a review of the work. Each woman is supposed to bring a section of completed work or a sample of a needlework translation of the design. We'll know then whether this process we've set in motion is going to work at all and whether the women can actually work on their own.

In the meantime, I was interviewed by a woman who has done a number of articles on me over the years. I used the opportunity of the interview to launch The Birth Project *in the media—or, as the interviewer said, "to drop a pebble into the water and see how many ripples it will make."*

A *woman named Mary Ross Taylor, who had helped organize the Houston exhibition of* The Dinner Party, *came to visit me. We discovered that we have a mutual interest in empowering women and that we both had the feeling of wanting to work together.*

On *Wednesday night I'm having a meeting with some women in the community to talk about their birth experiences. My interest in making images using the birth process as a metaphor for the creation of the universe is leading me by the nose. I'm making connections with other women and seeing my ideas about an artist being the voice or the visionary for a community coming to life.*

I have never had a baby, which has both advantages and disadvantages in relation to this work. After all, artists have certainly not personally experienced everything they've painted—one needn't have been crucified in order to be qualified to paint the crucifixion. One works from observation, impression, and empathy as well as from direct experience. In terms of the birth process, I rather suspect that never having had a child allows me to see the whole experience more objectively and also in a larger, more universal, less personal perspective. But in order to educate myself, I am becoming a conduit for other women's experiences, listening, absorbing, studying, and learning about the range of birth experiences women have had.

Pattern for *Creation of the World,* ©Judy Chicago, 1980. Ink on paper, 30½'' x 66''.

This black and white pattern of *Creation of the World,* which I adapted from my tapestry cartoon, became the basis for a series of works on this theme—quilts, embroideries, needlepoints, and petit points. At this point in the project, I envisioned a series of basic patterns that could be translated into different sizes and techniques.

This is a center detail of the first *Birth Project* work, *Creation of the World Q 1,* executed by Sally Babson. It combines appliqué, quilting, and embroidery. Overall size: 41½'' x 74½''.

Gerry Melot, who executed another version of this image, explained it:

"The image is of a woman lying on her back giving birth to the world; it is a very powerful image of womanhood, an image that is not seen very often. It tells a new story of creation while still incorporating the theory of evolution; there is a sea with fish that become the sky and birds which in turn become the infinity of space. There is a primordial scene in the woman's very pregnant belly and a human fetus growing out of her body. Visually, I would suppose the focal point of the painting is her vagina, located almost at dead center.

"The most interesting aspect of the image, for me, is the fact that the woman's face is completely hidden from view. I think it is an important feature of the work. I have spent many hours wondering why Judy didn't include her face, and I have come up with several reasons. One is that it is not our faces that make us different from men, but our vaginas; that is why the vagina is the focal point."

Needleworker Gerry Melot, Houston, Texas

Detail of pattern for *Creation of the World.*

At my publication party, a woman came up to me. She was a saleswoman at the store where Sally and I bought the cotton for the quilt. She told me that when she saw the pattern, she called her boss and said, "There's someone here who's doing work that is an imitation of Judy Chicago's." When I wrote the check, she called back and said: "She's not imitating her."

Detail of primordial scene, *Creation of the World Q 1.*

This version of *Creation of the World* was executed in cotton appliqué. Once the appliqué and the quilting were completed, I drew and painted directly on the top of the quilt. The primordial scene, a detail of which is reproduced here, was stitched directly over my painting. Sally Babson used two strands of Zwicky silk in the satin and stem stitch to render the forms in thread. Some of the little creatures were embellished with specialty fabrics donated by Los Angeles dress designer Holly Harp. The embroidery was done last.

The more I explore all this, the more upset I become with the fact that the birth process, so central to human existence, is virtually a "taboo" area for open human expression. Little attests to or explains or symbolizes or honors or renders this primary experience, so I'm practically starting from scratch. It certainly is a challenge to address a subject which has so minimal an image bank to draw upon. Art usually grows from art, but this time art is going to have to grow directly from experience. I am making myself into a creative vehicle for the expression of one of the most fundamental and important life experiences of the human race.

Monday, September 29

I'm getting deeper and deeper into the birth material. Last week I had the evening meeting where women spoke about their birth experiences. It was spellbinding and very moving. It made me wonder why there has been so little art about birth. As I quipped at the meeting, "If men had babies, there would be thousands of images of the crowning [the moment when the baby's head first appears]." It can be a dramatic and deeply moving experience if the woman is awake participating in the birth.

The Birth Project

Saturday, October 4, 1980

I'm in New York for the opening of The Dinner Party; *I'll be here several months. I've been thinking about how the work I've been doing in California relates to New York and the obvious life struggle that is so clear on every city street. The kinds of issues I've been dealing with don't seem to quite relate or fit in. But then, on the other hand, birth happens to everyone.*

I spoke to Sally the other day and discovered that we had received over 300 letters after the article on The Birth Project *appeared, most of them from stitchers who want to work with me. If the response to that one article is this large, it suggests that I have stumbled into an area that has enormous potential. As word spreads about what I'm doing now, it is possible that a large work force will emerge, which would enable me to create hundreds of images to be executed and shown all over the country. That would mean building a national network that would allow me to supervise the production of all that art. The response to* The Dinner Party *proved that there is a large audience for my art, and now it looks like there may be a large group of people interested in participating in my art-making process as well. The way I feel is, if it won't work, I will learn soon enough; then I can always go back to traditional art-making.*

Right section, *Creation of the World Q 2,* ©Judy Chicago, 1982. Executed by Judy Kendall, Mt. Shasta, California. Painting, quilting, and embroidery. Overall size: 40'' x 70''.

Detail, *Creation of the World Q 2.*

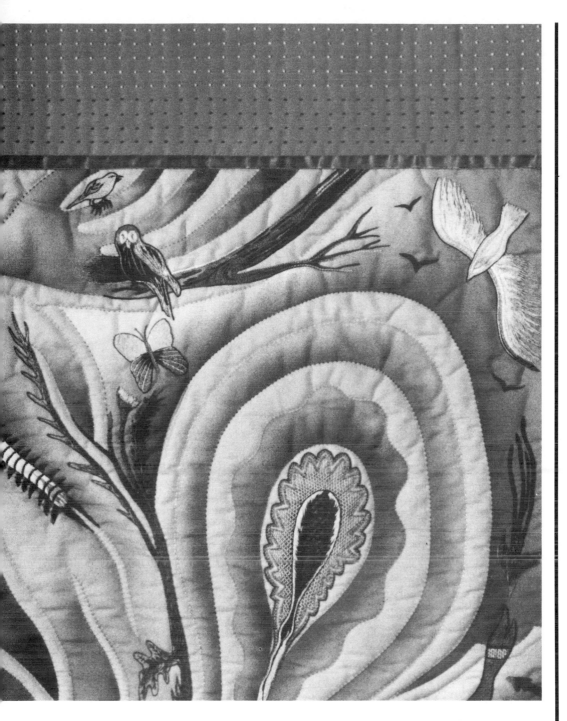

This version of *Creation of the World* was executed by Judy Kendall, from Mt. Shasta, California. Sally and I had decided that the pieces would need more preliminary work by us, including my actually applying the image to the fabric by painting or drawing it, instead of just providing patterns. I would also establish the color range, thus making sure that there would be certain esthetic controls.

Judy Kendall was not able to attend reviews very often, so we had to communicate through the mail. After an extensive period of correspondence, we sent her a piece that I had sprayed onto fabric, then drawn on over the painting. I chose thread colors that related closely to the paint, thinking that no matter how she used those tones, they would all work together with my painted image. Nonetheless, she had to make many alterations in the embroidery colors as we went along so that the painting, quilting, and stitching remained integrated.

The image was outlined and quilted in a variegated DMC embroidery floss and stitched over my hand-drawn details in DMC thread. Among the stitches used were outline, split, chain, long and short, varieties of the leaf stitch, bargello, couching, laidwork, and bullion knots. The border is chiffon over polished cotton, tufted in rows of French knots that are half an inch apart and gradually fade from gray to pink.

Even though I had painted the image and controlled the color and thread range, I did not want to predetermine the final form of the piece. Rather, I wanted to establish a base for the needleworker to elaborate upon, but within a certain visual framework. The fact that one pattern produced so many different interpretations demonstrates that, even though all the needleworkers worked on my images, the results were a unique fusion of their talents and mine.

Judy Kendall and I celebrate the completion of the quilt we created together.

Creation of the World Q 3 combines painting and embroidery. I sprayed the image onto black cotton and hand-drew all the creatures and the primordial scene. Jane Thompson embroidered the image and couched silver around the edges of the form. Sally Babson had previously quilted the whole piece with silver thread, but I felt that a couched silver line would help relate the embroidery to the painted image. Jane removed the quilting when necessary and, otherwise, couched over the quilted lines. She also found a way to fuse her embroidery with my painting.

I sprayed this piece on black cotton with white Liquitex. That caused many problems for Jane because the silk thread frayed very badly when the needle went through the paint, and many of the details were embroidered right over the painted surface. Fortunately, Jane's incredible technical skill redeemed my feckless use of an inappropriate paint. I learned later that Versatex, a fabric paint, would have been much better.

Detail, *Creation of the World Q 3*, primordial scene, ©Judy Chicago, 1984. Embroidered by Jane Gaddie Thompson. Sprayed acrylic, hand drawing, quilting, and embroidery in silk and metallic thread. Overall size: 30'' x 63½''.

Spray-painting *Creation of the World Q 3*.

Jane Thompson's description of this image perfectly expresses my intention in creating it.

"Out of this woman is borne the universe; on her belly is a primordial scene, rich with softly rolling hills and a river teeming with life. This piece is a celebration of woman's power.

"I began by following Judy's shading on each form, then outlining many of the forms with a tiny, subtle line of black silk sewing thread after the embroidery—mainly a random, overlapping satin stitch—was finished. I figured out a method of shading in the primordial scene in order to make the water appear to be alive and flowing, which I accomplished by making the concave areas dark and the convex

22

areas light and by shading back and forth as well as lengthwise.

"I used several different kinds and weights of silver on the quilt. The lighter-weight silvers I used directly in my needle for stitching, just as I did the one-ply silk floss. For the heavier weight of silver braid, I couched the laid thread with a light-weight silver thread.

"I have loved this image and this piece from the very first moment I laid my eyes on its beauty. It says to me that out of great pain comes great joy; it shows the wonder and mystery of life." Needleworker Jane Gaddie Thompson, Houston, Texas

Jane Gaddie Thompson's hands.

Birth

The Dinner Party is officially open in New York as of today. Mary Ross is very interested in what I am thinking about in terms of a national art-making network—how to do that is what we have been discussing, although it's been quite difficult in the middle of this week, as it has been really mad: interviews, people, parties, pressures.

Thursday, October 30

I'm on the plane back to California, struggling to deal with a terrible review about The Dinner Party *in a national publication that just devastated me; I feel like a flayed animal. Meanwhile,* The Birth Project *seems to be developing almost on its own. There are more people who have written about being interested in working with me than I can deal with. Mary Ross and I are going to launch the project in Houston in February. I am also planning to introduce the idea of* The Birth Project *in Chicago, where* The Dinner Party *is soon going. I laid the groundwork for it when I was there doing interviews on* The Dinner Party. *When I go back there in March I'll have a meeting. If enough people are interested, I'll start some projects there.*

There were quite a number of women at the meeting I held to discuss the birth experience. Many of them came because they had never had the opportunity to discuss what had been a major event in their lives. The age range of the group was striking; there were young women who had benefited from the changes in attitude that had produced the alternative birth movement, and there were also women the age of their mothers and, in some cases, their actual mothers. The older women remembered their experiences vividly, making it clear that the "amnesia" which is supposed to follow childbirth does not happen to everyone. Here are some of the stories I heard.

I really know very little about the birth process, even after having gone through the experience of childbirth twice. The first time, the doctor I went to was very backward; he gave me castor oil. My labor didn't start until the next afternoon, and then it was incredibly fast. I was home with my mother, and I said, "Mom, I think we better go." I vacuumed the floor while she was getting dressed. I went to the doctor's office, and he said, "I think you better go to the hospital." They barely had time to get me prepped and on the table. They strapped me down, and they gave me gas at the moment it was happening! I recall nothing except my screaming, their taking the gas off my face long enough to tell me to quit screaming, and then putting the gas back on my face.

In my second birth, I was at least awake, though I was so full of drugs I missed the whole experience; I missed it because of the people in control—the male doctors.

Sally

During my first birth I went through my first ten hours of labor with no anesthetic. When my membrane first ruptured, I rang for the nurse and told her I'd wet the bed, as I thought that was what had happened. I was actually told to get onto the gurney, and I could not; I had fainted. But I could feel them throw me onto the table, strap me down, and put a mask on my face. When I came to at 4:30 p.m. the nurse said, "Your child was born at 9:30 this morning." I do remember the episiotomy; it was on both sides.

Kay, Sally's mother

When I had my daughter, I was so busy being a law student, I really didn't have much time to think about it. I was anxious to have my child and get everything in order and get back to my law practice. It never occurred to me that being involved in the birth process was important. When it was time for her to be born I just got sicker and sicker, and they finally toted me down to the hospital and put me in the room and started giving me IVs. There were twelve people in the labor room. There was one little thirteen-year-old girl, scared out of her wits. She got out of her bed and crawled under my bed. I was terrified that she was going to rip the IV out of my arm. They finally retrieved her, and then somebody came and collected me and X-rayed my tummy and brought me back. I was in the hospital for four days and very ill, without anything happening. Finally, on about the fourth day, they got smart; they gave me the right shots to make the baby come. I had the baby very quickly, but during those four previous days I did not see my husband. I didn't see my mother at all (she was here from Iowa to help with the birth and all). It was a very lonesome time. They should not do that to people.

Mary Ann

I remember when my labor started. I was walking up a hill and I had a pain. I went home, I went to bed, and I knew it was happening. I lay in bed and suddenly my body took over; I lay there for three hours. Then I got up and cleaned the house, just like the books said. About one o'clock in the morning, I realized that I should go to the hospital. My husband started massaging me, but I suddenly knew that this was *my* experience, and that no one else could do anything about it. In the Lamaze classes, the whole emphasis had been that you would do this as a duo, and I realized that it wasn't going to be like that; it was *my* body.

We went to the hospital. I went into the alternative birthing center; there was a picture of Berthe Morisot's *Mother at the Cradle* on the wall, and it seemed a good sign to have the work of a woman artist in the room. Then I sat on the bed. I remember all these primitive feelings; I could see millions of women throughout history in little shacks by rivers, all alone, or strapped down in hospitals. That's one of the biggest things that happened to me—that connection with other women throughout all time. I went into the delivery room and I had to push for two hours and twenty minutes. During that time I squatted on the floor, which felt fabulous. But the main thing was the power that I felt in that moment and in the whole process. Anyway, I kept pushing and finally Toby started coming out, and they said, "Stop now." And I said, "You fool!! What are you saying? I can't stop now." So I kept pushing and his head came out—and he lay there for that incredible moment. And then they put him at my breast and I nursed him.

Ann

What would happen if one woman told the truth about her life?

The world would split open.

—Muriel Rukeyser (12)

After hearing all the personal testimony, I decided to expand my investigation of the birth experience by sending out a questionnaire to more than a hundred *Birth Project* participants. Here are some of the questions we asked. I incorporated what I learned from the answers into the *Birth Project* art.

Why did you want to have a baby?

How did you feel about your body?

Describe your birth experience.

What was the best part of pregnancy and birth?

Did pregnancy and birth affect your relationship with your partner?

What side effects did you experience?
a) Frequent urination
b) Heartburn
c) Excessive sweating
d) Change in skin texture, hair
e) Vaginal infections
f) Constipation
g) Hemorrhoids
h) Nausea
i) Vomiting
j) Ankle swelling
k) Spot bleeding
l) Varicose veins (legs, labia, etc.)
m) Change in emotional states

What physical changes have become permanent?
a) Uncontrolled urination
b) Varicose veins
c) Prolapsed uterus (fallen uterus)
d) Hemorrhoids
e) Change in breast texture
f) Vaginal changes

Friday, October 31

I'm back in California, and I now realize how the time in New York took it out of me; I'm planning to rest a little, then plunge back in. I'll soon know what happened to the pieces I started here; I want to see whether or not people can sustain work on their own, seeing me only every two or three months when I review the work they did. Mary Ross and I have been discussing our future working plans; I've revealed more about my overall plan of work for the next period and my idea of slowly building a network to support the image-making and then the distribution of those images nationally. I'm thinking about how to both create and distribute images so that they reach an even wider audience than The Dinner Party.

Late in the summer of 1980, I witnessed a birth. Here is my journal entry about that experience:

It's mid-afternoon; I have just witnessed my first birth. Karin Hibma and Michael Cronan had a well-prepared, natural birth in a hospital, with a woman doctor and a woman resident. It was really quite incredible— just what I needed to see to continue to work on these birth images. Probably the best thing I did was to tape-record the sounds. I had planned to wait until the actual delivery room, but it was a good thing I did it before that because they wouldn't let me take my recorder in there, only into the labor room. So I got a good hour of labor sounds—all the way until the last half hour, when there weren't that many anyway, since the pain diminished once the head crowned. I feverishly made sketches and shot tons of Polaroids, some of which came out. I'm just not the best photographer in the world, that's for sure. There were a lot of blurred images because Karin moved, and when the baby was actually emerging the doctor was blocking my view, so I couldn't see much. But there were certainly lots of vivid visual images that sunk into my consciousness: the expression on Karin's face, the glazed look that came over her eyes during the height of the contractions, the darkening of the pelvis as she pushed.

Detail of face from *Birth Q 1.* ©Judy Chicago, 1983. Quilted and embroidered by Roxanna Rutter, Berkeley, California. Overall size: 45½'' x 74''.

"I stitched the facial features with DMC cotton floss, using the long and short satin stitch. I then couched an outline to accentuate the forms." Needleworker Roxanna Rutter, Berkeley, California

Detail of face from *Birth Tear Q,* ©Judy Chicago, 1983. Embroidered by Dorothy Cavanaugh, Mary Kidd Fogel, and Mary Ann Seamon, Houston, Texas. Quilting by Sally Babson, Benicia, California. Overall size: 57½'' x 78''.

"We outlined the head in a reverse braided chain stitch made of six strands of DMC floss interlaced with three strands: we worked the facial features in the stem stitch with three strands and the hair in a running stitch with three strands whipped with six strands of thread." Needleworker Mary Ann Seamon, Houston, Texas

Detail of face from *Birth NP*, ©Judy Chicago, 1984. Needlepointed by Jo Chester, Joyce Gilbert, Joan Hargis, Peggy Patton, and Karin Telfer, Houston Texas. Needlepoint over painting on 18-mesh canvas. Overall size: 46¼" x 81".

"The outline was done in two rows of chain stitch using #5 DMC perle cotton. The face was done in the long and short stitch and the eyes and mouth in basketweave with Medici yarn. When the face was done, suddenly the canvas became alive, and we began referring to it as 'her.'"
Needleworker Joyce Gilbert, Houston, Texas

Detail of face from *Birth E 4/6* (unfinished). ©Judy Chicago, 1984. Embroidered by Marcia Nowlan, Fairfax, California. Overall size 12" x 21".

"I stitched the face in the split stitch, using one strand of DMC floss. I tried to emphasize the sense of determination I perceived in the image. I felt that her expression was a metaphor for my own life: I had to be *very* determined in order to carve out the time to develop a regular stitching rhythm."
Needleworker Marcia Nowlan, Fairfax, California

These are face details from some *Birth Project* works—two large quilts and a needlepoint, one small embroidery—from four of my images of women giving birth. Their features are contorted, their heads thrown back, their expressions those of creatures caught in an experience not of their making. Yes, of course, some women have a choice about becoming pregnant, but whether a woman chooses to give birth or not, once she is in the throes of labor, her individuality counts for little; she becomes caught up in the universal act of "giving life." She can do this with control and passion or be totally unconscious and unable to participate—but once begun, the birth process is unstoppable. I have tried to express, in these faces, some of the feelings I believe women experience.

Journal entry, continued

Looking at that dripping, engorged cunt, with the lifeless umbilical cord hanging out afterwards, was really something—a view of the vagina I've certainly never seen before, nor have many other people. It was interesting that Karin became totally disconnected from her body when the baby was in her arms. There she was with her legs spread, the center of her body covered with cloths. She and Michael were holding the baby in their arms while the doctors cut and groped and stitched and the blood poured out and the placenta emerged and this bloody, gaping hole just oozed.

All the while, "maternity" surrounded the upper part of Karin's body and suffused her, the baby, and Michael in a kind of unearthly glow that was in total contrast to the animality of her bleeding, cut, lower body. I was shaking by the time I left, though I was very proud of myself because, in spite of my emotional state, I had been able to handle the tape recorder, tapes, camera, and film without error.

Her husband was really good, a real ally in the struggle, but what a lot of pain! At one point, I really understood why some women choose (and so many doctors want to administer) painkillers. It takes a lot of courage to go through natural birth, especially one as long as Karin's—on and off about eighteen hours, I guess. I was there for the last three or three and a half, the most intense part. She had to have an episiotomy, and there was an enormous amount of blood.

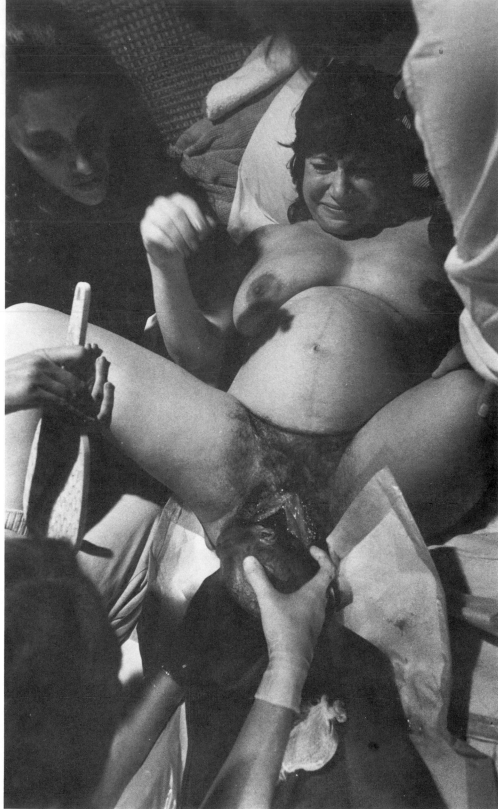

This photograph (by Andrée Abecassis) of Leah Potts Fischer, giving birth to son Mischa, perfectly captures the anguish and joy of the act of birthing in a positive, woman-centered environment.

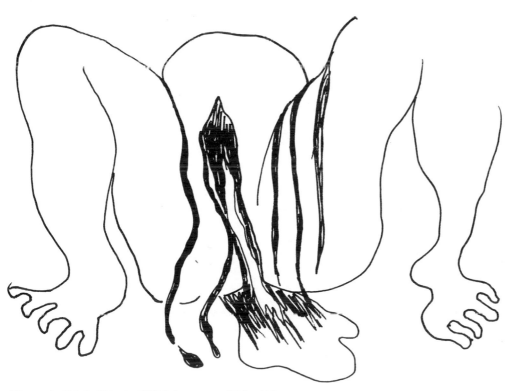

Karin Pushing, ©Judy Chicago, 1980. Ink on paper, 8¼" x 11".

I did these drawings while I was at the hospital during the birth of Karin's and Michael's child. Watching Karin holding her legs in her hands while she pushed inspired this image. Although I didn't include them in the drawing, Karin was wearing the most wonderful pair of knee socks. Unfortunately, they got covered with blood.

Afterwards, ©Judy Chicago, 1980. Ink on paper, 8¼" x 11".

After the baby was born, I was shocked by the way Karin's vagina looked. She had had an episiotomy and there was blood everywhere. I couldn't believe that a woman's body could sustain such trauma.

Monday, November 3, 1980

Last night, Karin and Michael came over to see the pictures and tapes I had made of their baby's birth. I sat there and watched Karin feed the baby while she went on and on about all the details of her blissful days of child-tending. She was always a slim woman, and I wondered if she minded what had happened to her physically—her body was larger, her features were coarser, and her breasts were huge.

I just couldn't believe that taking care of an infant could be all the bliss she said it was. Many women I had talked to had confessed to a whole range of feelings, but they all said they could only admit to the "negative" ones years later, as they felt too guilty to say anything except "everything is wonderful" at the time. I can't imagine how one feels when there's no room to acknowledge what has to go along with the wonder, joy, and happiness; there must be rage and feelings of entrapment and loss of identity. But the "myth of motherhood" seems to hold everyone in its sway, and the silence on the subject historically isolates every woman in what must be a prison of unexpressed emotion. I certainly have my work cut out for me in trying to bring truth to a subject shrouded in such secrecy and mythology.

Karin Hibma and Michael Cronan with their son, Nicky, whose birth I witnessed.

29

Last week I finished two Birth Quilt designs, and yesterday Sally and I started developing some ideas for reverse quilts. My drawing will be on the back, and the quilting will be done from behind on turquoise or green fabric to create a reliefed effect.

The time in New York has really left me feeling confused. It's clear that I'm not going to be embraced by the art world as a result of having accomplished not only a large body of work, but this monumental piece, The Dinner Party, which is beginning to feel like an albatross around my neck. I feel myself being forced into a greater level of "otherness" than I've ever experienced before, and I'm definitely having a failure of nerve. But I have to go forward; what else can I do? Go back to being an isolated artist in my studio, making useless, impotent products? I already have a warehouse full of work I can't show or sell. Perhaps I'll feel better after Saturday, when The Birth Project meets in Benicia. I'm afraid that people haven't done any work and that all my dreams and ideas will be irrelevant. My plans are built on a decentralized work process which I supervise. But if people need my day-to-day presence in order to produce, as they did in the Dinner Party studio, then this idea of mine won't work. Have I over-extended myself based on too little real evidence? I guess I'll have to wait and see.

I drew this Birth pattern on vellum, and Shari Knapp silkscreened the image in reverse onto the back of the fabric to be quilted. Sally then prepared the pieces by placing batting between the colored cotton facing fabric and the muslin on which the pattern was screened. We chose three colors of cotton for the front fabric strips for appliqué and DMC thread for the quilting and embroidery in matching tones. I did not specify which of these techniques (other than quilting) should be incorporated into the work, leaving those decisions up to the stitchers.

There were twelve in the original series; only five were completed. One of these, quilted by Phebe Schwartz, from Bellingham, Washington, was left

Pattern for *Birth Quilt,* ©Judy Chicago, 1981. Ink on vellum, 17'' x 30½''.

without a border when she joined the Peace Corps and went to Africa. Mary Ewanoski, of Goleta, California, completed her piece. It is shown with the matching quilt that Mary stitched.

In addition to Mary Ewanoski and Phebe Schwartz, other people who executed versions of the *Birth Quilt* were Rita Borden, of Glastonbury, Connecticut; Lynn Holyoke, of San Francisco; and Elizabeth Van Horn Taylor, of Berkeley, California.

This is a detail of the quilt Mary Ewanoski executed. Overall size 21'' x 34''.

"I used two strands of DMC floss and a regular running stitch to quilt along the lines of the image. After quilting the body, I turned the work over and appliquéd the border in one piece using a second color of cotton fabric. The appliqué stitches were done with one strand of DMC in the blue background color.

To do the border on Phebe's piece, I did rows of quilting around the piece, using the wavy lines on the silk-screened side as a guide for the quilting."

Needleworker Mary Ewanoski
Goleta, California

Detail of quilt Phebe Schwartz executed and Mary Ewanoski completed. Overall size 20½'' x 33''.

"When the pattern and fabric first arrived, my stomach fell. Silk-screened on muslin, a woman spread-eagled and oozing off the edge of the piece—this was it; birth in graphic detail. My God, I thought, is this what it's like to give birth? The image hit my core being, made my body feel the force of the event, made all my muscles contract. I was shocked—the impact was too physical. I knew I needed to take time, get to know the image, before I could work on it."

Needleworker Phebe Schwartz
Bellingham, Washington

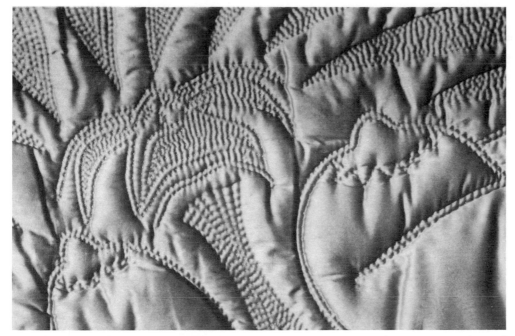

Section of *Birth Q 2*, ©Judy Chicago, 1982. Quilted by Linda Gaughenbaugh, Davette Gregg, Mary Anna Harris, all from Sacramento, California. Overall size: 49½" x 82".

Sally and I went to see a beautiful quilt show. I was particularly struck by some of the border patterns on the quilts. I decided to try and design a border specifically for what we referred to as the "Sacramento Quilt"—a large, reverse quilt which depends entirely on variations of light play on the surface for its visual effects, as the red fabric is quilted with the same color thread. I thought I could accentuate the rhythm and texture of the surface with a dynamic border.

I showed sketches to the stitchers, Linda, Davette, and Mary Anna, who liked them but requested that the corners meet in a certain way. After trying this idea out and discovering that it wouldn't work, I came up with what I considered a graceful, mitered corner. It is always difficult to make the corners of idiosyncratic patterns line up and not look awkward, and it often requires what I call "fudging"—i.e., making something appear to be symmetrical when it's not. At the next review, the quilters demanded to know why I had changed the initial corner idea, and only an hour-long demonstration at the light table convinced them that I had really done the best I could.

I first drew the image in reverse on a piece of muslin. Sally then basted that together with batting and the red polished cotton we had chosen for the front. The quilting was done from the back, which caused the needleworkers some difficulty in keeping the stitches a consistent length, as they couldn't really see what they were doing and had to turn the quilt over frequently to check. This was hard to do because it was on a quilting frame.

The needleworkers used a running stitch for the reverse quilting, then added front quilting for emphasis. The stitching was all done in two strands of DMC. The cording was done after the quilting and helped to define the forms. The piece is based on the traditional trapunto quilt, which was stuffed from behind after the quilting was complete. Sally helped the quilters adjust the padding so that there were smooth transitions between the stuffed and unstuffed areas. This involved almost shaving the batting as it was inserted in order to get it to flatten gradually.

Detail of *Birth Q 2*, showing border design.

This detail aptly demonstrates reverse quilting, a traditional technique in which the quilting is done from the back, producing a reliefed or sculptural visual effect.

Detail of my design for the border on *Birth Q 2*.

Tuesday, November 18, 1980

The work itself is moving along, though it is still not certain that high-quality work will actually emerge from this process. There's always a difference between initial enthusiasm and the long haul required for making art. It certainly does require a lot from me to keep the projects going, and it is very demanding, both emotionally and esthetically—but it's the work I've cut out for myself. It's doubtful that I'll be able to do much else once it's in full swing.

One thing I noticed during **The Dinner Party** *is that people kept referring to their "real lives" away from the studio. For me, of course, my real life is in the studio, and one of the things I'm investigating in this project is how the fact that my art is being worked on at home, in the participant's "real lives," will affect those lives. There is no question that for many of the* **Dinner Party** *workers, the opportunity to participate in my art-making process changed their lives. But it also created a lot of tension between them and their families and friends, who usually didn't understand what they were getting out of the experience. I wonder if the presence of the work in the needleworkers' homes and the chance to witness the day-to-day process will have an impact.*

Birth, ©Judy Chicago, 1980. Ink on vellum, 37″ x 72½″.

This is my original line drawing for the *Birth* image. At first, I made different-size blueprints and photocopies and gave them to the needleworkers, usually with fabric Sally and I had bought. But I soon discovered that, since color is one of my strengths as an artist, their color choices were not as good as mine—so I began to color-control the images. Then I realized that when I allowed the needleworkers to transfer my patterns to the fabric, their lines were not as fine as mine. So before long, I was giving out hand-drawn, hand-painted, and color-coded projects.

At this point in the project, I was thinking about designing the images in terms of traditional needlework patterns. Historically, needlework has been an interpretive art, and needleworkers have worked from artists' designs. But most of the patterns and designs available today are quite unoriginal and degrading to women. The subject matter is usually neutral and certainly has no relationship to women's lives.

Roxanna Rutter working at home in Berkeley, California.

This project began in the fall of 1980. A group of young artists and art students took a full-scale pattern and fabric at the first meeting. They were an enthusiastic lot, but they were never able to really agree on an approach to the piece. Eventually one of their members, Roxanna Rutter, completed the piece alone.

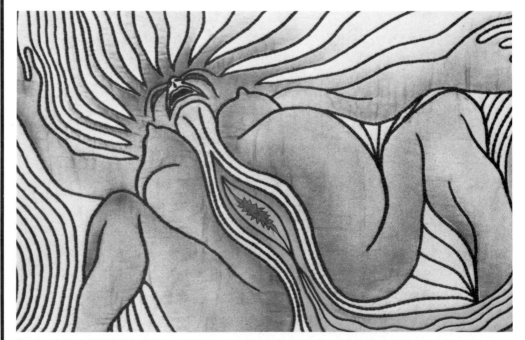

Center of *Birth Q 1*. ©Judy Chicago, 1983. Executed by Roxanna Rutter, Berkeley, California. Sprayed paint, appliqué, couching, and embroidery. Overall size: 45½″ x 74½″.

Pattern for *Birth Embroidery* project, ©Judy Chicago, 1980. Ink on vellum, 11½'' x 20½''.

I adapted and altered the original *Birth* pattern; then Shari Knapp silkscreened the pattern onto cotton for the *Birth Embroidery* project. This project, like the small *Birth* reverse quilt series and other multiple projects, was intended for people whose life situations and/or needlework skills were not, in our estimation, suitable for more individualized pieces. This might have been because they lived far away and would only have mail-in reviews, which, I thought, would limit communication; or because their time was quite limited even though their interest was high; or because their needlework and/or art background was minimal.

The image was screened onto either brown or blue fabric in contrasting ink colors (i.e., blue on brown, brown on blue), and I enclosed instructions and a color range of DMC threads. Sally prepared the pieces by basting each of the silkscreens onto a backing fabric, after which they were embroidered on frames. Here are some details of different interpretations of this image.

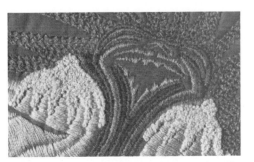

Detail, *Birth E 3/6*. Embroidered by Jennifer Pawlick, Webster, New York.

Detail, *Birth E 2/6*. Embroidered by Beverly McKinzie, San Jose, California.

Sally worked closely with Beverly McKinzie in the development of this piece.

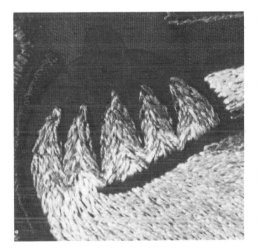

Detail, *Birth 5/6*. Embroidered by Charlotte Anderson, West Hartford, Connecticut.

"I had difficulty relating to the image I worked on because I have never given birth, although my friends have related to me the joys experienced in birth and during the natural childbirth process. However, the image seems to depict birth as something painful."

Needleworker Charlotte Anderson
West Hartford, Connecticut

Meanwhile, people are gobbling up my images as fast as I can make them. I feel trapped between the desperate need and hunger of women and the terrible sense of negation by men. So, what do I do, stuff my face? That really helps a lot. It's just that I feel as if I have no time alone anymore, and if I do, then I get upset because I need help to get work done. It's a vicious circle. The reason I need help, of course, is that I've taken on so much. And the results seem so intangible. So far there are a number of works in progress, but their completion depends entirely on other people, which, of course, makes me anxious.

The images are very powerful. I know that. The way I'm conceiving them to be needlepointed, quilted, or embroidered is intended to soften them, to make them easier to handle—by whom? Am I doing this because I am being a mother, providing for all these needy women? God, I'm all mixed up.

Women are coming out from the woodwork to work with me; they're so eager, and I'm so scared they won't come through. I'm putting what I cherish most—my images—in women's hands and letting them take them away. It was one thing to have them work in my studio under my nose; it's quite another to paint these wonderful works and then hand them over to virtual strangers. And yet the only way I'll be satisfied with the work and the only way the needleworkers will really be able to work to my satisfaction is to have me underpaint the forms.

The Crowning

Wednesday, December 10, 1980

I'm back in New York; The Dinner Party's still mobbed; it's still generating controversy. I'm getting recognized on the street, in restaurants and stores.

I've been drawing almost every day, working on black paper, doing birth and creation images—and today an entrapment image, trapped by biology or by the need to be connected to life. I have almost never really allowed myself to need another person, to depend upon another person. I've always deprived myself of that so as not to get "caught." But I understand how one can be caught by life, and it's partly that that I've been trying to explore. Birth and its subsequent responsibilities are a metaphor for being "caught" by the life process, something most women seem to both crave and fear. But once the baby is born, choice is at an end.

I've also been working on another image of The Crowning. *I did one during the summer, but now I'm trying to develop it further. I'm planning one* Crowning *project— a series of batiks in blues and purples to be executed by people around the country.*

At an early meeting, Dianne Barber approached me about incorporating batik into some of the images. I was reluctant to do so, as I felt that batik was very imprecise. But she was quite insistent, arguing that my Crowning *pattern in particular would lend itself to batik. She did some samples for me,*

Aztec Goddess Tiazolteotl. Aplite, speckled with garnets (13).

This Aztec sculpture is an exquisite example of one type of birth image that recurs in many nonindustrial societies. I like to think of it as a depiction of the crowning.

The Crowning, ©Judy Chicago, 1981. Prismacolor on rag paper, 24'' x 33''.

"Judy Chicago's *The Crowning* is an image of a woman about to give birth. It is a stark, powerful image. Her head is down; she seems to be concentrated on the task at hand. Her vagina is the focal point. Her hair flows out over her head like the branches of a tree. Her toes are spread and extended like roots connecting her to the earth, the source of all life."

Needleworker Gloria Van Lydegraf
Chico, California

Detail, *The Crowning Q 8/9,* ©Judy Chicago, 1982. Quilted and embroidered by Rebecca Hanner, Pilot Mountain, North Carolina. Batiked by Dianne Barber, Jenner, California, from Judy Chicago's drawing. Overall size: 32'' x 48½''.

This piece in the series of batik quilts based on *The Crowning* was executed by Hope Wingert, of Benicia, California. The background was quilted, the uterus appliquéd with metallic fabric, and the outline satin-stitched with DMC. The border is a piece of ribbon that Sally and I found which perfectly matched the colors of the quilt. Overall size: 28" x 43½".

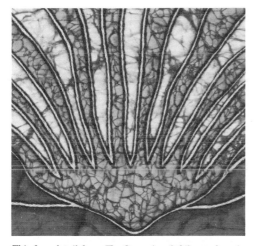

This face detail from *The Crowning Q 3/9* was done in needle lace by Rheda Schultz, Madison, Wisconsin, who quilted and embroidered this version.

Detail of petit-point crown appliquéd on another version of *The Crowning*, a batik quilt by Nora Bullock, Kutztown, Pennsylvania.

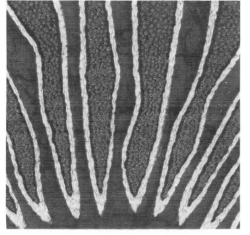

Hair detail: *The Crowning Q 4/9.* Quilted and embroidered by Helen Cohen, Palo Alto, California.

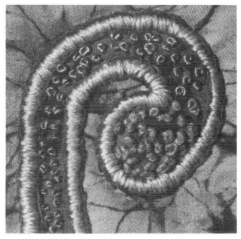

Detail of fallopian tube, *The Crowning Q 5/9.* Executed by Judy Wallen, Port Alexander, Alaska.

and I became interested. Dianne then produced a number of these crowning images in related colors. When she brought them to me, I was distressed by the way the batik process had produced an uneven outline around the body forms. So I meticulously painted precise outlines on all the pieces, which I then asked the needleworkers to cover with stitching. I sent a limited range of colors of DMC embroidery floss and suggested using quilting, embroidery, and, in some cases, appliqué. My suggestions for the development of each work depended in part on the skills of the needleworker.

"The first image I worked on was *The Crowning*, and I grew to love it. I was especially fond of the curve of the arms and the way the knees seemed to express the strength required to give birth."

Needleworker Dianne Barber
Jenner, California

Another needleworker, Joanne Lanicotti, from Edison, New Jersey, worked on a batik quilt version of *The Crowning*. She expressed her feelings about the image in a poem excerpted here:

Huge muscles hump
   over my shoulders
The tendons of my
   thighs
Flex in and out
My neck turns toward
   the stars
Water laps around my
   ankles
I become
The Power
Of the Universe.

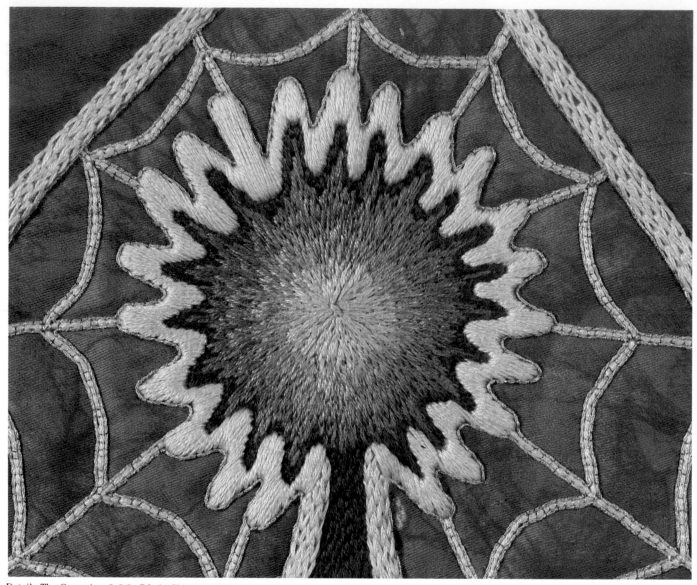

Detail, *The Crowning Q 9/9*, ©Judy Chicago, 1982. Quilted and embroidered by Gwen Glesmann, Washington, D.C. Batiked by Dianne Barber, Jenner, California, from Judy Chicago's drawing. Overall size: 28¾'' x 44''.

My initial ideas for the series of batik quilts based on *The Crowning* changed and evolved as the individual pieces were completed. The detailed embroidery in this version, executed by Gwen Glesmann, would have been lost if I had made the separate pieces into a large quilt; therefore, in order for it to be appreciated, we exhibited it as an individual work.

"All the needlework is done using DMC cotton floss—one strand for the quilting and two to six strands for the embroidery. The embroidery was done in four basic stitches—chain, satin, long and short, and couching. Judy suggested adding gold thread, which accentuated the spiderweb quality of the uterus shape.

"I had trouble relating to my image for a long time. Not having any children or any plans for having children, the image did not inspire any special feelings in me. However, my whole involvement in stitching this piece became a celebration of my own rebirth and the incredible joy of bringing myself out of the oppressive roles I have been taught and peeling away the layers of self-doubt which had surrounded me." Needleworker Gwen Glesmann, Washington, D.C.

Gwen Glesmann and I during a review of *The Crowning Q 9/9*.

Another version of *The Crowning* was executed in Waterloo, Iowa, coordinated by Martha Sanford. In some projects, the group process seemed more the focus than the art itself, although without the art there would have been no process. For me the art was always the most important, but I recognized that for some of the needleworkers, especially those in remote areas, the opportunity to work with other women on art that related to their experiences was the paramount motivation. The process these women went through is told in the documentation that accompanies the piece they executed, which tells a story to which many viewers seem to relate.

After Dianne Barber batiked this piece from my full-scale drawing, I outlined the image, which was quilted, embroidered, and embellished by the group in Iowa that Martha Sanford coordinated. The crown contains hair from the group members, and the outline is enhanced with small ceramic objects made by one of the group, Geraldine Boruta.

There must have been something about the *Crowning* image that stimulated people's imaginations. Here is an excerpt from another poem, written by Martha Sanford of Waterloo, Iowa, who coordinated the quilting and embellishment of a large batiked piece which the group referred to as ''Mom.''

Mom, as we came to call her,
has the topography of a mighty
    river
running from her source
to a rich full delta—her spine
from the center of her brain
to the delta of the birth canal

> I am a woman
> I am a woman
> having a baby
> I am a woman
> having a baby
> all by myself—alone

I remember watching my
first son being born
my feet up in metal
stirrups, my spine therefore
my body relieved of any
sensation, because of drugs

> Now, years later, as
> I look at our piece
> I feel as though we
> transformed that
> most marvelous
> sensation into a
> work of art and
> I rejoice at our
> accomplishment

Mom is a great source
of joy, and each time
I stand back and look
at her I'm overwhelmed
by her beauty and by
my own part of that beauty.

Needleworker Martha Jane Sanford
Waterloo, Iowa

RITA JACOBMEYER

The ''Mom'' group—back row (left to right): Martha Jane Sanford, Audrey Schmitt, Anne Wardell, Martha Waterman, Judy Bennor, Mary Ellen Kelly; front row: Lili Church, Kathy Herman, Geraldine Boruta, Connie Greany, Nancy Dieball Galloway—with quilt in progress.

Thursday, December 18, 1980

I am thinking about exhibiting **The Birth Project** *in small units, from one to five or six works, each of which can be rolled up in a tube, will be inexpensive to ship, and will be simple to hang. Even people who are not experienced in handling art could put up a show, which would mean that* **Birth Project** *art could be accessible to libraries, hospitals, birthing centers, and women's centers as well as museums and galleries. And imagine—if there were one hundred works, and each one went to one hundred places where one hundred viewers saw the art, that would be a million people who would be seeing, probably for the first time, an image of birth.*

Installation view, *The Crowning Q 6,* ©Judy Chicago, 1983. Overall size: 57'' x 88¼''.

My *Crowning* image became the basis for a number of works: embroideries, quilts, needlepoints, and even a crocheted and a knitted piece. The work is uneven; some of it is spectacular, while other pieces are somewhat clumsy visually—the result of a great range in the skill levels of the needleworkers. But all the pieces that I decided to exhibit have something unique about them. In some cases, it is the human process by which they were made that is most important, while in others the technical accomplishment is staggering. And then there are some pieces in which image, technique, color, and visual acuity all work together splendidly.

One of the earliest projects was coordinated by Ann Piper when she was teaching a women's studies course at Diablo Valley College in Pleasant Hill, California. Neither she nor most of her students had much needlework background. Sally taught them and helped them, although she had never really worked with a group before. The piece is appliquéd, quilted, and embroidered.

Sally instructing the DVC group. (Left to right) Sally Babson, unknown, Ann Piper, unknown, Anne Stafford, Kim West.

Sally working on the DVC *Crowning* quilt.

"I have never worked with a group of people before. The first meeting with them was literally about teaching them to thread a needle. And there was food everywhere, food and wine. Finally, I said: 'How about we take a look at this piece?' We started cutting out pattern pieces that first night; they really didn't know what they were doing.

"I'd never organized a group; it was the first time I realized that there are certain people in groups that naturally gravitate toward the head of the group and want to take control. There was never any direct confrontation, but then I am one who avoids direct confrontation at all costs. Judy was telling me, '*You* need to take control.' That was frightening for me; it has been frightening for me all along in the whole project, not just on this quilt. I went every week, but too many times I found myself alone, so I quit going. I said, 'If you need me, call me.' But by that time they were doing the same stitch over and over again, and they didn't need me.

"After they finished the outline many of them dropped out, and finally there were just two of them left. Then I realized if we wanted that piece finished in a reasonable time, the only way it was going to get done was if I sat down and did it."

Sally Babson

Betty Hallock attempted to translate the *Crowning* image into a knitted piece. She did an incredible job of gridding the pattern in preparation for the knitting and figuring out how to accomplish the task technically. Despite her efforts, however, the result didn't have sufficient visual grace.

Betty Hallock at work in Burlingame, California.

"My 'crowning' took one year to do. During that time I had to educate my friends to the fact I was doing something important and was not to be disturbed. On occasion, I worked all day Sunday because I had a problem that needed solving, and only experimentation helped me to arrive at a solution."

Needleworker Betty Hallock
Burlingame, California

The Crowning ST, ©Judy Chicago, 1982. Crocheted by Chrissie Clapp, Red Bluff, California. 58" x 86".

Chrissie Clapp translated my *Crowning* image with an unusual crochet technique that produced a surface which is rich in color and texture.

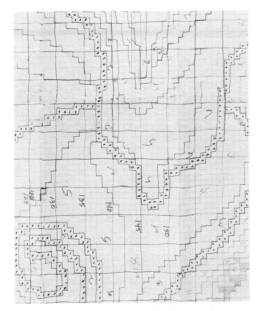

Section of Chrissie Clapp's graph of my mock-up.

Same section crocheted.

"I took Judy's pattern and charted it on graph paper. I then made a color sketch for her painted mock-up and dyed the wool yarns with acid dyes. I made many samples for both the color fades and the crochet technique. The piece is worked in single crochet over a core thread added to provide strength and continuity, particularly for a row that had several color changes; some had over fifty changes. The color changes were accomplished while crocheting each vertical row. On each right-to-left row, the threads were all pulled to the front when not in use; on each return row, they were pushed to the back to maintain an even surface. Some areas which required more detail than possible with this stitch were embroidered with a duplicate stitch. The piece is bordered with a backward double crochet stitch that I call a ridge stitch. There are over 70,000 stitches in this work of art." Chrissie Clapp

One of the more unique versions of *The Crowning* was executed by Chrissie Clapp in a crocheting technique she developed herself. Working from my full-scale, painted mock-up, Chrissie first gridded the pattern, then crocheted it. Her translation of my color fades was quite unusual and gives the image an undulating quality that greatly enhances it.

Chrissie first submitted samples to show me how the image would look in the unusual crochet technique she developed. Halfway through the piece it was ruined by her dog, and she had to start again. Undaunted, she incorporated everything she had learned the first time into her second effort and was able to improve her technique. One problem she encountered and solved was how to prevent the crochet from pulling in on itself as she worked, which would have greatly distorted the image.

Chrissie and I discussing work.

"Working with Judy changed a lot of perceptions I had about how people become artists. It has to do with far more than talent. It has to do with vision, perseverance, and dedication. I also learned about my own limits, and I feel that because of that, I've grown a lot. I have gained more self-confidence, especially in relation to trusting my own judgment."

Needleworker Chrissie Clapp
Red Bluff, California

39

These two pieces demonstrate even more clearly how one image can be used in very different ways through the needlework. On the left is a small embroidery of *The Crowning,* executed by Elisa Skarveland, Pt. Reyes Station, California, in small, exquisite stitches. The quilt on the right is much larger, executed in reverse appliqué and quilted by Jacquelyn Moore, then of Mendon, now of Hopedale, Massachusetts.

The contrast between the two is a good illustration of what has always been very common in needlework—the use of a basic pattern, which is then enlarged, reversed, reduced, or transformed by the needleworker. In *The Birth Project,* it was Sally and I, working with the stitchers, who established most of the techniques we used. We wanted to include as many as we could, partly because it was challenging to explore them and also because we wanted to demonstrate what can be done with traditional textile techniques if visual rigor is brought to bear. The exactness of Skarveland's stitching and the near-perfection of Moore's reverse appliqué honor and continue the long and generally neglected tradition of the needle arts.

Center detail of *The Crowning E 1,* ©Judy Chicago, 1983. Embroidered by Elisa Skarveland, DMC floss on silk. Overall size: 19½'' x 29¼''. This piece was embroidered directly over my drawing in the split and chain stitches.

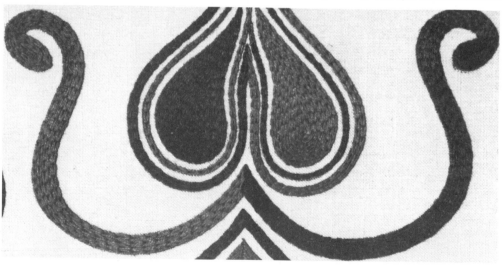

Detail of *The Crowning E 1.*

Elisa Skarveland worked on this embroidery for almost three years. Every time I would become exasperated with the slow pace of her work, I would be mollified by the beauty of her stitching, which was done directly over my drawing on fabric.

Elisa Skarveland embroidering Judy Chicago's *The Crowning E 1,* Pt. Reyes Station, California.

The Crowning Q 5, ©Judy Chicago, 1982. Reverse appliqué and quilting by Jacquelyn Moore, Mendon, Massachusetts. 56½" x 89".

Reverse appliqué is a quilting technique widely used in Central and South America as well as in the United States. Sally had been trying to convince me to do a flipped image, which, she said, was a very traditional quilt design. But I felt that it was too decorative. She kept after me about it, insisting that the *Crowning* image was the most appropriate for this kind of treatment. I finally tried it and, much to my surprise, liked the results.

I first transferred the images to fabric. Sally then basted a layer of contrasting-color fabric behind my drawings. Jackie Moore carefully cut away the top layer of fabric so that each of the four images appeared in the contrasting color beneath. She then turned all the cut edges under and stitched them down by hand. Later, Jackie quilted the image along all the edges.

Jacquelyn Moore with *The Crowning Q 5,* at home in Mendon, Massachusetts.

"I delivered a child at home in my own bed, and I did hold my legs open with my hands in order to expedite the birth, so I know this image of the crowning to be an accurate portrayal of childbirth."

Needleworker Jacquelyn Moore
Hopedale, Massachusetts

Jacquelyn Moore at work.

"To quote my 86-year-old Albanian grandmother, 'Women's fingers are like diamonds—precious.'"

Jacquelyn Moore

41

At the right is a section of a large needlepoint that was still in progress at the Benicia studio at the time I was working on the book. It was our first needlepoint project, begun in January 1981. I spray-painted it, then Lynda Healy and I finished painting it by hand. It has had a long and difficult history, with a changing cast of stitchers, long periods where little work was done, and ego struggles that nearly destroyed the piece. Through it all, a few of the early stitchers kept on working, some one day a week, others more, but they never gave up—they kept on stitching even though the piece took over four years. More than once I wanted to end the project, but they wouldn't hear of it.

The photograph reveals my painting beneath the needlepoint, done entirely in basketweave in six strands of DMC floss—an incredible technical achievement, one that shows what spectacular color needlepoint can produce.

Benicia needlepoint group (left to right): Susan McMillan, Janis Wicks, Lael Cohen, Maggie Eoyang, Jeanette Russell.

"For me, this piece brings beauty and meaning into the world; I hope She will touch men and women's lives deeply, remind them of the force of life, the power of beginnings, the awe of the bringer and the brought."
Needleworker Maggie Eoyang
Berkeley, California

The center section of *The Crowning NP 1* (in progress), ©Judy Chicago, 1985. Needlepointed by Maggie Eoyang, Susan McMillan, Jeanette Russell, Janis Wicks, and guest stitchers Jean Berens, Susan Bloomenstein, Lael Cohen, Penny Davidson, and Ann Gibson. DMC floss on 18-mesh canvas. Overall size: 50" x 86½".

"The blending was done on top of Judy's sprayed painting, which acted as a color guide. We also had a pattern that Judy had coded in terms of the position of the colors and how they should move from one to another. But, still, we were on our own and had to rely on our intuition as well as a basic plan to achieve the blends.

"First, we arranged the threads to be blended from dark to light in color; colors close in values blend most successfully. We began by putting five strands of the darkest color and one strand of the next value in the needle, then gradually replacing the strands with lighter and lighter tones, being careful to leave an uneven edge between the stitched colors so the transitions would not be noticeable. To emphasize areas, we used unblended tones; to make transitions, we used more neutral colors between stronger ones.

"After the initial stitching was completed, we overstitched randomly with one or two strands to break up any visual lines or unevenness."   Needleworker Janis Wicks, Walnut Creek, California

Center section (including border) of *The Crowning NP 5*, ©Judy Chicago, 1984. Needlepointed by Jan, Maria, Marian, and Sharon Lo Biondo, Vineland, New Jersey. Paternayan and Medici yarn and perle cotton on 18-mesh canvas. Overall size: 30" x 48".

This work was executed by the Lo Biondo family in Vineland, New Jersey. The kind of struggles that took place within the Benicia needlepoint group were not their problem—their struggle was with me. Sophisticated stitchers and owners of a needlepoint shop, they had difficulty with the lack of certainty that I, as an artist, am quite comfortable with. I try something, and if it doesn't work, I change it or throw it out and start again. This is in sharp contrast to the way many stitchers work. But ultimately we resolved our differences, and the piece was successfully completed because we all shared a commitment to the work itself.

"We are most proud of working as a family—possibly the only one, we think, in *The Birth Project*. We stitched most of the body with six strands of DMC in the Hungarian stitch, worked horizontally. The head and hands were done in the star stitch, the fallopian tubes in basketweave with one strand of Paternayan, the uterus in an open star with one strand of perle; the crown in the tent stitch with one strand of Paternayan, and the center with six strands of floss. The outline was done in a variation of the stem stitch with two strands of perle, and the border was done in the upright cross with three strands of DMC. We combined stitches to achieve the rich textural effects Judy wanted."

Needleworkers The Lo Biondos
Vineland, New Jersey

Wednesday, December 31, 1980

This weekend I am having a meeting with the needlepoint people, and then I will begin painting needlepoint canvases, something I've never done before. Next weekend I'm going to do reviews and see where I am. I also want to start work on some new images next month.

Monday, January 5, 1981

The Birth Project is developing by leaps and bounds. I've spent the last few days working with Sally and Diana Gordon, a woman with a needlepoint business here in Benicia. Between us, we're developing the needlepoint part of the project, which I didn't do in The Dinner Party; I actually worked very little with needlepoint then.

I knew that historically, needlepoint has been used in large-scale, ambitious projects. But recently, it has sunk to the level of kitschy kits which thousands of women stitch on their laps while watching TV. Although I love most forms of needlework, needlepoint was not my idea of a technique suited to "high art." Moreover, I have never painted a needlepoint canvas. But Diana, who had been an artist, convinced me that needlepoint had a great deal of visual potential, and the idea of exploring the technique's possibilities and pushing needlepoint into a whole new scale appealed to me. Diana offered to help me with the painting, and, though I really knew very little about the technique, I decided to try.

Kathi Haas at home in San Antonio, Texas.

Kathi Haas needlepointing *The Crowning NP 3.*

Kathi Haas needlepointed *The Crowning NP 3* in shades of yellows and golds in Paternayan yarn on 18-mesh canvas over the painting Lynda Healy and I did from my pattern. She used Paternayan yarn and a bargello and brick stitch. The amazing thing about this piece is the way Kathi changed the scale of the bargello stitch so that it fit into the different areas of the body. She did extensive samples for both the color and the stitches she used. The border repeats the colors used on the canvas. After Kathi completed the piece, Janis Wicks adjusted the outline with embroidery stitches over the needlepoint to even out the lines.

Left side of *The Crowning NP 3* (including border), ©Judy Chicago, 1983. Needlepointed by Kathi Haas, San Antonio, Texas. Paternayan yarn on 18-mesh canvas. Overall size: 28¼'' x 45''.

"The first stitches I took were between the breasts; I let the outline of the body dictate the 'waves' I created using the vertical bargello stitch. I really was working an uneven flame stitch all across the body (arms, legs, hands, head, breasts, buttocks). The size of the stitch (vertically) depended on the location in the body part; for example the stitching on the largest part of the breasts and buttocks covered five warps, and the smallest on the toes and fingers covered only two or three warps."

Kathi Haas

Frannie Yablonsky's interpretation of *The Crowning* is unique. She combined DMC floss and yarn and integrated a variety of different stitches to achieve a rich surface and an energetic image.

Looking over work with Frannie Yablonsky.

"The woman's body is worked in six or seven strands of DMC floss in square format stitch designs. Exceptions are the uterus, worked in French knots, and the fallopian tubes, in basketweave. The woman's face and hands are done in 'mosaic.' Breast, shoulders, arms, wrists are stitched in 'crossed corners.' Feet, stomach, legs, hair, and thighs are worked in the 'scotch stitch,' which is varied in size and register.

"The background bands are worked in free-form bargello following the contour of the individual bands. The bargello is surrounded by basketweave; the background between the hairs is solid basketweave. The background is all wool fibers—one or two strands, depending on the different wools used.

"Methods used in blending the colors depend on the area worked. In the fallopian tubes, I mixed the six strands of DMC progressively. Example: six red, then four red/two pink, then two red/four pink, etc. In the majority of the blends the color was laid on in a more intuitive fashion, with little counting of strands in the mix except that the total count was always six or seven in the needle.

"In developing the stitch patterns, I tried to choose stitches which in and of themselves would express the feeling of Judy's painting."

Needleworker Frannie Yablonsky
Somerville, New Jersey

Together, Diana and I have planned a series of different-size needlepoint pieces to be executed over the next several years. We plan to use mainly 18-mesh canvas in order to achieve fine blending and a tight visual surface, with less texture and more pictorial quality than is usual in needlepoint. Maybe I'll end up changing my mind about this technique.

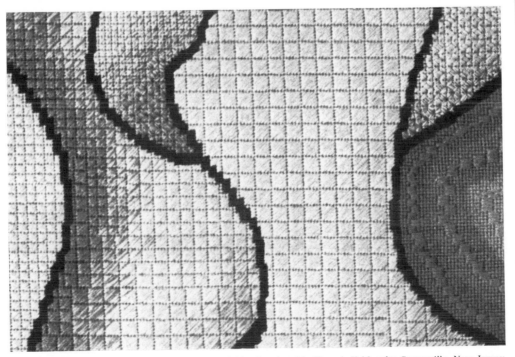

Detail, *The Crowning NP 4*, ©Judy Chicago, 1984. Needlepointed by Frannie Yablonsky, Somerville, New Jersey. DMC floss and Paternayan yarn on 18-mesh canvas. Overall size: 31" x 51".

The Crowning NP 4, ©Judy Chicago, 1984. Executed by Frannie Yablonsky, 30½"x 51".

"Today, in the midst of breathing techniques, fetal monitoring machines, and obstetrical procedures, the fact that birth is a celebration is often lost. Prints of these images should be on the walls of labor rooms to remind the birthing woman, doctors, nurses, and families of the celebration of giving birth."

Frannie Yablonsky

Exploring Needlepoint

Tuesday, January 13, 1981

It has been very hectic; last weekend we did reviews. Every two months seems like the right time interval for the reviews— long enough for people to accomplish a good deal of work, but not so long that they lose contact with me or the larger sense of the project. And it was very clear that everyone really looks forward to these reviews.

Sunday night, I held a meeting for people interested in the administrative aspect of **The Birth Project.** *It's obvious that it will require a considerable amount of work to keep track of all the individual projects (especially if interest stays as high as it is now) and to maintain regular communication with all the needleworkers. At the meeting, I made it clear that what I was after was a national project, set up either formally or informally in different regions from which I could generate and exhibit about one hundred works. To accomplish this, we need a solid system—and there were some enormously capable women at that meeting. There was also a woman there named Diana Gordon, who designs needlepoint canvases here in town. She's going to transfer three of my large images to needlepoint canvases. When I return from New York, I'll paint them and they'll be stitched according to my color code.*

One thing I was interested in doing was pushing the traditional scale of needlepoint. I knew from my needlework research during *The Dinner Party* that large-scale pieces were not uncommon historically, but most contemporary needlepoint is pillow-size. More than one stitcher responded to the 30" x 40" canvas I sent her (small by my standards) that "it was *so* big." Those canvases could be worked on standard frames, however. We had to develop the large frames for the bigger pieces because there were none available commercially.

We developed special frames for working the large needlepoint canvases, which were constructed by Diana Gordon's son Bill. These frames disassembled so they could be shipped to stitchers in different parts of the country.

It often amazed me that just as a need appeared, so did a person. That was the way it happened with Lynda Healy, who had a small business painting needlepoint canvases. No sooner had Diana Gordon and I planned a series of needlepoints than Lynda volunteered to work on *The Birth Project.* Painting needlepoint mesh is altogether different than painting on artist's canvas. I kept trying to pile on more paint than you're supposed to, and invariably I would plug up the holes. Then Lynda and I would have to painstakingly unplug each of the

324 holes per square inch with an awl. Sometimes we couldn't get them all, and then the stitcher would have to struggle to get her needle through the clogged-up holes when she worked the piece, probably cursing me the whole time.

Painting the large *Crowning* needlepoint canvas with Lynda Healy.

With Lynda Healy in my studio.

"January 31 was our starting date for actually stitching *The Crowning.* I went to Diana's at 10 a.m. We talked for a while and then unfurled the newly painted *Crowning*—beautifully intense colors that will be fantastically rich when sewn. We spent the whole afternoon sewing the canvas onto a huge frame Diana's son built. It was physically difficult because the selvage was thick, and we had to use big needles and string.

"There was plenty of good food, and the talk afterward was great. Each of the dozen or so women took a turn introducing herself. A few of them really poured out touching stories.

"Sunday morning, Diana made us eggs and toast. Then we began stitching the blue lines of *The Crowning*, ringing a ceremonial bell as each of us put in her first stitch." Needleworker Susan MacMillan, Petaluma, California (journal entry, 2/6/81)

Establishing or "coding" the color for each piece required developing palettes for the different threads. Generally, thread charts are not grouped by color families like a painter's palette, which is laid out according to the spectrum from yellow through red to purple, then blue and green. In order to do color coding, I first had to take the threads and position them by value and hue. Once I had my "palettes" I would either specify color by number, do a series of colored pencil swatches to be matched with thread, or work on a black and white pattern of the image, identifying which color went where.

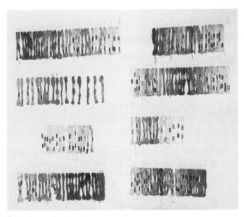

My thread palette.

Color coding for petit point was the most difficult task of the project. Both *Creation of the World* petit points, one executed by Rhonda Gerson of Houston, Texas, and the other by Jean Berens of Milwaukee, Wisconsin, were done in DMC floss, and only one strand would fit through the holes of the 40-mesh silk canvas. It was almost impossible to tell what one strand of a color would look like; unless the tone was very strong, it would practically disappear on the image.

Coding color with Rhonda Gerson (left) and Joyce Gilbert (right) of Houston, Texas.

Janis Wicks at work on *The Crowning* in front of my color-coded pattern, used as a guide in blending.

Montage of *Creation of the World* images (left to right): (1) *Creation of the World NP 3*, ©Judy Chicago, 1983, needlepoint by Lael Cohen, Berkeley, California. (2) *Creation of the World NP 4*, ©Judy Chicago, 1984, needlepoint by Lee Jacobs, Houston, Texas, and Chrissie Clapp, Red Bluff, California. (3) *Creation of the World PP 1*, ©Judy Chicago, 1984, petit point by Rhonda Gerson, Houston, Texas. (4) *Creation of the World PP 2*, ©Judy Chicago, 1984, petit point by Jean Berens, Milwaukee, Wisconsin. (5) *Creation of the World NP 2*, ©Judy Chicago, 1984, needlepoint by Gerry Melot, Houston, Texas.

This page contains a montage of different translations of the *Creation of the World* image into various scales of mesh. Lael Cohen (1) used four strands of DMC on 24-mesh canvas and restricted herself to one stitch—the continental. Chrissie Clapp (2) of California completed a piece on 18-mesh canvas begun by Lee Jacobs in Texas; they used Paternayan and Medici yarn to achieve a more textural effect. Rhonda Gerson (3) and Jean Berens (4) each executed a petit point on 40-mesh silk; although they both used one strand of DMC in the tent stitch, the results are strikingly different, in large part because of my color choices. Gerry Melot (5) needlepointed on 18-mesh canvas using blended DMC in a variety of stitches.

The effect of such dramatic difference in scale in the mesh is emphasized in this photo-montage. The petit points, both 5″ x 9″, while much smaller than the needlepoints, all 18″ x 37″, are shown larger than life to create this photograph. The grids at right show true scale difference.

All the pieces were done over mesh that I had drawn or painted. I took my original drawing and reduced it, then transferred the small-scale photocopy onto silk mesh for the petit points. Lynda Healy helped with the transferring and painting on the larger mesh canvases.

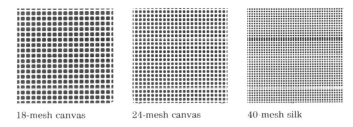

18-mesh canvas   24-mesh canvas   40-mesh silk

These drawings illustrate the gauge of the different types of mesh used in these pieces. The numbers refer to the vertical threads per inch.

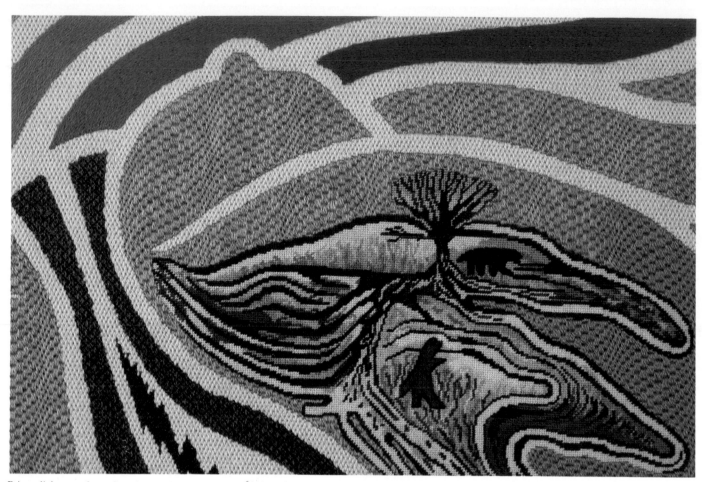

Primordial scene from *Creation of the World NP 1,* ©Judy Chicago, 1984. Needlepoint by Helen Eisenberg, Berkeley, California, and Mickey Lorber, Des Moines, Iowa. Yarn on 18-mesh canvas. Overall size: 34'' x 69''.

Helen Eisenberg, working in California, and Mickey Lorber, stitching in Iowa, collaborated on this rendition of *Creation of the World.* The piece and the large frame it was worked on went back and forth from the West to the Midwest. Helen did the woman's body (in the Chinese jade stitch, with two plies of Paternayan yarn), the background (in the brick stitch with two plies of Laine-Colbert wool), and the rainbow (in the stem stitch with one ply of Paternayan). Mickey Lorber worked the primordial scene (in the continental stitch, with Paternayan yarn).

Working with Mickey Lorber at a review in Chicago.

"I climbed the tree of life with my needle.

"The primordial scene proved to be quite difficult. I had to work it upside down. Every few stitches or new color had me running to the opposite side of the frame to study the visual movement of the scene. I worked and reworked many sections in three strands of Medici yarn and one of Paternayan using the continental and basketweave stitches."

Needleworker Mickey Lorber
Des Moines, Iowa

Working with Helen Eisenberg in California.

"I attacked this canvas as though I were dealing with a great big mother giant. I wanted her body to vibrate emotion. I knew the stitch I would use: the jade stitch, with the pattern repeated every seventy-four stitches. The flesh had to look as though it had been cut out of one consistent pattern. I put in one row of the pattern with perle cotton #8; the pattern climbed to the upper right, and all work was counted from that master row."

Needleworker Helen Eisenberg
Berkeley, California

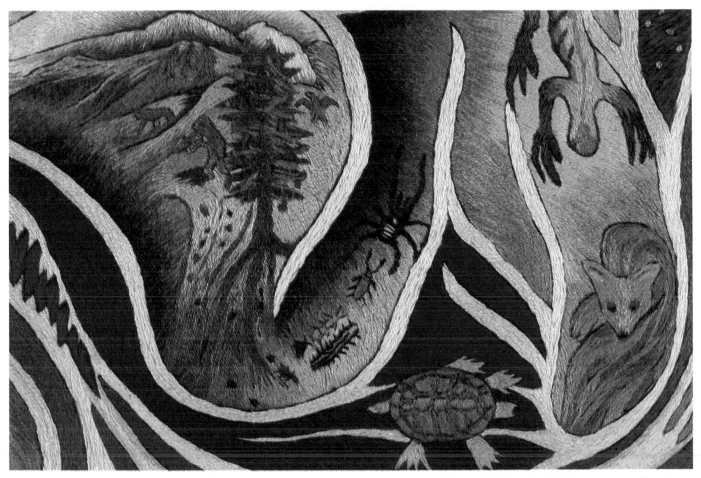

Center of *Creation of the World E 1,* ©Judy Chicago, 1981. Embroidered by Pamella Nesbit, Sebastopol, California. DMC floss on cotton. Overall size: 8¼" x 16".

"I embroidered this piece using single- and double-strand DMC cotton floss. Later I added silk and cotton sewing thread and gold and silver metallics for detail. The stitches I used were the stem (outline) stitch, a modified long and short for shaded fill-ins, the satin stitch, and French knots. The border is a combination of the stem stitch and Igolochkoy (Russian punch-needle). The image itself is so wonderfully organic. It was absolutely joyful to me to form the woman's body as if it were actually growing out of the earth. I took these forms as far as I could with my thread. As I progressed with the piece, Judy just kept pushing me farther and farther along. I wanted to be finished many times before the work was actually complete. As a result of her pushing, I seemed to become more involved with the meaning of the image—the woman as the giver of life, the woman as the earth, as the universe itself, and even as God.

Working with Pamella Nesbit in Benicia.

"Finishing this piece was a form of birth. Judy was my coach, and she pushed right along with me. I began the piece on January 16, 1981, and finished it October 2, 1981—like all births, it took nine months."
Needleworker Pamella Nesbit
Sebastopol, California

Pamella Nesbit worked on this piece over my hand-drawing and Eileen Gerstein's stenciled colored transfer from my original pattern. Because Pam had art-school training, she could render my most delicate line in thread. The difference in scale, technique, and execution between this embroidered scene and the one in the Eisenberg/Lorber needlepoint is another example of the visual range of needlework techniques.

Applying to *The Birth Project:* From Sample to Participation

Tuesday, January 13, 1981

Slowly, out of the chaotic process in which this work began, a form or forms are emerging. I really don't want to over-control things, as a kind of organic development is taking place, with people sorting themselves and their feelings out as they begin to see how much space there is for them. Basically, what seems to be happening is that those people who are really capable of doing supervised, but self-sustained work, are making themselves known through repeated appearances at meetings. New people are arriving, groups are slowly forming, and people are finding their way into the art-making projects as they develop or are making suggestions for spin-off projects that I am encouraging.

We are developing needleworker application procedures based on our experience here. This basically involves giving each applicant a form to fill out and providing her with a sample pattern of one of my designs. She can then stitch this sample in any technique she chooses, in whatever color she wants. Each completed sample will provide me with information about the applicant's needle skills, her visual acuity, and her color abilities. Based on this information, Sally and I should be able to assign or design a project that is consistent with the women's abilities.

At an early needlepoint meeting, I spontaneously began to draw on needlepoint canvas, giving the pieces to interested needleworkers who could then demonstrate sample stitching on them. Even though many of them had brought examples of their work, I wanted to see what they could do with the kinds of forms I typically use. The enthusiastic response to these hand-drawn samples led me to design a pattern that we could send out as part of our application procedure.

At first, the demonstration of needle skills was enough to secure a project for any applicant. But as I began to do more individualized pieces, and as early projects began to falter, we decided that we needed more information about a prospective participant than simply whether or not she could stitch. This led us to develop something we called our "tell-us-more" letter, in which we asked the applicant a series of questions—e.g., whether she really had the time necessary for *Birth Project* work; whether she could sustain extended work of a year or two; and how she felt about (1) working on my images, (2) volunteering her time, and (3) knowing that all finished work would belong to Through the Flower. The reason these questions were so crucial was that we were discovering that many of the women who wrote to us were very unrealistic about anticipating their available time and usually tended to take on too much work. Moreover, if they did do a piece, I wanted their expectations to be clear.

Helen Eisenberg's abilities were very evident in the stitching she did over my hand-drawn image on needlepoint canvas. I could see that she was an accomplished stitcher by the number of different stitches she used and the fact that she was able to be quite accurate in rendering my forms.

Looking at the display of samples at Through the Flower, Benicia, California.

People from all over the country submitted samples. The array of translations of my simple black and white design again demonstrated how one "pattern" can produce extremely diverse results. Not all the people who did needlework samples ended up doing projects.

Frannie Yablonsky submitted a needlepoint sample, along with extensive documentation about her process. Her sample was stitched in DMC floss using the tent, basketweave, and mosaic stitches. The thorough documentation she included testified to her rigor as a needleworker, and the sample demonstrated her skill. Frannie's sample showed me that, in addition to skill and rigor, Frannie had a good sense of color and the ability to blend. The latter was especially important, as blending is a central element of my work.

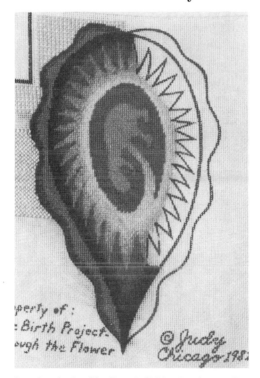

Sample submitted by Frannie Yablonsky, Somerville, New Jersey.

The letter Frannie sent with her sample indicated a lot about how seriously she approached needlework and her interest in participating in *The Birth Project*.

Dear *Birth Project:*

Enclosed is my finished needlepoint sampler and three pages of documentation. Please let me know when my sample will be reviewed. I have also sent some photocopies from a needlepoint book on basic stitches, in case Judy is interested.

I hope I will be chosen to be a participant in this exciting project.

Sincerely,
Frannie Yablonsky

Page Prescott became involved with *The Birth Project* as a stitcher, but ended up as our last research coordinator. She submitted a sample done in an unusual embroidery technique; it combined strong texture with delicate stitching. After she had completed the application procedure, she was assigned one in a series of silk-screened *Creation of the World* multiples. At first the work on the piece looked interesting, but then it became obvious that the stitches she was using did not relate to the form.

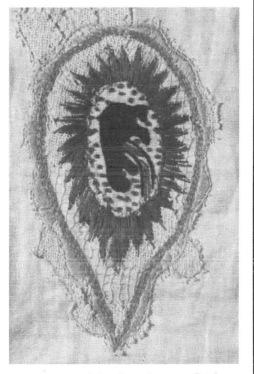

Sample submitted by Page Prescott, Petaluma, California.

One problem experienced by a number of needleworkers was a failure to understand that the thread had to be used to render the form, not to decorate it. Page never was able to adapt her stitching technique to the image. Finally, Sally and I told her we didn't think the piece was going to work. She was very disappointed, but quickly rallied and decided that if she couldn't be in the project one way, she'd try another. She did a very effective job with the research and has also been a big help on this book.

This process will also allow some time to pass, which means that every applicant can have a chance to try out stitching a design of mine and also have time to think about whether she really wants to make the kind of commitment that Birth Project *work requires.*

I designed this pattern to indicate, once it was stitched, whether the applicant could maintain a clear and regular line, do sharp points, and fill solid areas of color.

Often, when a sample arrived that caught my attention, I'd get very excited and rush to the phone. I did just that when I saw Jane Dadey's appliquéd and quilted sample, which was twice the size of the pattern.

"The best part of *The Birth Project* was having Judy call and say, "HI, THIS IS JUDY CHICAGO. I REALLY LIKE YOUR SAMPLER!"
Needleworker Jane Dadey
Marquette, Nebraska

On Friday night we had another open meeting; fifty people came. We have instituted the application procedure, which we hope will sort out the people who just come to "touch the star" from those who really want to work. After the meeting, I must say that I wondered whether all this was such a good idea. I have almost no time to myself; the response is so enormous that I already feel overwhelmed. It would be so much easier (meaning more within my control and less scary) to just go back into my studio alone—but it would be so utterly impossible after all I've been through and all I now know.

An early and very chaotic meeting.

Last night, I woke up panting and crying after having a dream about fleeing from a man who was trying to destroy me. In the dream I challenged him, refused to go with him, and frantically tried to escape from him, running everywhere looking for help—an apt symbol for my desire to run away after the beating I took from male art critics about **The Dinner Party.**

Susan Fisher and Eugenie Taber, from Kalamazoo, Michigan, submitted a unique sample. The two stitchers used four techniques in one sample, thus demonstrating that, between them, they had an impressive range of skills. The best part was that they got the different sections to line up in the middle—no mean feat.

Detail of sample submitted by Susan Fisher and Eugenie Taber, combining several types of embroidery and needlepoint.

Eugenie Taber (left) and Susan Fisher (right) with the embroideries they worked on after they had successfully completed our application procedures.

"I make no claims to having learned anything about needlework at anyone's knee. I hated it when I was a kid, perhaps out of the common experience of scorning 'girl stuff'. I sewed and mended, but enjoying embroidery only came as a result of knowing that my work was accepted and the results appreciated." Needleworker Susan Fisher, Kalamazoo, Michigan.

"I'll leave the poetry to the poets and simply say that I consider the birth process to be one of the most normal and natural things in a woman's life, and that's why I wanted to be involved in this project." Needleworker Eugenie Taber, Kalamazoo, Michigan

One of the more interesting techniques demonstrated in a sample was that of filet crochet—usually associated with doilies, tablecloths, and curtains. I was wild to try to design for this technique, which was rarely if ever used in "art," as I had always loved and felt badly about the doilies casually heaped in piles in every antique shop I'd ever visited.

Detail of sample executed in filet crochet, submitted by Diane Duncan Rasmussen.

Candis Duncan Pomykala and Diane Duncan Rasmussen, one hour before Diane's wedding. During the time they were involved in the project, both sisters got married.

"Candi, my sister, had already applied to and been accepted to work on *The Birth Project;* working on the project has helped us to share an activity, support each other's work, and not compete. When I was six years old, I began being trained in hand-sewing. The summer I was eight, our neighbor gave me lessons in crochet. I learned to make doilies of fine thread, using tiny steel hooks. Later, I learned to knit, embroider, needlepoint, macramé, tat lace, embroider over drawn threadwork, sew, spin my own threads, and weave fabric. But I like crochet the best." Needleworker Diane Duncan Rasmussen, Tinley Park, Illinois

JULIET MYERS

One day we received an unusually beautiful embroidery sample from a woman in Canada, Ann Gibson. I was pleased at the prospect of extending participation across the border and based upon her sample, I developed a piece for Ann to embroider. I wanted her to approach it as if it were a drawing—laying the threads on the fabric as one would lay the strokes of a colored pencil on paper.

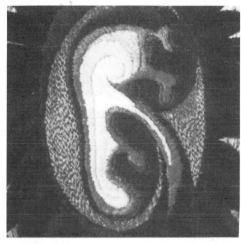

Detail of sample executed in embroidery by Ann Gibson. The quality of Ann's stitching and the beauty of her blending were perfect for my images.

Ann Gibson and I at review.

"My background in needlework is virtually nil, though I have always been attracted to it and have a small collection of fairly nice pieces, gleaned mostly from grandmothers and aunts and elderly friends whose own progeny weren't much interested. I knitted a lot at one time and have always sewn. As for embroidery, I have completed two pieces: the first, about fifteen years ago, was a crewel kit someone gave me. A couple of years ago I designed a piece based on a drawing of mine, but I never completed the piece. The second completed work was my sample for *The Birth Project,* and my third was *Thou Art the Mother Womb."* Needleworker Ann Gibson, Vancouver, Canada

I did a colored-pencil drawing and an outline painting on black silk to be embroidered by Ann, using the drawing as a guide. On the drawing, I included color notes and suggestions on how to lay the thread in sequence to achieve the same kind of blending as in my drawing. However, I was not simply interested in a "painting in thread," but rather in a transformation of the image through the sheen and surface of floss on fabric.

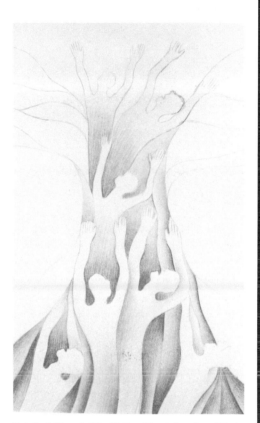

Detail of *Thou Art the Mother Womb* drawing, ©Judy Chicago, 1982. Colored pencil on vellum. Overall size: 20" x 20".

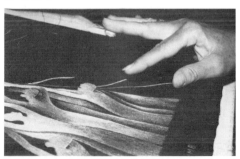

Ann Gibson stitching.

"I believe that we're all born 'artists,' with an acute awareness of and sense of the interconnectedness of everything. We are given wonder; it's free; we begin with it. Our responsibility is to hang on to it as best we can and nurture it in others."

Ann Gibson

I woke up this morning feeling trapped and as if I'd started something I'll be sorry about. This is stupid, I know. I have records of whom I've given work to; I have signed agreements—and I'm still getting freaked out because I'm afraid that these women won't come through, that they'll let me down. And that's why I feel trapped—because I already feel let down by the men, fundamentally let down by the way they've treated me throughout my career and, most recently, in relation to The Dinner Party. *I feel punished, shut out of the art system, and made to feel ashamed of what I've created. And so I've turned full-face to women, but I'm filled with fear and anxiety and doubt. It is my own lack of trust of women that I am confronting and my own dislike of women that I am encountering.*

It's quite a different thing to give out simple black and white patterns than to give out hand-painted fabrics and paintings and drawings that took me days and weeks of work. One solution is not to go so fast—to wait and see what will happen. But the project is moving at its own rate; I can move at a fast pace and still not keep up. But I'm getting totally freaked out by giving away my work to people I don't know in the hope that they will stitch it, quilt it, needlepoint it in a way that I like.

The image embroidered by Ann Gibson was derived, in part, from my investigation of creation myths combined with my sense of both Woman and the Earth as the begetter of life. A Babylonian myth I quoted earlier provided the title of the piece:

Thou art the mother-womb, The one who creates mankind. (2)

Ann Gibson's description of the image seems perfect:

"Judy's image seems based on a volcano in the middle of a wonderful, vital eruption. The earth is opening up and, with great spasms, delivering life. The flames are figures leaping out of the mysterious center and reaching into the void. It is Earth, the Mother, giving birth.

"I started out doing a long and short satin stitch, but I ended up combining that with a split stitch in a very unorthodox manner. I embroidered like a painter, mixing threads as if I were mixing color on a canvas, laying one thread beside another so that, to the eye, they appear blended. The outline is done in chain stitch using one to three rows of chain, depending upon the width of Judy's painted line." Ann Gibson

Thou Art the Mother Womb, ©Judy Chicago, 1984. Embroidered by Ann Gibson, Vancouver, Canada. DMC floss and silk thread on silk, 20'' x 20''.

Detail from *Thou Art the Mother Womb.*

58

Captured by the Species Burden E 2, ©Judy Chicago, 1984. Embroidered by Susan Fisher, Kalamazoo, Michigan. DMC floss on silk, 18'' x 24''.

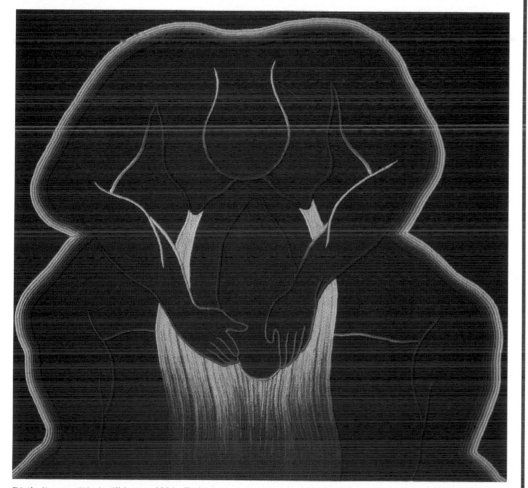

Birth Power, ©Judy Chicago, 1984. Embroidered by Sandie Abel, Madison, Wisconsin. DMC floss on silk, 15'' x 15''

These two pieces, done on black silk, deal with both women's power and women's containment. *Captured by the Species Burden,* embroidered by Susan Fisher, depicts a female figure being sapped by the umbilical cords which bind her to her children, draining nourishment from her very being. *Birth Power,* embroidered by Sandie Abel, presents a woman whose reproductive power is both fiery and self-absorbing. The stitcher describes it:

"Birth Power's colors are those of intense heat, searing fire. Yet the feeling it conveys is not one of anguish. The aura surrounding the figure seems to radiate the pain away from it, transforming the heat from pain into power. And the fire beneath the figure, flowing from the breasts, is a steady, vigorous heat the heat of a furnace or forge.'' Needleworker Sandie Abel, Madison, Wisconsin

Working from my drawings, both Susan Fisher and Sandie Abel embroidered these pieces with DMC floss. In *Captured by the Species Burden E 2,* Susan Fisher blended the thread colors so that the tones change almost imperceptibly. Sandie Abel used a very different blending method for the flames in *Birth Power.* The colors seem to leap up like flames themselves, creating the sense of fire.

Fisher chose the long and short stitch for the blending, a woven stitch between the hairs, and the couching stitch for the outline. Abel used the split stitch for the flames and the padded satin stitch for the outline, which was first sewn in split stitch and then overlaid with the satin stitch.

Tuesday, January 27, 1981

On Sunday, Mary Ross and I went to Chico, California, to meet with a group that wanted to do a large quilt project. Several women had come down here in November to plan it with me. They went back and organized a group and scheduled this meeting, but made no plans about what would happen there. Somehow, I guess, they thought I would arrive and wave my magic wand; it was very depressing.

We were both bummed out by the low energy level of the group, but we realized that the struggle in women's groups in small towns is what this is all about—and that is where we have been going, to small towns, needlework shops, and women's groups. I now have one project going in a women's studies class, and we're presenting The Birth Project *at a needlepoint shop this week. I'm going to the places where women gather and offering projects so that women can form groups in places where there is no support for them and no access to the existing women's support network. The image-making provides a focus and a basis for getting together and into the feminist process. This process begins as soon as the women begin to work on my images, whether individually or in a group. They are forced to confront their own birth experiences, their ideas about art and about women. Whether real art can come out of this is yet to be determined.*

In November 1980 I held a large organizational meeting for people interested in *The Birth Project*. Over one hundred people arrived, and the day was sheer chaos. Among the group were two or three women from Chico. One of these women told me that there were more than fifty people interested in participating in and around the Chico area. In response to this, I designed a project which involved a large, group quilt and a number of smaller, border quilts which could be done by individuals who lived too far from Chico to work as members of the group.

The group of fity people turned out to be a small group of eight or ten, many of whom still weren't sure they really could "give time." I'll never understand how women think things get done; they somehow must imagine that they can go from "wanting" to "having done" without actually ever sitting down to the sometimes boring, usually repetitive tasks involved in "doing."

I changed the project to accommodate the smaller group, giving them an image I had sprayed and Sally had prepared for quilting. I thought it wouldn't be too much work for them. But I knew that there would never be twenty-four border quilts, and I wondered whether there would ever really be a finished group project.

(Left to right) Christina Nichols, me, Lynn Schmidt, Gloria Van Lydegraf, Kom Dixon, and Alicia Erpino. Working with some of the women from Chico on the large quilt and the small embroideries that were originally intended as border pieces.

I hand-drew the spiral onto the sprayed fallopian tube for the stitching on this part of the "Chico Quilt," which combined my sprayed painting with quilting and embroidery.

Installation view of the "Chico Quilt" project, ©Judy Chicago, 1983. Executed by Paula Busch, Chrissie Clapp, Kom Dixon, Alicia Erpino, Roberta Fountain, Carol Hill, Benita Humble, Jo Murphy, Christina Nichols, S. Lynn Schmidt, and Gloria Van Lydegraf. A multi-media installation. Overall size: 45' long.

Eventually, I decided to combine the group quilt and the four embroideries originally intended as border pieces in an installation that chronicled the evolution of this project.

The building that housed Through the Flower Corporation and provided a home for *The Birth Project* (a project of Through the Flower).

In addition to studio space, production facilities, a darkroom, and an office, Through the Flower offered a changing exhibition program of *Birth Project* art, as well as lectures and events, during 1982 and 1983.

With Marleen Deane, who supervised the renovation of the entire 11,000-square-foot Through the Flower building, now the owner of Benicia's finest restaurant, First Street Foods.

I've decided that I'll need a building by the end of the year for the office, storage space, and a small production facility where patterns can be made and pieces can be prepared for exhibition. Benicia, California, will be the base for The Birth Project, and we'll see when we go to Houston whether establishing regional centers will work or not. The shape of this project is emerging ever more clearly and, with it, the shape of my life.

I realize that I'm addressing the whole relationship of art and community, artists and society, in this work; I'm convinced that women stand no chance to really participate in culture unless the nature of culture changes and the definition of art and what constitutes being an artist changes along with it. I feel totally apart from the art world; there are not many people in that world who can understand my work. They're so embedded in that system and see no alternative. So I've been forced to find alternatives, since that system has been closed to me.

I'm absorbed and fascinated by the work, and I'm handling the fact that I need so many people on so many levels. I can be so hard on everyone involved with me and so hard on myself.

Projects That Didn't Work

Thursday, January 29, 1981

We went to a needlepoint shop last night and presented the project; it was a big flop. I guess we'd better continue the way we're going—responding to letters and requests. That way, people who are already interested and somewhat knowledgeable about my work come to us, rather than our trying to solicit volunteers.

Thursday, February 5

I produced all this work this week, and again I feel ambivalent about it. I feel anxious and full of doubts. Perhaps its just a result of working in this new way, opening up my life and my work to other women so completely, having to trust them with what is most fundamental to my existence. Do I trust women? At what level? With my person? With my art? With my life and ideas? I don't know. Right now, things have sort of slowed down. I don't know whether that's because starting this application procedure has turned people off, or because people are busy working on their samples, or because no new articles have come out to generate a new round of interest. Whatever, things are slow, and I'm doing all this work that's intended to be completed by other people, and I feel anxious and somewhat disconnected. So I'm going straight to the studio this morning; I hope that will help. I think I need to take a break, ease up, not deprive myself the way I do—I never allow myself to rest and instead just push, push, push.

During the first year of *The Birth Project* I began to encounter the problem of women starting pieces and not completing them. Since I am a person who rarely says I'll do something unless I mean it (except for social engagements, which I too frequently break), I found this *very* difficult to deal with. I particularly didn't understand it professionally, as one of the basic tenets of professionalism is completing any task one undertakes.

But, of course, I was working primarily with people who were not professionals. Most of the needleworkers stitched in their idle hours, fitting their work in and around the demands of their lives. I do the opposite—squeezing my personal life and needs into the little crevices left over in my workdays. My expectations for a time commitment to the project were based on my own lifestyle. It was a long time before my expectations began to accommodate the reality of most women's lives.

The woman who started this work had a baby shortly after she started working with me. While she was pregnant, she kept assuring me that she would have "plenty of time to stitch," particularly after she quit work in the latter months of her pregnancy. But she did not count on being sick or tired or overcome by inertia as the months drew on. Nor did she plan on the endless hours that a newborn child requires—or the sleepless nights—or the exhaustion at the end of every day. But she tried. She picked up her needle and stitched a little here, a little there, whenever she had a few odd minutes and wasn't too tired or when the baby didn't wake up early from her nap. The trouble was that this interrupted stitching caused her to forget where she had worked the previous time she had picked up her needle and thread. But when she came for a review and valiantly protested that she didn't want to give up the piece (as she tried to hold back her tears), I could see how her fragmented life was causing the rhythm of her stitching to be broken—and consistent rhythm is what produces part of the beauty of an embroidered surface. Still, she kept insisting that she would be able to complete the work, and I was unable to see early enough that this just wasn't true. So I let her keep the piece, even though the stitching was going too slowly.

Finally, six months after the birth of her first child, she came to a review and gave back the work. She said she felt that the baby had destroyed both her time and her sense of individuality and that she felt completely overwhelmed. Moreover, she had become pregnant again and knew that a second baby would end any possibility of extra time. Reluctantly, she handed me back the embroidery, and I wept at the loss to her and to me.

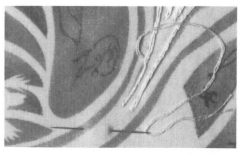

Detail of *Creation of the World* (unfinished), ©Judy Chicago, 1982. Silk-screen, hand drawing and embroidery on wool. Overall size: 14½'' x 23¼''.

We left the needle where the stitcher had placed it when she finally realized that she was not going to be able to complete the work.

Because this happened frequently—women misassessing their capabilities and their lives—I decided to present this unfinished work as a symbol for women's uncompleted lives. This image celebrates woman's fecundity and her power to bring forth new life. How ironic that this very power often causes us to lose control of our own lives.

Another project that blew apart was one which Sally and I were very attached to. A group of women from Oklahoma applied to the project, first submitting a group sample and, later, a series of samples that demonstrated an impressive range of textile skills. We met some of the group members at a review in Houston. They struck us both as an enthusiastic, energetic, and talented bunch of women.

I decided to design a large project, a Goddess Garment, that would challenge the skills of this group. Sally and I did a full-scale mock-up and sent it to them, requesting that they do translation samples demonstrating how they would execute each section of the piece. Some time later, I traveled to Oklahoma to see them. I arrived to find the group without a place to work—the only space big enough to set up the 12-foot piece was the rectory of the church ministered by one of the women's husbands, an amusing, if somewhat discouraging, situation. Moreover, when I looked at the small mock-up they had done to show me their ideas, I was absolutely flabbergasted. The imagination in their sample had been replaced by a cautious, uninteresting interpretation of what Sally and I had already produced. I was very disappointed and told them so. Unfortunately, at that time I really had no idea what a shattering effect my criticism often had on the needleworkers. I am a professional artist, and accepting criticism is something I learned to do long ago.

The project never really got off the ground after that, though the group tried and so did I. They made sample after sample, but too often the ideas in the sample couldn't be translated into reality. The final outcome was unfortunate for everyone, particularly so because I liked these women so much.

It finally became evident to both Sally and me that, after a year and a half with no tangible results, the piece was just not going to be realized. We "ended" it—but that was not the end. The group decided they would keep the piece, even though the large mock-up had been made by Sally and me and the group's contribution was limited to two small mock-ups and a series of samples. By this time, having been through all this before, I was not sympathetic, and our lawyer began legal proceedings immediately. Ultimately, a series of telephone conversations between me and several of the group members caused them to realize that they had to send back the work. They did, but not without it leaving a bad taste in everyone's mouth.

This group never succeeded in translating this large mock-up for a Goddess Garment, which Sally Babson and I had put together specifically for the skills demonstrated by the group in their samples.

Friday, March 13

This has definitely been a difficult week for me. There were a number of emotional scenes during the reviews. On Saturday, a woman brought up the issue of the change in the contracts. Last September, when I started The Birth Project, *I offered people a contract which said that the needleworker(s) and I would jointly own the work and split any profit there would be if the works were sold; that was when I saw this work as private work to be shown in galleries and museums. Anyway, when the response to* The Birth Project *turned out to be so large and wide-reaching, I changed everything and put the whole* Birth Project *into* Through the Flower, *primarily in order to be eligible for grants and donations. That of course changed the whole issue of profit, as* Through the Flower *will own all the finished works and, as a nonprofit organization, cannot legally give people—the needleworkers or me—profits from the sale of the work (if there ever are any). I explained all this very carefully during the January reviews, and everyone assured me that they weren't involved in* The Birth Project *for money. Well, lo and behold, this woman had suddenly had a change of heart; she brought the whole thing up, and we had a stormy session. Although I empathized with her, I never would have let an emotional scene like that take place in the middle of the reviews, except that I felt terrific pressure because of the presence of a Canadian journalist.*

The whole situation at the review became even more complicated because of another woman who had also started work in September. She's working on an extraordinary white-work version of Birth on handkerchief linen.

Wanda is an expert needlewoman, but she has no sense of how to use her skills for anything but decorative purposes. Working with me is opening up a way of imbuing her techniques with meaning, and her piece is quite breathtaking, even at this early stage of development. At the last review, we projected that a certain amount of work would be done by this time, and it wasn't. But I never really had a chance to notice that because of the scene the first woman started. Suddenly, Wanda stated that she had been so upset by the change in contract in January (which she had never mentioned before) that she had been unable to work. I was so threatened by the possibility that she wouldn't complete the work that I didn't stop to think that I had already offered her a special deal—that we could complete the work based on the original contract or that I would trade her a painting of mine for her embroidery work. What I now realize was that the whole scene was probably a cover-up for her not having done the work she had promised. Well, there were lots of tears and confusion, but no real confrontation about her not having completed her work. Wanda left seemingly placated and swearing she'd go back to stitching immediately. I hope so.

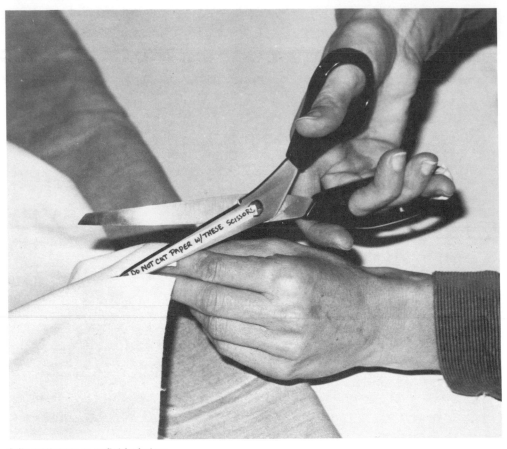

Sally cutting up an unfinished piece.

Yet another project that did not work out ended up in an unpleasant mediation procedure which Wanda, the needleworker, insisted upon. Our lawyer, Iris Mitgang, and Sally were there, along with Wanda's lawyer, the mediator, and me. The whole thing lasted two hours; then Sally cut up the piece with the scissors that say, "Do not use these on paper." Wanda's resistance finally capsized in the face of the fact that there was no resolution other than destroying the piece. She suggested it herself, when the mediator asked her to tell the story of what had happened. When asked what she thought the options were, she suggested, among others destroying the piece. She meant it as a threat, I think.

When I told my version of the story, and the mediator asked me what I wanted to do, I said "Destroy the piece." About ten minutes after I proposed destroying the piece, it dawned on me that the mediation was essentially over, for we had both agreed that destroying the piece was an option we both could accept, although I don't think Wanda ever thought that I would do that.

Wanda left in a huff; Sally cut up the piece; and the mediator wrapped it up in a cloth and carried it, like an aborted fetus, to the garbage can. In a moment of rage, I scrawled "Abortion" across the top of Wanda's folder. Unfortunately, over the course of the project, about one-quarter of the work I began was never completed. Usually the unfinished projects blew up, but sometimes Sally and I ended them because the stitching was not working or the pace was too slow.

Detail of *Creation of the World Quilt* (project terminated).

After I had spray-painted this piece, Sally basted a beautiful piece of linen over my painting. The linen was then cut through to expose the painting, and I drew a series of forms on the painted surface to be embroidered. For a while the piece looked wonderful, but it moved along at such a snail's pace that it simply lost the energy that is so essential for art to feel vital. So we terminated it.

Detail of *Birth Tear NP 1* (project terminated).

In this piece, the problem was not the stitcher's fault but ours. After Lynda Healy, who had painted needlepoint canvases with me, left the project, I had no more needlepoint canvases to give out, but I had many requests. Then a woman from the Midwest applied who painted canvases commercially and wanted to try painting some from my designs. I said OK, and in fact, gave one that she had done to Jan Leone, a fine stitcher from Florida. But as the piece progressed, it just didn't look right, primarily because I hadn't painted it, and it looked more like a needlepoint kit than a work of art. Somewhat reluctantly, Sally and I ended the project.

Are There Any Men Involved?

I am on the plane back after spending the week in Houston. Last night we held an open meeting, and 125-150 people showed up, including one male needleworker. People are always asking me "Are there any men involved?"—as if their presence were needed to validate the project. I am, however, continually disappointed that more men don't volunteer, so I was happy to see this guy.

Over the years in which I've been involved with participatory art-making projects, I've thought a lot about the fact that it's so much more usual and acceptable for women to volunteer for men's activities than for men to voluntarily work in an environment where women predominate. After all, women always volunteer their time to museums that show primarily men's art, musical organizations that present only men's music, churches that worship a male god, and hospitals where male physicians are the authorities and the female nurses are oppressed. And even though I tend to provide a more humanized and egalitarian environment and process for people, I'm often viewed as "difficult" or "intimidating," whereas men who run their enterprises in vastly more authoritarian ways are not criticized like I am. But I guess the double standard dies hard.

I asked several of the husbands of the needleworkers to share their feelings about the project, as I felt it might answer the frequently asked question, "What do men think of all this?" Only one—Bud Nesbit, husband of Pamella, who executed six embroideries over the four years of her involvement in *The Birth Project*—replied.

"What has impressed me most about *The Birth Project* is the emotional investment so many of the participants have been willing to make. This is not something I would be likely to do, and I believe that, in general, it would not be fundamental to the functioning of a group of men. In my dealings with the project staff and stitchers, I have seen (and heard about) confrontations in which intimidation (at having to reevaluate something as integral as self-esteem), frustration (at having to work under someone as difficult and demanding as Judy Chicago), and satisfaction (at keeping a commitment or making a deadline) were all experienced and shared openly within the group. I can't say whether the project could have succeeded in any other way, but the longer I knew the people involved in it, the more impressed I became.

"Because Pam's art career has always been something we've built into our life together, the demands of the project have not had a significant impact on our relationship. The long hours spent working on each piece, the emotional highs and lows, the weekends lost to reviews, and the Fridays spent in Benicia while I took care of our son while she stitched did not introduce any new strain. Initially, my only concern was that Pam would be unpaid, working on a piece designed by another artist. Later, when it became clear that Judy had structured the project to give appropriate credit to the stitchers, and as I came to appreciate the education Pam was receiving by being a part of the project (both technically and in terms of her perception of art), I supported her participation completely (as she had supported me through graduate school). There was never a time when either of us felt her commitment was a mistake.

"I have been to at least four *Birth Project* openings, and the pieces I have seen there have invariably impressed me, in terms of both the images and the technical skill. However, I am aware of many emotional reactions by women viewing the art and I am surprised at my own lack of such a reaction. While I have never thought of myself as having a 'male viewpoint' about anything, this 'nonreaction' may indeed be the result of my seeing the project through a man's eyes. Whether this is actually the reason, or it is the result of an undeveloped artistic sense or my uncertainty as to the basic premise of feminist art, is something I have not yet decided."

Bud Nesbit
Sebastopol, California

Bud Nesbit with his wife, Pamella, and their son, Christopher.

Over the years, there have been a number of men involved in *The Birth Project,* some more intensely than others. There have also been men who supported the project through contributions of money, labor, materials, and expertise. In addition to Stephen Hamilton, our exhibition designer, and Michael Cronan (who established the graphic format for our exhibitions), other men have participated. Jon McNally was our first and only photographer during the early years of the project. Jon helped set up our darkroom, did all the early photographs of both the process and the art, and began the documentary photo program that chronicled the ever-expanding *Birth Project* network.

Jon McNally, who was the *Birth Project* photographer from 1980 to 1982.

Lynn Francom, who did all the electrical work at the building and the lighting for our exhibitions.

"I've been involved on a limited basis doing odd jobs, paid and unpaid, depending on my need for money at the moment. My favorite job has been lighting each exhibition of completed works. Being in the gallery by myself, soaking up all the beauty around me, has kept me involved. The art is so beautiful, so inspiring, and has created such indescribable feelings for me."

Lynn Francom
Benicia, California

Scott Lewis, who worked as our curator for over a year.

"One day late in my senior year, I went to a showing of Johanna Demetrakas' film *Right Out of History: The Making of Judy Chicago's The Dinner Party*. Afterward there was a lecture by the needlework supervisor, Susan Hill. I saw something in that film that I couldn't believe: strong women and nonsexist men working together to make something meaningful and beautiful. I had a feeling of great joy.

"Susan Hill told me that it was still possible to become part of the Benicia community. She encouraged me to go to Cleveland, Ohio, where *The Dinner Party* was opening, and meet Judy. I read Judy's autobiography, *Through the Flower*, in two sittings and borrowed a car to drive to Cleveland from my school in southern Ohio. After getting lost and driving around Cleveland like a maniac, I finally arrived at the house where the meeting was to take place. There I met Judy Chicago. I immediately knew that I wanted this woman to be my teacher and mentor. She agreed to my request to come to Benicia for two months. I went and stayed for a year, working many fifty- to sixty-hour weeks for *The Birth Project*.

"Working with dedicated people in Through the Flower taught me many valuable lessons, but one thing stands out for me. I learned that I can affect this world by sharing my values and concerns. This is one of the greatest powers a human being can possess.

"As far as my being male, here's how I view that. I have a penis just like I have a liver and a small intestine. I don't allow my penis to determine my life or the work I do, just as I won't let my small intestine control me. I believe that men, like women, are locked into roles and conditioning. I believe that the patriarchy enslaves men as it does women, although not to the same extent. My hope is that in helping to free my sisters I will eventually be able to help free my brothers."

Scott Lewis
New York, New York

One man's response to *Birth Project* work was expressed in a review of our first exhibition in Houston:

Men's refusal to acknowledge and explore the mysterious process of giving birth as the wonder it is has denied women the chance to celebrate this core female experience as a worthwhile and fulfilling achievement. Only in the past twenty years have there been strides made in the deplorable conditions under which most women have been forced to give birth. Obviously men will never experience the process of giving birth, but Chicago's work opens up the possibility for men to understand the different components of birth from soul-rending pain to the transcendent state of joy. As our knowledge and understanding grow, so will our respect and admiration of women.

—Geoffrey Westergaard (14)

At one of our pot-lucks in Houston, we decided to include the spouses or partners of the needleworkers—"significant others" is what we called them. It really changed the quality of the evening to have the men there. It probably demystified a lot of our process for the men, but afterward all the women agreed that once was enough. Instead of the kind of intense discussions we usually had, the evening was more like a social event. Nonetheless, everyone felt glad that we had done it, as it satisfied a lot of curiosity about the project and about me.

"After dinner, Judy had us sit in a large circle. I'll never forget that night because I felt close to everyone there and proud to be a part of the project. I think all our guests began to realize why we wanted to work with Judy. Her dynamic organizational abilities were evidenced in the way she directed the flow of discussion and drew people out. While we were discussing the developing exhibition program and how we would handle possible critical rejection of the art, I said something to the effect that people might be repelled by the starkness of the images. 'Judy,' says I, 'your images are so stark and powerful; you don't pussyfoot around or beat around the bush.' Everyone, including Judy, burst out laughing. I *never* blush, but I turned ten shades of deep pink. I certainly was wearing my Freudian slip that night."

Needleworker Libby Vincent
Houston, Texas

Expanding *The Birth Project*

Wednesday, March 18, 1981

The time is just going by so fast, it's incredible. It seems like a constant struggle lately to make space for myself. I am very tired emotionally. It takes a lot of energy to generate creatively, and I just don't have it now. I'm working in the studio, but I feel like I'm not able to go real deep and come up, like a deep sea diver, with the real treasure—too much talking; too many meetings, discussions, and plans; not enough endless quiet. But what can I do? Run away to a desert island? One thing that is helping is that, finally, samples are arriving, and some of them have been executed in interesting and unusual needlework techniques. This gives me the opportunity to actually conceive of work in relation to the variety of techniques people demonstrate instead of just handing out work that Sally and I have preconceived. It also means that I can expand the number of techniques used in the project.

Mary Ross Taylor suggested that I present *The Birth Project* in Houston, which I did at a slide lecture early in 1981. We already had some slides of the early work, and I showed these and discussed my ideas for extending the participatory nature of the project to people around the country. When I was finished, I asked how many people would be interested in working with me; about 150 hands went up. I felt simultaneously overwhelmed and scared. How could I ever accommodate so many people's wishes? At that time, I didn't realize that there would be quite a large gap between those who "wanted to" and those who actually "did." Eventually, ten projects were completed over the course of three years.

Presenting *The Birth Project* to an interested audience in Houston, Texas.

At our Houston space: Pat Morton, the *Birth Project* administrator there, and Mary Ross Taylor, who organized the Houston wing of *The Birth Project*.

"When I went to Judy's publication party in the fall of 1980 and saw Sally Babson quilting the *Creation of the World*, I thought it would be great to sponsor *The Birth Project* in Houston. And knowing that other cities that had brought in *The Dinner Party* had nonprofit groups like our TACO, I thought those groups would be natural sponsors for *Birth Project* work in their cities—but that didn't take place.

"Judy gave a slide talk in Houston, and the room was packed. I thought I would know a lot of people, but I recognized few faces among the diverse crowd. The fact that most of the people there were not among my own circle of friends indicated that there was even more interest than I had anticipated. I felt nervous at the thought of organizing all these strangers and wished that more of the familiar *Dinner Party* network were there.

"The project outgrew us at every step. We took calls and answered letters, then responded as quickly as we could. We were inventing the procedures for this developing creative network and using them at the same time; sometimes that got very hectic and awkward. I flew back and forth helping to organize in California, then taking plans to Texas. Out of hundreds of inquiries, Houston ended up with some seventy-five participants, stitching, researching, and helping with communications. I actually underestimated the interest, not only in Texas but around the country. We didn't have the resources to respond to all the people who wanted to get involved. It occupied all our energies to support the stitchers with newsletters, a directory, and regular contact. If we'd been able to pay a staff, we could have made an even greater impact on Houston as well as other cities. But even with limited resources, the project grew.

"My goal in Houston now is to find permanent sites for some of the art from *The Birth Project*. The art will be an endless resource and a legacy of the energy that Houston put into the work."

Mary Ross Taylor

68

SOUTHWEST STITCHERS SHOW THEIR STUFF

BIANCA INDELICATO

Pat Morton in front of the wall of samples submitted by Texas needleworkers and the DMC thread charts I used for reviews in the Houston space.

Sally prepared some of the pieces I'd been painting, and the doubts I had about the forms I'm using disappeared. The minute my sprayed images were batted and backed and prepared for quilting and embroidery, they began to be transformed, and I knew that they were conceived properly. The softening that took place, even before any needlework actually began, was perfect. So, conceptually, I think I'm on the right track. The next thing is the labor force—have I assessed it properly? Are there enough women out there capable of self-motivation to be able to produce enough work over the next three years to have an impact? Unless there is enough work of a high enough quality to travel all over and have a large effect, this won't work. And there have to be enough women who can carry through without my constant presence; that is a real unknown right now.

Shortly after beginning to investigate the subject of birth, I decided that I'd like to develop an archive which could be used both as a source for my image-making and as educational material in relationship to the exhibition of *Birth Project* works. We were receiving numerous letters from people with research skills who were interested in helping. We began by assembling material on creation myths throughout the world, and then we branched out to investigate a range of subjects related to the birth experience.

In Benicia, the research was coordinated first by Beth Rose and later by Page Prescott. In Houston, where some of the most intriguing material was unearthed, Patt Hull coordinated a group that included the noted bibliographer Lorene Pouncey. She introduced me to an extraordinary book entitled *Iconographia Gyniatrica* (15), a pictorial history of gynecology, which stimulated many ideas for images.

MARY MARGARET HANSEN

Lorene Pouncey and I discuss research.

"I liked the independence I felt doing research, finding amazing, interesting items about women, birth, various cultures. It was rewarding, not only finding the information, but knowing that it was going to be used by Judy in creating the images and as a source of information for the documentation. The researchers all cranked out a lot of copy, some profound, some horribly sad, and much that was truly beautiful."

Houston Research Coordinator
The Birth Project
Patt Hull
Houston, Texas

69

Unusual Techniques: Macramé and Smocking

Tuesday, March 30, 1981

I have been working steadily in the studio, and the work is going well. Soon there will be between forty and fifty projects under way, which is pretty incredible considering that I started only last July. However, in one sense I started a long time before that, as the labor force that is now coming forward grows out of all the years I've been making images that affirm women's lives.

There has been another round of articles and therefore a whole new round of letters of inquiry—about ten letters a day now, all from people who want to work. More samples arrive daily; some of them are just fabulous. I am beginning to design specifically for the samples and the techniques they embody, and it is very interesting. One sample came that was done in a technique I could not identify—it turned out to be macramé.

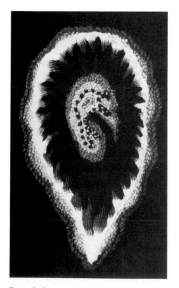

Sample in macramé submitted by Pat Rudy-Baese, Milwaukee, Wisconsin.

For me, one of the most intriguing aspects of needlework is its capacity to render form in a highly visual way. That is why I adore Renaissance tapestry, which is flat and pictorial, and dislike most contemporary weaving, which is generally sculptural rather than pictorial in nature. I love the fact that thread can render form like the sharpest pencil or smallest brush, and I enjoyed the challenge of demonstrating that fabric doesn't *have* to sag, that quilting can be as rigorous as geometric painting, and that techniques like filet crochet have a visual potential way beyond their customary uses.

When Pat Rudy-Baese submitted a macramé sample, I did not at first recognize the technique. Once I realized that this was, in fact, macramé, I was really intrigued and wondered whether I could design an image that was appropriate to what Pat had showed me macramé could do. I did a full-scale black and white pattern, transferred it to hymo, color-coded it, chose among the yarn samples Pat did, and then sent the piece to her. I must admit that my unfamiliarity with macramé often made it difficult for me to understand many of Pat's mail-in questions, but we did manage to communicate despite her lack of art background and my ignorance of macramé. The main problem we encountered was in the color changes inside the forms. There was no way, Pat insisted, that the color could be blended and we almost came to blows about the "unacceptable" stripes in the body. Finally another midwest stitcher, Mary Ann Hickey, taught Pat how to blend out the stripes by embroidering over the macramé—an untraditional though essential solution.

I call this piece *Birth Tear/Tear* (pronounced "tare/teer") because it deals with both the tearing of the vagina that often occurs during childbirth and the fact that the children, who are being both born and nurtured, are tearing at their mother, which naturally makes her weep. Pat had a strong sense of the meaning of the image from the first time she saw it.

At Pat Rudy-Baese's house in Milwaukee, Wisconsin.

"After Judy visited my house for a review, I spent three days removing areas of knots that didn't look good. The feared unmentionable happened—I made a hole in the backing. I left it alone until the disappointment passed, proud of myself for not deciding I was a failure because of it. It wasn't carelessness, it was too much stress on the horizontal threads of the backing material. I resisted an impulse to call Sally Babson and ask advice—to ask, in effect, to be rescued. Where's my self-reliance? Besides, what can she do? She's in California, and the hole is in Milwaukee." Pat Rudy-Baese

Detail of macramé sample by Pat Rudy-Baese.

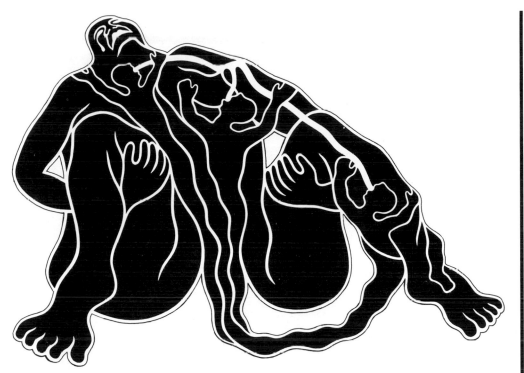

My original full-scale pattern for *Birth Tear/Tear.* Ink on paper, 30'' x 39''.

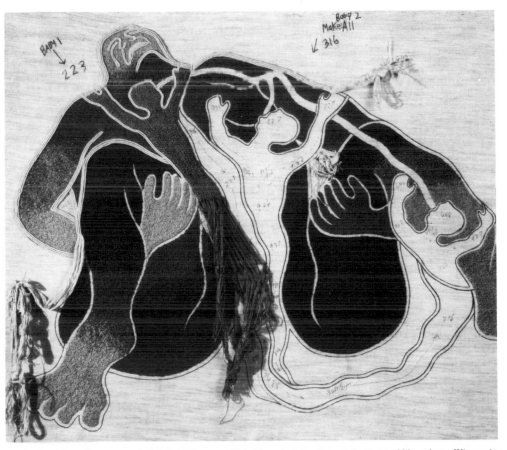

Birth Tear/Tear (in progress), ©Judy Chicago, 1984. Executed by Pat Rudy-Baese, Milwaukee, Wisconsin. Macramé, 32'' x 37''.

Wednesday, April 8

Every day I've had too much to do. I feel like my friend, the writer Lucy Lippard, who replied to the question "What do you do?" with "Too damn much." I work in the studio every day, including Sunday, finishing patterns and designing embroideries. Yesterday morning I went over to Diana Gordon's to establish the thread range for the beginning of the blended color areas on the needlepoint canvas. There was a scene there; everyone had her own ideas about how the blending should be done, and the discussion escalated into ego struggles and tears. By the time we started for a meeting of embroiderers in Marin, I was a total wreck.

Fortunately, they were great. Four works are in progress there, and there are a number of other people who want to start work. We had a long meeting and dinner, and I fell asleep in the car and woke up hungry and depressed this morning. Today I am working with people all day at the studio, reviewing work that can't wait until the next formal review in June, plus I am starting some new work. I feel pressured from all sides, and I am glad I am going on the road soon because I will probably get a little break then.

Pat Rudy-Baese explains what macramé is and how we adapted it to this image:

"Macramé is a very old fiber form. Sailors used to do it to pass the time at sea, making things from their ropes and fishing lines. Unlike embroidery, which is relatively flat, macramé is usually three-dimensional. As far as I know, using macramé knots on a backing, as we have done, is a unique use of this technique. This backing allowed me to discipline the knots and control the color.

"A macramé knot is made up of multiples of two, three, or four cords, which are continuous from one knot to another. Because of the nature of these knots, which are made of continuous cords, it was very difficult to change colors. By anchoring the knots on a hymo backing, I was able to alter the color as Judy indicated, though I did have to add top embroidery to soften the transitions from color to color.

"The body is done in Josephine knots. Though difficult to do, this knot is intricate and regal and hence appropriate for the woman, whom I consider queenly and royal. The child is executed in full square-knot sennets. Working closely with this image has made it clear to me how unique is woman's ability to bear children and how that uniqueness is used to discriminate against her rather than to show true respect for her."

Pat Rudy-Baese

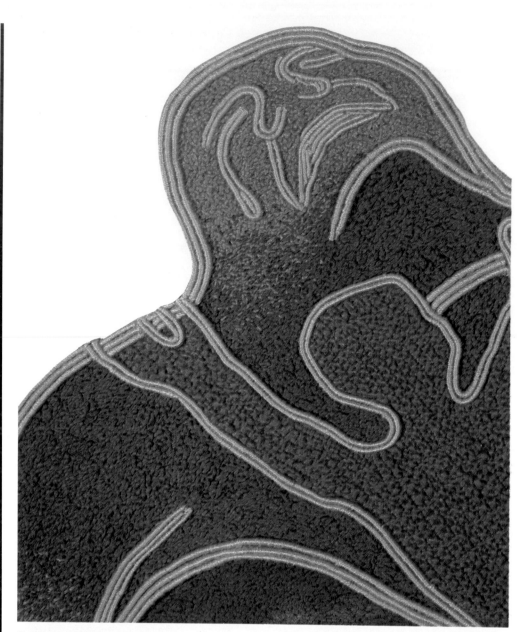

Detail from *Birth Tear/Tear*.

Detail from *Birth Tear/Tear*.

Another piece done in an unusual technique is *Smocked Figure,* which combines smocking and embroidery, executed by Mary Ewanoski from my drawing.

"One of the questions I was most frequently asked by people who saw this work in progress was why the figure had her hands over her face. I didn't know what Judy had in mind, but her image of a weeping, pregnant woman reminded me of something my mother had told me. I was the third of five children in a traditional Catholic home, and my mother, as a convert to the Church, was very conscientious in obeying its laws. One day she told me that when she found out she was pregnant for the fifth time, she cried.

"The color in the outline of the figure begins as an earth brown at the feet, becoming brighter as it moves up to the head and hands. It was done in three rows of chain stitch over a satin stitch. The satin stitch acted as the foundation over the uneven surface of the smocked pleats.

"I started with a flat piece of linen, 54 inches wide, using iron-on transfers to mark the fabric with rows of dots. It took six packages of smocking dots pieced together to make a transfer large enough to cover the fabric. After ironing on the dots, I gathered each row with a running stitch. These basting threads were then drawn up to create the pleats for smocking. Then Sally basted the outline of the figure on top of the pleats from Judy's drawing and I worked from Judy's color study for the embroidery.

"I stitched the pleated fabric on a frame, though smocking is not customarily done that way. But it seemed necessary because of the size of the piece and the fact that it had to retain its shape through a long process of handwork. The cable stitch on the interior of the figure was awkward and tiring to do on the frame, however. Each pleat had to be picked up with the needle and raised above the surface of the other pleats so that it could be stitched. There is one row of cable stitch every 3/16 inch over the entire length of the figure."

Mary Ewanoski

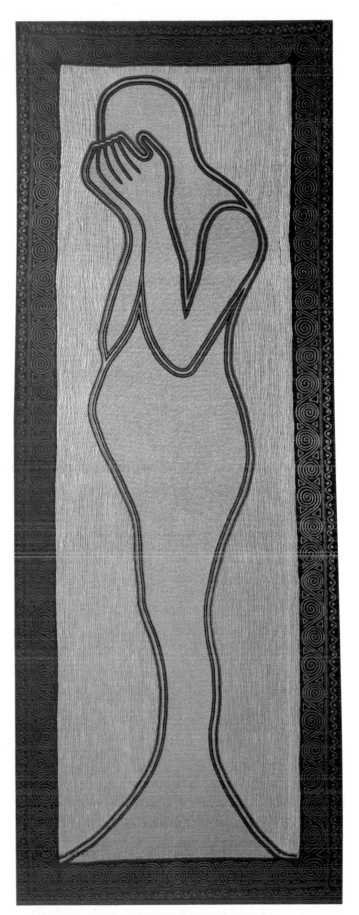

Smocked Figure, ©Judy Chicago, 1984. Executed by Mary Ewanoski, Goleta, California. Smocking and embroidery on linen, 61½" x 22".

Detail of *Smocked Figure* showing pleating, embroidery, and cable smocking.

"At one of the reviews in Benicia, another needleworker told me that the texture of this stitch reminded her of chain mail. I thought that was an interesting comment because the thread tension I had to maintain while doing the stitch and the taut, ungiving nature of the finished surface gave me the feeling that I was binding the figure as I stitched it."

Mary Ewanoski.

Detail showing embroidered border.

"Judy's border design was inspired by pictures of traditional shepherd smocks and the embroidered designs that were traditionally done alongside the panels of smocking. I used the simple feather and chain stitches and achieved Judy's stipulated color fades by mixing the threads as I stitched."

Mary Ewanoski

I had always been interested in exploring smocking; it's one of those needle techniques that's only been used in a limited way, primarily for clothing. Shepherds in Ireland and Wales used to wear smocked garments, and then they were adapted for children's clothes. Mary Ewanoski, who worked on an earlier project, expressed interest in a smocked piece, and I was thrilled at the prospect of pushing this technique out of its usual context and using it as an expressive medium for art. I designed an image with a visual quality that could not be separated from the way it was done.

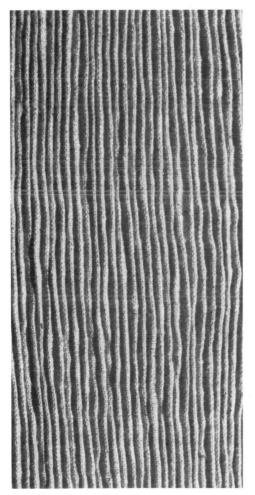

Detail from *Smocked Figure*.

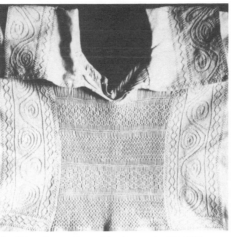

Traditional use of smocking in man's shirt (16).

"One reason smocking is no longer used to create work garments is because of the time involved. With the advent of the industrial revolution, work clothing could be manufactured cheaply and quickly by machine."

Mary Ewanoski

Judy Chicago reviewing Mary Ewanoski's samples for *Smocked Figure*.

"I don't have an art background or formal needlework training, though I've always done needlework. Because of this, I approached my *Birth Project* work cautiously, as I didn't have a lot of confidence in my own abilities. I trusted Judy's judgment, figuring that her experience and training gave her an edge in making decisions about color and scale. It was interesting to watch her do this during reviews. She could look at something and just say, 'This stitch doesn't work right here, try it this or that way.' I also found that even when I had my doubts about her ideas, they usually worked."

Mary Ewanoski

Tuesday, April 28, 1981

I've been on the road doing a variety of things—lecturing, dealing with **The Dinner Party** *again (I'm so tired of it), doing interviews, and having a little respite in Galveston, where I did a series of landscape studies. I began to find very clear rhythms in the landscape forms and discovered that if I could capture those rhythms, I could make an otherwise abstract form recognizable. When I was working on some of the* **Creation of the World** *images, which incorporated landscape references, I was unsure and tentative—just the opposite of the kind of authority I'm now beginning to develop in my forms. So I want to study the landscape and spend some more time studying nature so as to become more sure in my hand.*

Birth Figures: Was It My Fault?

One day I returned to the studio after a trip to review *Birth Project* work and interview some of the needleworkers. In several successive interviews, I asked the women about their birth experiences; I was struck by the number of times I heard them answer that when something had gone wrong during their pregnancies, they had blamed themselves. I was quite puzzled by this, as the problems in their pregnancies were strictly physical. One woman had a history of miscarriages (which later turned out to be the result of complications from an earlier surgery), another's placenta had partially dislodged from the uterine wall shortly before birth, another woman had had a stillbirth, and the last one had given birth to a deformed child (which died shortly afterward). Although it was obvious that all of these occurrences were outside their control, I had sat with them and heard each of these intelligent, educated women say the same thing: "I felt that it was somehow my fault." On the way home I couldn't get their words out of my mind. I made some sketches of pregnant figures whose attitudes toward their pregnancies reflected the feelings I had heard described. A few days later I showed the drawings to Sally, and she liked them very much. She had also heard women express those kinds of feelings and, moreover, had had them herself when she was pregnant.

Study for *Birth Figures,* ©Judy Chicago, 1982. Ink on paper, 8'' x 10''.

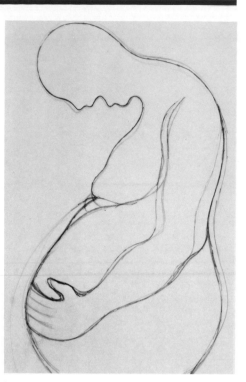

Section of drawing for *Birth Figure #2,* ©Judy Chicago, 1982. Pencil on vellum. Overall size: 74'' x 24''.

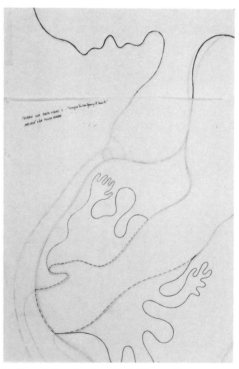

Section of drawing for *Birth Figure #4,* "Terrified She Was Growing a Monster," ©Judy Chicago, 1982. Ink on vellum and tissue. Overall size: 74'' x 24''.

"When Judy first showed me her sketches, I liked them very much because I know that every pregnant woman looks down at her belly sometimes and says, 'Oh, my God, what has happened to my body?' But translating the sketches into actual fabric pieces was very difficult. I made fabric patterns from Judy's full-scale drawings; then Judy and I made colored mock-ups, using fabrics we had in the studio. Judy wanted to get a sense of how the forms looked in colored materials rather than white paper. After that, we began to work directly with real fabrics, cutting them and placing them on the shapes I had originally cut out from Judy's drawings. Despite the fact that the linens cost $25 to $35 a yard, we kept trying different arms, bellies, and bodices until the floor was covered with expensive body parts.

"I had to devise a way to give these flat forms some body but still ensure that they would lie flat. I experimented with different combinations of backing fabrics and finally used pellon, fleece, muslin, and felt. I basted all these layers together for each piece, laid the fabric figure on top, and tacked it right where all the fabrics join—almost like quilting, but not quite. I drew the needle up and caught the threads where they were joined together. Then I turned each one over, carefully pulled the edges all the way around, and basted them to all of those layers."

Sally Babson

We decided to do a project together based on my sketches. I made some large-scale drawings, and we then mocked up the figures in fabric. Some weeks later we chose a series of colored linens which Sally cut and pieced. Throughout the weeks we were working on them, everyone who saw the *Birth Figures* responded very strongly, even when they were rough and unfinished. I wondered if that was because a lot of other women also felt that they were responsible for whatever happened in their wombs. It made me sad.

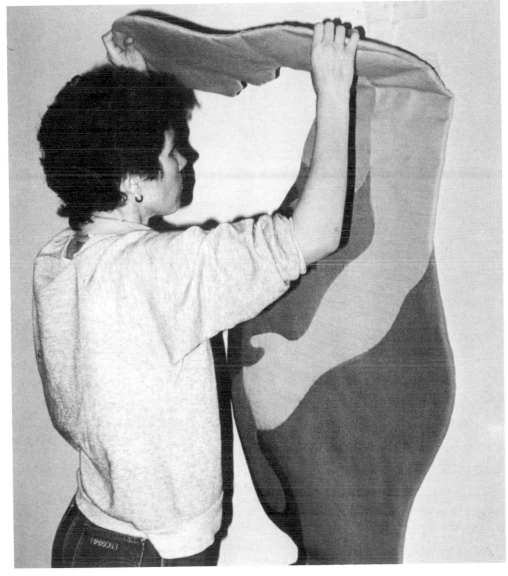

Sally installing *Birth Figures.*

"Once we had worked out the forms, then we had to figure out how to attach them to the wall. I inset Velcro in a grid form, making sure all the different materials remained flat and did not bulge in the front. We devised a template to travel with the figures so that the Velcro could be affixed to the wall properly."

Sally Babson

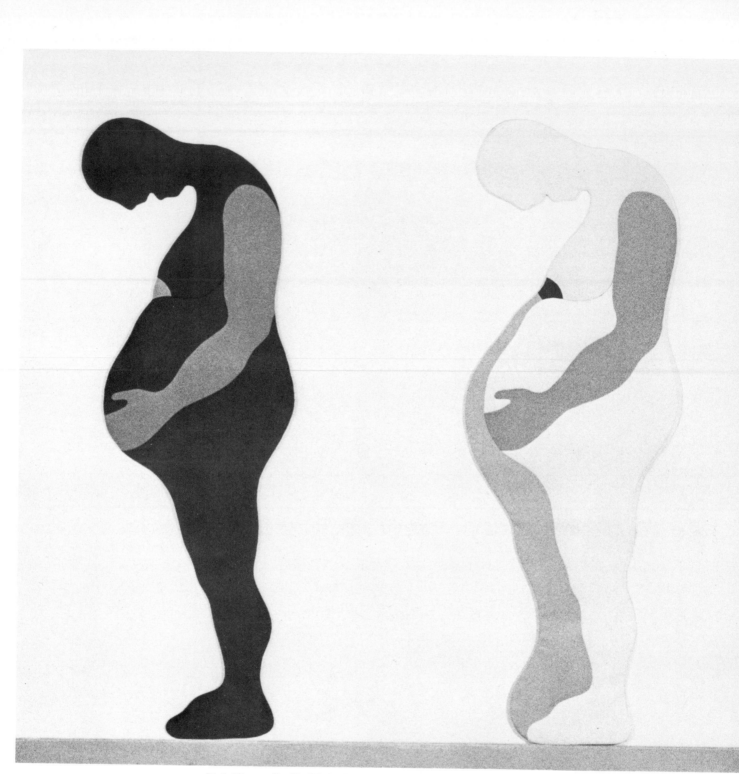

Birth Figures #1 - #4, ©Judy Chicago, 1982. Constructed by Sally Babson, Benicia, California. Overall size (installed): 19' long. Each figure is 74'' x 24''.

The *Birth Figures* present female forms in various attitudes toward what is happening to their bodies. One is staring at her bulging stomach in dismay; the next gazes at the milk pouring from her breasts; the third sees a monster growing in her womb; and the last figure ponders with horror the miscarriage that is carrying away the child she wants to bear. The figures were appliquéd and constructed by Sally Babson.

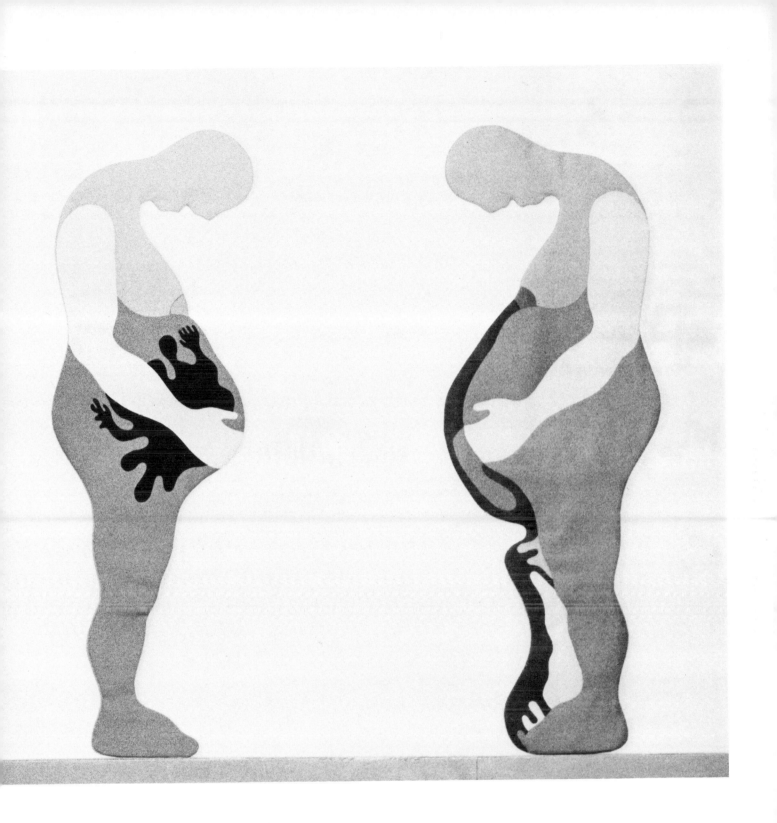

At about the same time as we were doing the *Birth Figures,* I designed another figure based on research done by Jan Cox-Harden of Lawrence, Kansas, who then worked on the piece. Her research originally focused on the swaddling of infants, which I really wasn't interested in. But reading all the information she sent suggested an idea to me—the figure of a woman whose form would be entirely swaddled, almost like a mummy—a metaphor for the containment of the self and the ego that childbearing requires.

Swaddled Infant, by Andrea della Robbia (1435—1525). Glazed terra cotta relief, Loggia Spedale degli Innocenti, Florence (15).

This ceramic relief depicts the way children were traditionally swaddled in the misguided belief that it was healthy for them.

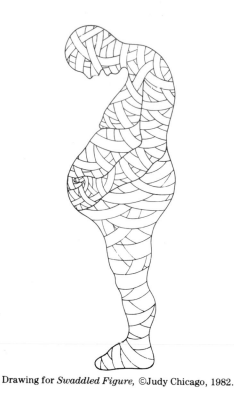

Drawing for *Swaddled Figure,* ©Judy Chicago, 1982.

Jan Cox-Harden weaving at home in Lawrence, Kansas.

Mock-up for head of *Swaddled Figure,* fabricated by Sally Babson.

Sally constructed this mock-up for Jan Cox-Harden so that she could see how Sally and I envisioned the translation of my drawn figure into fiber. Jan than submitted samples of fabric for the woven bands.

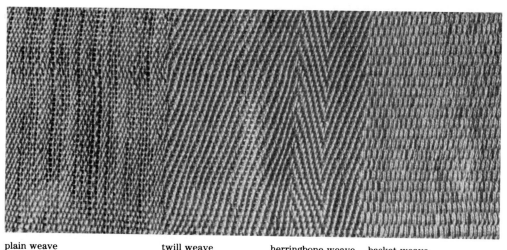

plain weave   twill weave   herringbone weave   basket weave

Samples for woven swaddling featuring four different types of weave, by Jan Cox-Harden.

Jan Cox-Harden did a series of woven samples for *Swaddled Figure,* experimenting with different types of fibers and patterns. Eventually we decided to combine plain and twill-weave linen, which resembled the type of cloth historically used for swaddling. Jan wove the fabric and cut out all the bands, pinning them in place according to my pattern. Then Sally constructed the figure, carefully cutting away all excess fabric and making sure that the surface of the figure was entirely flat.

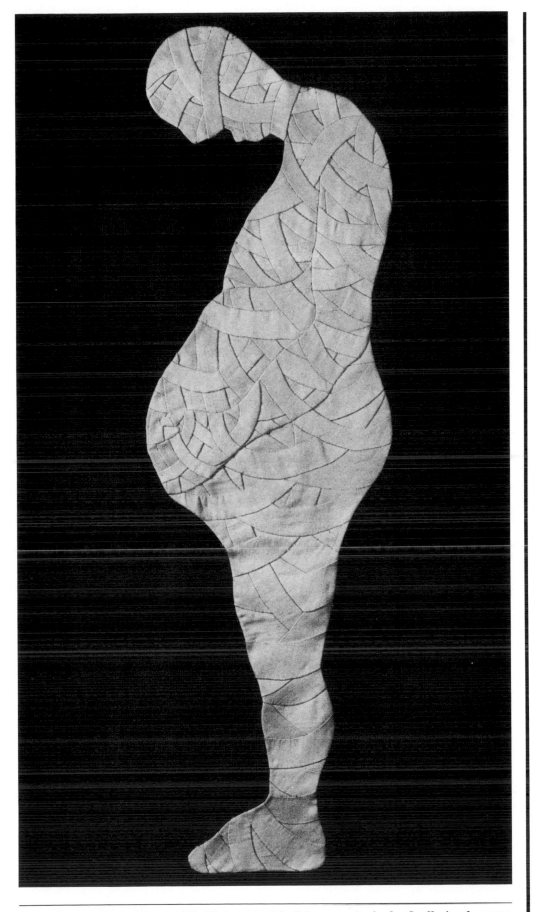

Swaddled Figure, ©Judy Chicago, 1984. Fabricated by Sally Babson; weaving by Jan Cox-Harden, Lawrence, Kansas, 76'' x 24''.

Sunday, May 3, 1981

I am back in Houston, and yesterday was the first day of giving out work here. In the morning I met with about five embroiderers, and in the afternoon I saw the same number of quilters and needlepointers. This seemed a small group in comparison to those madhouses in Benicia, but it allowed real dialogue and discussion. It took about five other people, however, to handle the logistics of each meeting—the recording, taping, paperwork and photography. It was amazing to see how much support work it takes for projects to get organized.

In the morning, after we had gone around and all the women had introduced themselves, I asked those who had children to talk about their birth experiences. They were all quite eager to speak, but for the most part their remarks were considerably more "covered" than at the Benicia meetings.

In the afternoon session, just as I was going to ask the people to speak about their birth experiences, I changed my mind and asked them to talk about the images. What came out was fascinating; there was a great deal of confusion about the differences between sexuality and birth, as well as what was pornography, the expression of sexuality, or an image that affirmed womanhood. It was, I must admit, painful for me to sit and listen to the women talk about the sexual nature of the images—particularly one woman, who associated them (as other people have done) with pornography and beaver shots.

The Birth Project in Houston

Journal entry, continued

By the end of the discussion about the images, everyone had begun to see the work in a new and more transformed way, which I felt was very necessary if they were going to be able to work on the pieces and handle the kinds of questioning and challenging from husbands and friends that the other participants report getting. Apparently they all get the same questions: "Why are you working for free?" "Why are you working on her work?" And comments like: "I don't like the image" or "It's pornographic."

After the discussion, I finally understood where those questions were coming from. I think that what I learned from yesterday was that the images have a lot of power and, according to some of the women, very accurately portray aspects of the birth process. People are unaccustomed to and made uncomfortable by seeing such images. But instead of bringing up the real issues, they focus on more obvious questions or attempt to invalidate The Birth Project *or the woman's involvement in it.*

Some years after this discussion, I received this statement from *Birth Project* needleworker Gerry Melot, who was one of the women who had experienced difficulty in separating my images from "soft porn."

The *Birth Project* needleworkers in Houston were the only participants outside of Benicia to have a space of their own where they could gather for reviews, events, and support. Because Mary Ross Taylor extended her organization (TACO, the umbrella for *The Birth Project* in Houston) as well as the building that had formerly housed her bookstore (the space we occupied), it was possible to maintain the Houston operation.

I really enjoyed working with this group of women. I think the fact that they had a "space of their own," away from their own homes, which was so clearly a *Birth Project* environment lent them a special feeling of connection.

The *Birth* needlepoint, coordinated by Joyce Gilbert, was worked on at the Houston space, on one of our special needlepoint frames. At first the space was not open to the public, but after we established our gallery there, visitors were able to watch the stitchers at work, which everyone really seemed to enjoy.

(Left to right) Peggy Patton, Karin Telfer, Jo Chester, Carol Strittmatter, Joyce Gilbert.

"I've become part of a group of women, brought together by the accident of a common interest, who care deeply about each other, who share concerns and support each other emotionally. Our commitment to the progress of this piece is what keeps us sisters." Joyce Gilbert

Another group that worked at the *Birth Project* space was the one coordinated by Mary Ann Seamon. One thing that struck me about many of the needleworkers was the way they related my imagery to the events of their lives.

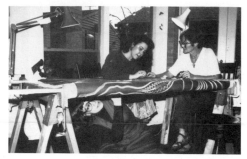

(Left to right) Mary Ann Seamon (under quilting frame) with Mary Fogel and Dorothy Cavanaugh after they had moved the piece to Dorothy's house.

"My feelings about our woman/quilt are strong earth feelings. They tangle endlessly with my grandmother's spirit and life, as well as my own relationship with her." Needleworker Mary Kidd Fogel, Austin, Texas

"The drawing is abstract, but I think the message is straightforward: the female is the source of life! It makes me feel good to work on this image, but when you put so much of yourself into something, it's difficult to part with it. In a way, I guess, it's like giving birth." Needleworker Rhonda Gerson, Houston, Texas

Rhonda Gerson working on a petit-point version of *Creation of the World.*

Many of the needleworkers became involved after they saw a newspaper article that appeared in a Houston paper. Lee Jacobs called her daughter, Gerry Melot, and both applied and were accepted as needleworkers.

From a newspaper article on Lee Jacobs and Gerry Melot (17).

Lee had completed only about half of her needlepoint when I discontinued the project because we just couldn't see the image the same way. Later, the piece was finished by Chrissie Clapp, who had previously executed two *Birth Project* works. Lee's daughter Gerry struggled for three years, amidst a series of personal traumas, to complete her needlepoint, another version of the *Creation of the World* series her mother had worked on. Throughout that time, her mother continued to be supportive of Gerry's involvement in the project.

Gerry Melot at home with the needlepoint she worked on for three years.

"When I first began working on *The Birth Project,* I had had three miscarriages and was using the project to help me deal with my frustrated desire to create a life.

"After I had worked on the piece for several months, I had another miscarriage. In the subsequent months, the image became very painful to me. But then I got pregnant again and did not miscarry, and working on the piece became a whole new experience. My prevailing fantasy was to be in the delivery room and be stitching my last stitch at the same instant my baby was born. Needless to say, I was more than a year away from finishing the piece when the baby showed up. Then I had to deal with diapers, crying, and stitching all at the same time."

Gerry Melot

Gerry Melot with her two "creations."

Human Beings
(or Why don't they pass the ERA?)

Men
　I have felt
　　you in my belly
Women
　I have felt
　　you in my belly
Funny
　you both felt
　　the same

Gerry Melot

"At a very early meeting in Houston, I commented that I had never seen such images outside of a *Penthouse* centerfold. At the time, Judy was not able to explain to my satisfaction the difference between her images and theirs. It is only through living with one of the pieces for three years that I have begun to grasp what it means. In my opinion, the women in the *Penthouse* pictures are submissive, just waiting for that big phallus in the sky. There is absolutely nothing submissive about Judy's images. There is a feeling of power and strength about each piece. It says: This is woman in her natural state, using her tremendous capability for creation. It occurred to me, while working on the piece I needlepointed, that women are really the more powerful of the species by virtue of their ability to give life. Maybe that is why men spend so much time trying to take life—it's really a frustrated desire to give birth."

Gerry Melot

A potluck at Rhonda Gerson's house. Houston and Benicia reviews were almost always accompanied by a potluck.

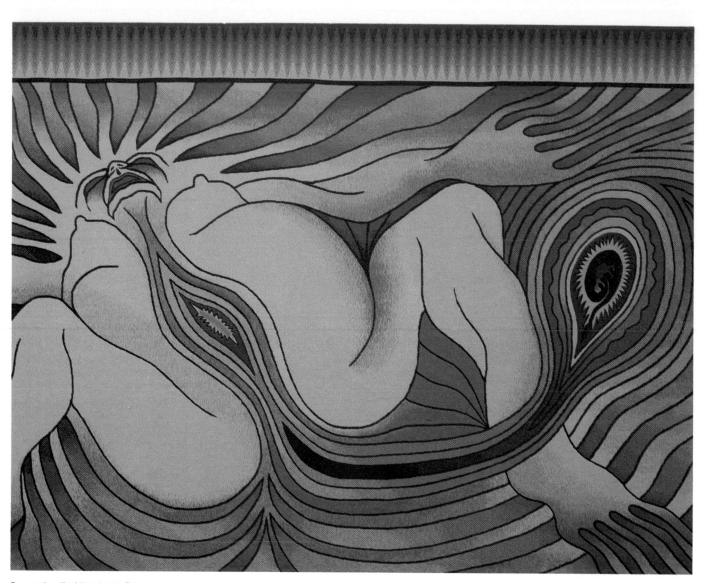

Center detail of *Birth NP*, ©Judy Chicago, 1984. Executed by Jo Chester, Joyce Gilbert, Joan Hargis, Peggy Patton, Carol Strittmatter, Karin Telfer, and Alvina Vaughan, Houston, Texas. Needlepoint and petit point on 18- and 24-mesh canvas. 46¼'' x 81''.

Ultimately, there were ten works of art completed in Texas, including these. Of the many people who attended my initial meeting there, less than twenty-five were able to sustain their involvement.

"This image shows a woman in the throes of labor. The woman's body was stitched in a split long and short stitch using three strands of Medici. The eyes and mouth were stitched in diagonal tent. The background was stitched in diagonal mosaic stitch using three strands of Medici. All outlines were done in two rows of chain stitch in DMC perle cotton 5 (No. 938). The vagina and the embryo were stitched separately on 24-mesh canvas, using four strands of DMC floss and the continental stitch, and were then woven into the large canvas. Four bands around the embryo were stitched in diagonal tent. The border was a flame-stitch bargello repeating six colors of Medici. Shading was achieved by blending two colors in the needle."   Joyce Gilbert

Detail of petit-point insert, *Birth NP*. Executed by Karin Telfer.

Birth Tear: The Violence of Birth

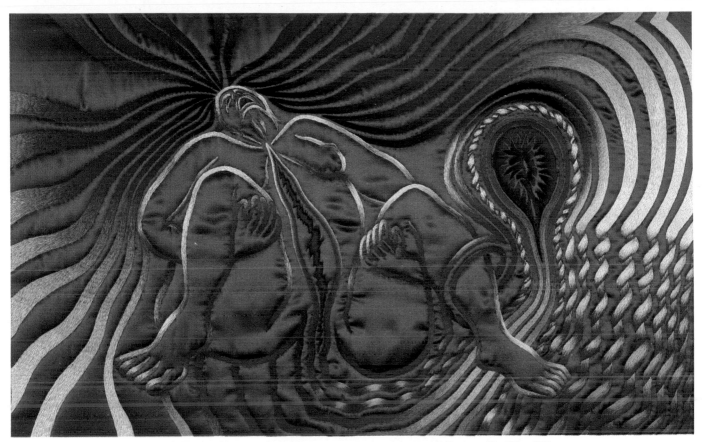

Birth Tear E 2, ©Judy Chicago, 1982. Executed by Jane Gaddie Thompson, Houston, Texas. DMC floss on silk, 15'' x 22''.

"I used two strands of DMC embroidery floss, except for areas of fine details, where I used only one strand. The body is done in a random combination of the outline, split, and back stitches; the face is done in the back stitch and the hair in the outline stitch.

"I divided the image into three parts: the woman, the hair, and the uterus-loop area. I placed an imaginary light over the woman and shaded her body accordingly. For the hair, I began at the head with the darkest color and shaded out to the lightest color at the lower left corner. Near the head I used shorter outline stitches, gradually lengthening the stitches and the bands of color as I proceeded outward, away from the head. The wavy line looping up over the uterus reminded me of an umbilical cord, round and gently twisted, full of magic and life. I decided to carry this idea through to the other lines on the right side of the image, with Judy's excited approval."

Jane Gaddie Thompson

Detail of *Birth Tear E 2,* showing the twisted forms Jane Gaddie Thompson likened to the umbilical cord.

Jane felt a great sense of identification with this image because of her own birth experience.

"It was a Sunday—the football game was on. After twelve hours, with no medication, the doctor came in and said, 'I think we're going to have to do a C-section.' But he waited until after the football game; I was really teed off. I was completely dilated but she was too big to move down. They got out binder cloths and tried to mash her down. There was a lot more pain than I expected. That's why this piece, *Birth Tear,* meant so much to me when I first saw it; I felt that Judy's representation of birth was perfectly realistic."

Jane Gaddie Thompson

There are three embroidered versions of the *Birth Tear,* and each one is quite different. I hand-drew the images onto silk for the pieces executed by Jane Gaddie Thompson (preceding page) and (jointly) by Rae Atira-Soncea and Kate CloudSparks (right). The embroidery, by Etta Hallock (far right), was begun very early in the project; Etta transferred the black and white pattern I gave her to fabric herself, which makes the quality of the drawing quite different. I specified the thread colors for all three pieces and did color studies for the piece embroidered by Rae and Kate.

Birth Tear 3 (in progress), ©Judy Chicago, 1984. Embroidered by Rae Atira-Soncea and Kate CloudSparks, Iowa City, Iowa. DMC floss on silk, 14'' x 19½''.

This piece was executed jointly by these two stitchers. Rae did the blended outline stitching in a variation of the long and short stitch. The blending was achieved through her unique use of as many as seven needles at a time. Kate used a long and short interlocking chain or satin stitch on the body, working back and forth over the surface. She used the thread to suggest anatomical forms, as she wanted the arms to show muscle strain.

Kate CloudSparks working on *Birth Tear* at home.

Rae Atira-Soncea outside her home in Ames, Iowa.

"Although I have never had a baby, the image has meant my Self to me—she is my universal experience as a woman, and she reassures me by her bigness, her strength, the set of her jaw. I have felt pain to that degree, joy of that depth and anger beyond that measure." Needleworker Kate CloudSparks, Iowa City, Iowa

"Working on this piece and dealing with the energy radiating from this woman, who is obviously torn, made me work through what my hospital birth was like, what my home birth was like, and how birth is dealt with in this country." Needleworker Rae Atira-Soncea, Ames, Iowa

Detail, *Birth Tear E 1*, ©Judy Chicago, 1981. Embroidered by Etta Hallock, San Francisco, California. DMC floss on linen. Overall size: 21'' x 24''.

"I started at the heart of the work—the tear—and worked outward. I used satin stitch for the tear and for the hair/aura, a combination of the French knot and the bullion stitch for the body, and the back stitch for outlines and for the face features." Needleworker Etta Hallock, San Francisco, California

JON McNALLY

Etta Hallock and I at an early review.

"One time when I went to one of my reviews with Judy, I was feeling emotional and started to cry. The piece brought up so many feelings—I felt just like the *Birth Tear*—I felt like I was completely open, everything was showing, and I felt raw." Etta Hallock

Am I pushing or am I dying? The light up there, the immense round blazing white light is drinking me. It drinks me slowly, inspires me into space. If I do not close my eyes it will drink all of me. I seep upward, in long icy threads, too light, and yet inside there is a fire too, the nerves are twisted, there is no rest from this long tunnel, or is the child being pushed out of me, or is the light drinking me? Am I dying? The ice in the veins, the cracking of the bones, this pushing in darkness, with a small shaft of light in the eyes like the edge of a knife, the feeling of a knife cutting the flesh, the flesh somewhere is tearing as if it were burned through by a flame, somewhere my flesh is tearing and the blood is spilling out. I am pushing in the darkness, in utter darkness. I am pushing until my eyes open and I see the doctor holding a long instrument which he swiftly thrusts into me and the pain makes me cry out. A long animal howl. —Anais Nin (18)

Hatching the Universal Egg and the *Tree of Life:* Universal Themes

Egg/Her, ©Judy Chicago, 1984. Embroidered by Pamella Nesbit, Sebastopol, California. Embroidery and paint on antelope skin, 21'' x 23''.

Tuesday, May 19, 1981

I've been home almost a week, and a lot has happened. I've spent the week getting settled, getting caught up, seeing what's happening with the building, and preparing to go to the studio, which I'll be doing shortly.

Last night Mary Ross, Margaret, Lynda, Sally, and I—the "core group" of The Birth Project—had a meeting. They had not done too well while I was in Houston, and I realized that I need to build a stronger group spirit, which I'm beginning to do. They all had ferocious ego struggles while I was gone, and both Lynda and Sally began resenting Margaret's authority. It was both quite humorous and quite human.

Wednesday, May 27

This month has just zoomed by. I can hardly believe it's over already. I've been working in the studio steadily. I prepared a new embroidery and did a painting on antelope skin. Generally I'm feeling okay, though I'm having my usual struggle not to eat too much. I'm also struggling in the studio and on the running path. I have generated so much work and have nothing to see yet, which is bothering me. Fortunately, a number of people will be bringing their work to the next reviews here, and that will give me a chance to see a lot of the work together. I do like the day-to-day struggle in the studio best, though. It's the deepest and most satisfying part of my life, even though it's so hard.

Pam Nesbit and I at work.

"I used single strands of DMC cotton, silk, and metallic threads, blending my stitches into Judy's paint strokes, merging the two, and delicately enhancing the painted surface."   Pamella Nesbit

This poem expresses my feelings about the female body, which is so often exploited, hurt, and ridiculed. The *Tree of Life* reflects my views and also embodies an ancient image of the goddess/tree.

My nipples are cathedrals,
My flesh is a miracle. I flow to
    the ocean
Where all the rivers of the earth
    come together.
My body is a holy vessel. I am
    fire and air.

— Grace Schulman (19)

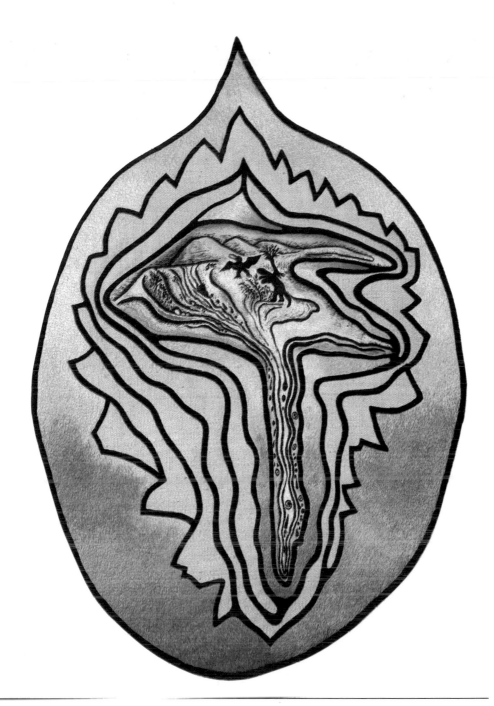

The Egg That Hatched Itself, ©Judy Chicago, 1984. Embroidered by Kathy Lenhart, Pittsburgh, Pennsylvania. Silk, rayon, and cotton thread on linen and silk, 26" x 17¾"

Both of these two pieces went through a number of evolutionary stages. The antelope skin I painted for *Egg/Her* was given to me by a woman in Houston who wanted to bead it after I painted it. When, after many months, her work was not progressing, I took the piece away and offered it to Pamella, whose stitching, I knew, was exquisite. It gave us an opportunity to further explore the mixing of paint and thread that we had tried in earlier pieces Pam had executed.

When I first saw the piece after Pam had begun work, I impatiently asked her what she'd been doing with herself, as I could see no stitching. Then I looked again and, with some embarrassment, realized she'd fused the thread with the paint so successfully that I could barely tell it was there.

Originally, *The Egg That Hatched Itself* was a small piece, hand-drawn by me, which was to be an insert in a larger piece. I can't quite remember how it became a scene in a large egg, but it was clear, after Kathy Lenhart had begun work on it, that it was becoming a piece unto itself.

"The primordial scene is the focal point of this piece and therefore the most detailed in stitching. Most of it was done in a random, overlapping satin stitch; the interior is all single-strand DMC floss or Marlitt rayon. The outlines are done in a combination of stem, split, chain, and raised chain stitches, and both they and the small figures are stitched in La Paleta silk. All the filling stitches are single strands, with considerable overstitching to achieve the blending.

"The egg itself is stitched in decreasing strands (from five to two) of DMC blending into Marlitt, with the colors blended in the needle, then overstitched for greater blending of the tones. Like the interior scene, it is worked in overlapping satin stitch. The dark outlines that contain the forms are worked in the raised stem stitch and are done in #8 perle cotton."

Needleworker Kathy Lenhart
Pittsburgh, Pennsylvania

89

This week I'm doing some hand-drawing on linen to be embroidered. The work I'm doing for embroidery is for specific people, selected through their samples. The first one is a very strong and powerful image, and I feel a little anxious about sending it to someone I've never met. The imagery expresses my feelings about the connections between the human race (as embodied in the female) and all of life.

Although I have a storehouse of images (I've been looking at the natural landscape for years, especially since I've been in Benicia), I feel scared as I begin to draw them. What I mean is that I've gone beyond all the familiar standards about what is good or bad in art, and I only know what I'm trying to say and whether or not I'm saying it. My creative process is purer than it's ever been. I don't think about anything outside of the work itself. Time stops as I struggle to express what I mean. The act itself has become everything, and I feel great about that.

Tree of Life (in progress), ©Judy Chicago, 1984. Embroidered by L.A. Hassing, Claremont, California. DMC floss over prismacolor pencil and ink on linen, 18'' x 23¾''.

L.A. Hassing, who is the only *Birth Project* needleworker to also have worked on *The Dinner Party*, embroidered this piece with single strands of DMC floss in the chain and split stitches. Her art background, plus her prior experience of working with me, provided her with the skill and the vision to translate my original colored-pencil drawing perfectly. Some friends of mine, who had seen my drawing before any stitching had been done on it, were quite concerned about its getting ''all covered up.'' I tried to explain that I had conceived of the piece as it would look when its surface was entirely made up of thread.

Detail of *Tree of Life*.

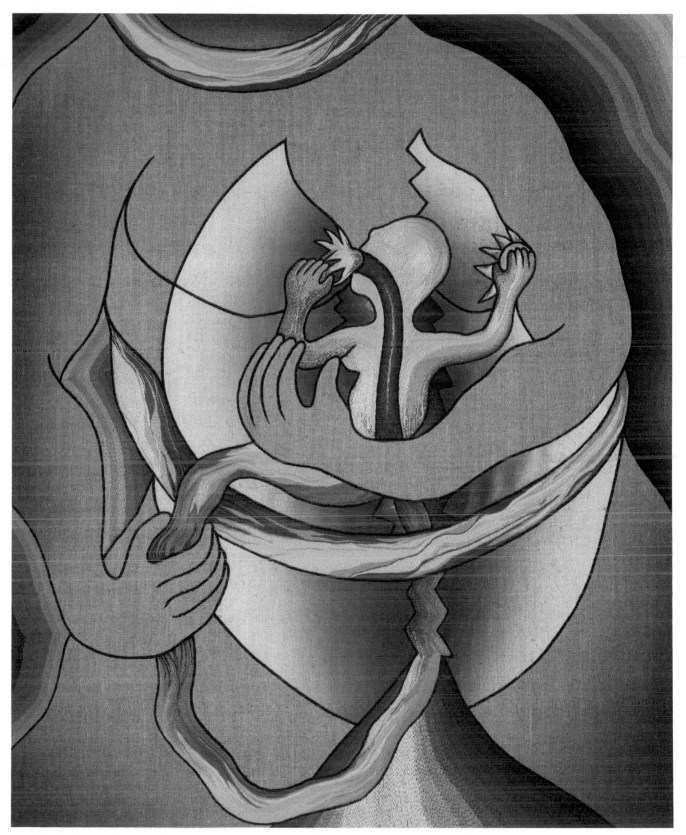

Hatching the Universal Egg E 2, ©Judy Chicago, 1984. Embroidered by Mary Ann Hickey, Chicago, Illinois. Airbrush, DMC floss over prismacolor pencil and ink on linen, 28½'' x 23''.

"I used my own adaptation of the split stitch and the chain stitch over Judy's colored-pencil drawing. The outline was couched with #8 perle cotton, and all the filling stitches were done with one to three strands of DMC floss. After the surface embroidery had been done and before I had completed the outline, Judy sprayed the egg and the background."

Needleworker Mary Ann Hickey, Chicago, Illinois

The series of embroideries grouped under the title *Hatching the Universal Egg* are derived from creation myths which describe life being created from an egg. Obviously, the ovum, the source of life, is actually and metaphorically the ''universal egg,'' but the many different versions of the myth attest to the fact that the way life arises has been mysterious and intriguing to many cultures.

I have used this image to deal with the female both as the provider of life and as the one who gets trapped by the needs of those she gives life to.

This is the myth that stimulated my drawing *Arising from Chaos*, as well as some of the other images in *The Birth Project*:

Eurynome danced towards the south, and the winds she set in motion behind her began the work of creation. Wheeling about, she caught hold of this new north wind and rubbed it between her hands, and behold! she created the great serpent Ophion. Eurynome danced on—she danced to warm herself, and she danced more wildly until Ophion, grown lustful as he watched the erotic dance, coiled about Eurynome's divine limbs and was moved to couple with her.

From this union came a child. Next, Eurynome assumed the form of a dove and laid the Universal Egg on the waves of the sea. She instructed Ophion to coil seven times around this egg until it hatched and split in two. Out tumbled all things that exist.
(2)

Arising from Chaos, ©Judy Chicago, 1981. Prismacolor and ink on rag paper, 11'' x 15''.

Laura Lee Fritz and I at Laura Lee's home in Inverness, California.

Hatching the Universal Egg E 1, ©Judy Chicago, 1981. Embroidered by Laura Lee Fritz, Inverness, California. Embroidery and paint on velvet, 20½'' x 24½''.

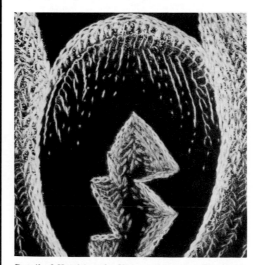

Detail of *Hatching the Universal Egg E 1.* The image of an egg has inspired poetry, mythology, and art throughout the world.

Laura Lee Fritz worked directly over my painting, which caused many technical difficulties. I had painted this early in *The Birth Project* with Liquitex, an acrylic paint, which hardened on the surface. Laura Lee managed to overcome this problem with a unique combination of feather, fly, stem, chain, buttonhole, and seed stitches, using single strands of silk thread and double strands of cotton thread.

''There is an aspect of the image which taps into my personal philosophy. The egg seems to be bringing itself into life; it really expresses the cycle of birth and death and rebirth.'' Needleworker Laura Lee Fritz, Inverness, California

I did a drawing as a color study for this embroidery, which I then outlined in paint on black silk and sent with the color study and thread specifications. Kris Wetterlund embroidered it in the long and short stitch, using two or three strands of DMC floss and then doing blending adjustments with one strand.

Hatching the Universal Egg E 3 (in progress), ©Judy Chicago, 1984. Embroidery by Kris Wetterlund, Minneapolis, Minnesota. DMC floss on silk, 15'' x 15''.

"In this image a female figure is giving birth to or hatching an egg. Her body is dark, while the area that surrounds her explodes with color. The cracking egg itself appears from between her strong, husky legs, and she embraces it with equally strong-looking arms. Her hair flies, and the beautiful colors flow around her to create an image that suggests that this birth or hatching is a special event. According to creation myths, the hatching of the universal egg was indeed a spectacular event. Some relate that it was from this egg that all things came, and others tell that when the universal egg was hatched, the sun was born." Needleworker Kris Wetterlund, Minneapolis, Minnesota

Kris Wetterlund and I at a review in Chicago.

"When I saw the *Birth Project* images I was deeply touched. Here was something that made the most natural sense to me—ideas and concepts that directly related to my own life." Kris Wetterlund

Art by Mail

In the fall of 1981, we received a letter from a needleworker in New Zealand expressing interest in my work. Early in 1982, she and I embarked on a project together—one that was particularly challenging because of the distance between us. With most other projects, I saw the needleworkers regularly at reviews, and even those who couldn't always attend in person managed to come at least once or twice. Additionally, as long as they lived in the United States, I could call them up or go visit them, but New Zealand was a long way away. That meant that all communication would have to take place through the mail, although early on we agreed that Pippa Davies would come to Benicia when the piece was close to being done.

I decided to include excerpts from our correspondence here because it makes the way I work with people very clear.

A series of letters between New Zealand and Benicia:

November 30, 1981

Dear Judy Chicago:

I am an embroiderer and have recently acquired and read your *Dinner Party* books. I have been involved in the women's movement here as the facilitator of a group. We have been working on expressing emotion, and your diary rang loud bells for me. I am full of admiration for the way you stick at it in spite of so many difficulties. Your new project sounds tremendously exciting, and the possibility of working on one of your designs is thrilling. Would the fact that I live in New Zealand be a hindrance?

Yours very sincerely,
Pippa Davies
Christchurch, New Zealand

January 20, 1983

Dear Pippa:

Welcome to *The Birth Project*. We are sending you an embroidery that I think suits your skills. Please read the instruction letter about handling the embroidery and all my notes on my drawing carefully. Then look at the image, study it, and let me know if you have responses to it or questions about it. Because you are so far away, I would like to limit our reviews as much as possible so we don't have to stress the piece by sending it back and forth too many times.

The first thing I'd like you to do is to develop samples in *every* area to be worked. You could, if you'd like, appliqué the egg rather than embroider it. But the other colored areas of the drawing are meant to be solidly stitched, and there needs to be an outline stitched after all the areas are filled. This outline should be higher than the filled or appliquéd areas. Your sample stitching should be enough to show me how the egg, the background, the stitched areas on the hands, and the outline will be treated. The outline should be clean and regular and should tie the different areas together; it needs to be done *last,* though I'll need to know *how* you'll do it soon.

After you send samples and we approve them, I'd like you to start stitching, communicate by letter about your progress,

send the piece once when it's halfway done, and then send it again when it's finished. I would like to receive the translation samples by May 15. Then I'd like the piece sent, half-finished, by November 15 and completed by March 15, 1984. If you think that is unrealistic, let me know.

We are enclosing a piece of black fabric to do sample stitching on and some DMC thread, one skein of each specified color; we're also enclosing two pieces of fabric for use on the egg if you decide to appliqué it. I'm sure you realize the appliqué would have to be done after the background stitching and before the outline, or you'll go crazy keeping the satin clean.

That's about all for now, except be sure to always stitch (even samples) on a frame, with the fabric tightly and evenly stretched. Let us hear from you when you get the piece, and who knows, maybe you'll be able to bring the embroidery here yourself when it's done.

All best,
Judy Chicago

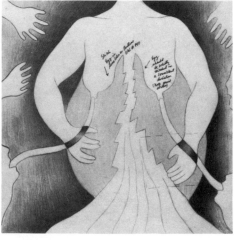

Study for *Hatching the Universal Egg,* ©Judy Chicago, 1982. Prismacolor on vellum, 19¾'' x 20½''.

This is the drawing I sent to Pippa Davies, along with the image painted on fabric, color specifications, and suggestions for the stitching.

February 21, 1983

Dear Judy,

I'll bring you up to date on what I've been doing. First I made a copy of your drawing so that I could plot the colours onto the background. Then I framed up a scrap of the black satin and transferred the sample pattern to this. I started first on the background and found no problems with that. It flowed smoothly and looks good. I did find it necessary to go back and rework it a little to bring my colours more into line with yours.

Then the appliqué: What I would really like to do is reverse appliqué, and I will experiment with that this week. By doing it this way, I could create an illusion that the hands and tubes are lying on top of the egg, and I could pad it a little from the back, trapunto style, to give a little fullness and roundness to the egg. I have not yet done anything about the outlining, but I'm thinking in terms of a couched cord. Could you ask Sally to send me any technical tips on appliqué work? All ideas will be gratefully accepted.

I am really enjoying the discipline of racing through the basic housework first thing in the morning so that I can get to work before nine, and the hours just fly by while I'm at it. The family are most supportive, and my husband is building me a new standing embroidery frame on which to do it. It looks most elegant.

Kindest regards,
Pippa

In response to our letter saying we didn't like the reverse appliqué sample:

March 11, 1983

Dear Sally,

Could you and Judy please reverse your decision about the reverse appliqué? I really do want to do it this way, as I think it heightens the effect that the hands are actually folded over the egg and would look better than top appliqué. If you decide against the reverse appliqué, I would like to know the details of your reasoning as to why it is not the right technique for this piece; then I could understand and accept your decision.

Your letter has made me realise how very important it is to me that some of my ideas be incorporated into this piece. I know that the concept and the design are Judy's and that she is a major artist. But I am more than a pair of hands pushing a needle; this is a major undertaking for me, and I need a share in its interpretation from paper to fabric. So please do not reject my ideas out of hand. I am emotionally invested in this lady too.

All the best to you and Judy.

Regards,
Pippa

April 12, 1983

Dear Pippa:

Sally and I are looking at your wonderful translation samples, and we are happy to tell you that we were wrong and are thrilled that you stuck up for yourself. You are obviously *Birth Project* material, as strong-minded, talented women make the best participants. Of course you are going to be involved in the conceptual development of this piece, in cooperation with us. You make a suggestion and we make a suggestion. You send a sample and we respond. Now, here are our responses to your new samples:

We both like the reverse appliqué, but Sally thinks, and I agree, that it is too padded for the image. Does it need that much stuffing? Or can you stuff it more lightly? The other issue is, which areas would be stuffed and which would not be stuffed? I would think that the egg lends itself to light stuffing, but I am not sure that anything else should be padded. It will distort the image in a way that I don't think would work visually. Or perhaps you could lightly pad the arms progressively so that the lower arm and hand are not so flat as they come up next to the egg. These are the kinds of visual details that are very, very important in *The Birth Project,* and they need to be thought through.

The other thing I want you to pay attention to is the way in which the cords meet each other and end. In the sample, the cord that goes up the arm, and makes the crease in the arm, ends with a very bulbous point that is neither graceful nor sufficiently elegant for the nature of this piece. You will need to think about shaving the ends of the cords down so that they come to a fine end; you will also need to think about where one cord moves into another. The intersections must be graceful.

That's all for now, Pippa. We both think the samples look great.

All best,
Judy

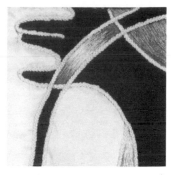

Translation sample: reverse appliqué.

When we first received Pippa's sample for the reverse appliqué of the egg, neither Sally nor I liked it. Sally wrote to her and told her so and also offered to appliqué the egg herself if Pippa was having trouble with it.

Translation sample: cording.

At first Pippa's cording was too gross, particularly where the points met. But as she worked, she was able to make the cords more delicate and taper the points. We completed the cording when Pippa came to Benicia to do the final work on the piece with Sally and me.

June 13, 1983

Dear Sally and Judy,

It was such a thrill to actually talk to Sally last week. I had been getting so frustrated by the two- to three-week delay between asking a question and getting a reply. I was so nervous about making an international call that I was shaking like a leaf.

You have no idea how much I appreciate your constructive criticism; I had thought that I might feel somewhat resentful, but I don't. I am just learning so much that I find I am looking forward to the critiques. Now about the samples: The padding—I removed the wadding and replaced it with felt; I feel that it is considerably improved, as the felt sits up against the edges more firmly and makes the levels better. It was tricky getting the size exactly right, and I don't think I have quite got it yet. The cording—I have at last gotten the message about "splitting" the cord at the wrist junctions, so I've unpicked those and replaced them. I have just realized that some of the joins aren't too good, but I am aware of that and will pay attention to it when I start the piece.

I think that is all; I hope so, anyway.

Kindest regards to you both,
Pippa

September 28, 1983

Dear Pippa:

I can tell from the pictures you sent that there are problems in the blending. The color needs to fade imperceptibly from tone to tone. How many strands are you using to embroider with? One thing you could do is go back over the embroidery with a single strand and try to blend out the inconsistencies. We are enclosing a couple of slides for you to look at (the work of other *Birth Project* embroiderers) so you will have a sense of what blending really means.

As to the issue of being finished, Pippa, one thing that happens often in *The Birth Project* is that many people think they are finished before they are. The blending is a long way from finished, and you must be prepared to both overstitch and probably take some of it out. It has to be consistent and beautiful, with no internal lines. Keep stitching; keep up the good cheer.

All best,
Judy Chicago

October 11, 1983

Dear Judy,

Thank you so much for your letter. You seem to have had something of a shock on seeing my stripey photos, and I realize I should have told you about them in my letter. The answer to the stripey effect of the stitchery lies in my method of working, and the photos were out of date even before I sent them. I stitched a ground layer of two strands (usually of two different colours), in approximately the right positions, over one whole side, as I realized that I would have to go back over it anyway. Having done the ground layer, I then reworked the whole side with single threads. I trust you will feel happier with the results.

I do realize that the piece is only provisionally finished, but I hope you won't feel that there is too much more work to be done on it when I get to California.

I hope you are happy with the appliqué too. I realize that some of the stitches are visible, but I feel that this is exaggerated by the white lines of the design and will, in any case, be concealed by the corded outline. I am feeling somewhat nervous about your reactions to the work so far. Natural enough, I suppose, but I really am looking forward very much to hearing what you think. I think that is all for now.

All the best,
Pippa Davies

After we saw the piece for the first time:

October 19, 1983

Dear Pippa:

Here's the good news: The blending does look much better; it is obvious that you know how to "paint with thread." Here's the bad news: The fact that you are so far away and have never seen other *Birth Project* work is causing you to make some decisions which, if we were in closer contact, you might not have made. I am glad you are coming to the next review.

What I mean about the bad news is that the weight of the stitches in the blended areas is very heavy. Moreover, when you stitched the background you did not leave room for some of the outlining that needs to go in the same areas—for example, around the hands. I don't mean the hands of the woman; I mean the hands that are reaching toward her. The edges are quite well done in those areas, but I think you will have to reconsider the weight of the cord you were planning to use for the outline. You will probably need two weights of cord: one for the outlines, where you have enough room to use a heavier cord, and another for the places where, in order to keep the form intact, you will have to use a lighter-weight cord. And please don't plan to finish this before you come. Plan to bring it close to completion and leave room for adjustments when you are here, even if you have to plan to spend a little more time with us in order to do that. This is a plan that has worked well for us because it allows time for me to bring my visual acuity to the completion of the projects.

About the appliqué: We are worried about what is going to happen to the body form once you pad the egg, although we know there is no alternative but to pad the egg. Will all those sags and puckers on the arms and breasts be exaggerated or minimized? The white fabric reflects the light and you see every pucker, which is not in keeping with the nature of an egg form. Sally suggested that you might need to pad the body—do one layer of felt behind it and two layers behind the egg. You will also have to taper the padding down the arms so that it goes flat at the wrists.

Best regards,
Judy

November 17, 1983

Dear Judy,

Good to have the piece back again; thank you so much for your comments. I must admit that I wondered about those hands at the edges. You will see that I have done some new cord samples for them.

Now the padding: I would say that the amount of wrinkling in the work depends to a certain extent on the final mounting. When "she" is stretched on my frame, there is virtually none. Sally's suggestion of two layers under the egg and one under the body sounds good. I will experiment and let you know how I get on. Looking forward to seeing you in February.

Regards,
Pippa

November 30, 1983

Dear Judy,

What a battle I've had with the body, as the accompanying photos will show. I've had padding in and out of those shoulders more times than I care to remember. However, the wakeful nights and hard work have produced an answer which I think will work.

I will leave it like this now. Further adjustments can be made when I see you. I am now planning to proceed with the cording, but I won't tackle any of the finer cords until I have heard from you. There is plenty I can do working with plain 10-strand cord.

Looking forward to hearing your comments.

Regards,
Pippa

December 28, 1983

Dear Judy,

Since I wrote last I have had another battle with the outlining of the crack. Doing each little section of that line with a separate piece of cord proved unsatisfactory. Eventually, I modified the technique of marking the cord, making it turn the sharp corners; it looks better now.

I'm planning to have a private viewing of *Hatching the Universal Egg*, for those who are interested, on the weekend before I leave for California.

See you soon,
Pippa

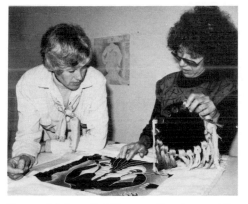

Pippa and I at our first "in-person" review—and the last review before the piece was complete.

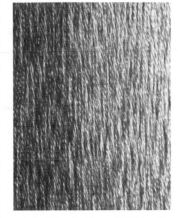

Detail of blending from *Hatching the Universal Egg E 4*.

Pippa worked out the problems in the blending by overstitching with single strands of thread. She completed the color adjustments in Benicia.

A thread palette.

Pippa organized her threads according to the color system I sent her, which allowed her to see the sequence in which the threads should be laid down in order to achieve even blending.

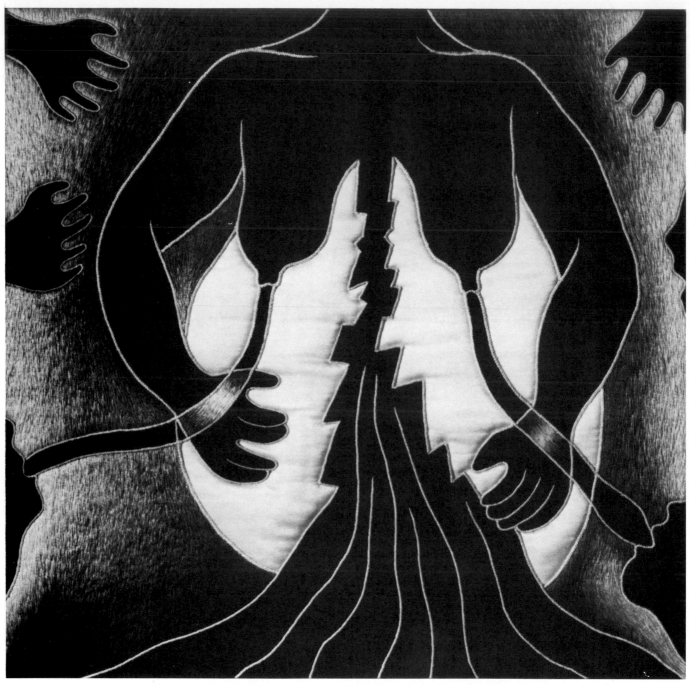

Hatching the Universal Egg E 4, ©Judy Chicago, 1984. Executed by Pippa Davies. Christchurch, New Zealand. Reverse appliqué, cording, and embroidery, 19½" x 20".

" 'She' is a faceless lady—Everywoman. The image makes a statement about all women and the price they pay as nurturers. As to the figure being faceless: 'She' has no personal identity, whereas the sources of the demands *do* have identity—i.e., the three faces. This implies that the mother is less important than her offspring, whose identities she helped establish.

"The piece certainly relates to my own experience. By the time my youngest was a year old, I felt empty, as if I had given all of myself away. I did not begrudge this, but I just couldn't find "me" any more. This image certainly expresses one of the consequences of giving birth."

Pippa Davies

Earth Birth: Merging Flesh and Landscape

The image Pippa Davies worked on was one that I created later in the project, at a time when I felt freer to work more directly. By then, I had abandoned my original idea of a series of basic patterns in favor of more individualized works. One of my personal favorites is *Earth Birth.* For a long time, I struggled to portray the landscape as I perceived it—as female in form. In this piece, woman, nature, and power are fused.

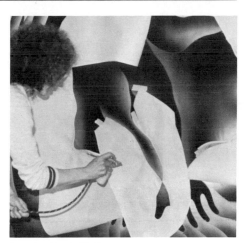

Spraying *Earth Birth.*

Jackie Moore wrote a poem about her experience of quilting *Earth Birth,* from which these lines are excerpted:

> I love Judy's strong women, and get angry
> and impatient with weak women.
> *feeling* protected by her, not protective of her.
> *seeing* only power and strength in her.
> *feeling* controlled and dominated by her
> as I hover over her to do the quilting.
> *discovering,* also, undulating waves of ecstasy,
> appearing gently as I quilt.
> *remembering* my birth experiences:
> the precise moment the child descends,
> akin to sexual climax—
>
> *wondering* how Judy can part with her creations.
> *feeling* amazement at her trust in us to do the work
> and not fail her.
> *wondering* if Judy wearies of tending our egos
> and who tends hers?
>
> *re-experiencing* both the pain and ecstasy I felt
> when in the throes of birthing.
> *reacting* with annoyance when I have to stop quilting
> and become a "mother"—
> *relishing* the hours that I can work undisturbed.
> *savoring* the deep satisfaction I feel
> just doing the work.
> *reflecting,* today, how all of my life has been
> lived within societies of women:
> *quilting* for Judy—women and birth.

Jacquelyn Moore

In *Earth Birth,* I wanted to create an image in which the female form and the landscape were merged. I sprayed the 5' x 12' fabric. Sally batted it and prepared it for Jackie Moore, of Massachusetts, who quilted it with tiny stitches that followed the forms. As she quilted, she changed the color of the quilting thread to blend with the tones of my sprayed painting.

I worked on this piece in intense twelve-hour spurts, then went home every night and collapsed. When I finished it, a terrible madness overtook me. Having been very deep inside myself for days, and having transformed those deepest feelings into this image, I was then overwhelmed with feelings of being ugly, gross, horrible, fat, grotesque, unable to control my appetites—all the negative feelings that sit right next to the power and strength from which this image emanated.

Judy in California.

Jackie Moore in Massachusetts.

Earth Birth, ©Judy Chicago, 1983. Quilting by Jacquelyn Moore, Hopedale, Massachusetts. Sprayed Versatex and DMC floss on fabric, 63'' x 135''.

Providing a Sense of Connection

There will be sixty projects by the end of the summer (if no more fall apart), but most of them are just inching along. The primary problem is women's work difficulties, which are manifested in bad work habits, fragmented lifestyles, inconsistent hours—all the stuff that came up in The Dinner Party. *But this time they're not in my studio being inspired, pushed, and confronted, but rather on their own turf, where no one's watching over them.*

Often there's a problem around starting. Many of the needleworkers seem terrified of ruining the work I send them; because of that, they're overly cautious and scared to make a mistake. This has made us see that we need to go a little farther with people after their samples are accepted and find out more about them, their past accomplishments, and their real schedules before we give them a piece to do. Then, during the first six months, all the work difficulties begin to appear. After that, it seems that having invested a certain amount of time and effort makes it more difficult for them to let the piece go down the tubes. But even some needleworkers who've been at it for a while encounter unexpected obstacles along the way. For every project that moves forward, one or two get stalled, and I get upset every time. It's something I have to learn not to do.

One of the most difficult aspects of *The Birth Project,* for me, was the continual uncertainty about whether there would be a sufficient amount of satisfactory work to justify both the time and energy I was expending. Moreover, this uncertainty continued throughout the development of each piece because sometimes a piece that looked wonderful would fall apart as the needleworker approached the end, as many of the women had trouble finishing. But usually, the main difficulties were at the beginning of the process.

When a person first applied to the project, she was usually very enthusiastic, but that did not always last.

Dear Birth Project:

I am a 41-year-old woman who feels frustrated, angry, and unheard. I have a nine-year-old daughter and have been a woman alone since I was three months pregnant. Pregnancy and birth hold deep meaning for me. To be able to express those feelings through needlework along with my sisters is something I need to do.

I can fully understand the need for commitment. You have my word—if I am accepted—that I will willingly offer a minimum of fifteen hours per week to *The Birth Project* and that this will be prime time, never leftover time.

I consider this a Christmas gift to myself.

Dear Judy and Sally,

I do not know how to begin this letter. The best way I can describe myself is that I am frozen in place.

I have lovely ideas as to what I want to do with the piece. It is not that I lack the time or commitment. It is just that my soul is tormented with doubt and a lack of hope.

Each time I attempt to work on the piece, I freeze. I should have reached out to you before, but I was immobile.

At first Sally and I were very sympathetic to the difficulties some of the women were having, and we tried to be extremely supportive.

Dear Theresa,

I am sorry to hear that you are having trouble stitching, but I want you to know that this is not unusual for the *Birth Project* needleworkers, especially early in their work. Please let us help you through the rough spots; we're all in this together.

Sincerely,
Sally

After a while, we began to hear so many excuses about why the needleworkers weren't working that they all began to sound alike: "My son got sick; my aunt came to visit; my daughter got married; my husband interrupts me every ten minutes and I can't work; I have three children who need tending to"—and it wasn't that these were not understandable reasons. It was just that the women had made a commitment which, given the nature of their lives, was not realistic.

Moreover, some of the needleworkers *were* working, despite the fact that they had the same demands placed on them as everyone else—but the difference was that they had made space for themselves in their lives. Their success made us impatient with those women who didn't "own their lives."

Many early reviews were spent, not in discussing the stitcher's work (as there wasn't much early on), but rather in talking about how the work related to the structure of her life. This letter from Marcia Nowlan, a *Birth Project* needleworker who faced many of these problems, is revealing:

Dear Judy,

I deeply responded to your idea about "fitting the work into your life rather than building your life around the work" as one of the reasons for my initial failure in the project. At first, I became defensive—how I have struggled with this issue all of my adult life! The given for me now is that I nurture six children—alone. After our discussion, I have decided to restructure my life and my psychic frame of reference to facilitate my involvement with my *Birth Project* embroidery. It has been one hell of a winter!

A month ago I finally began in delicate, single-strand chain stitches, and I am getting comfortable with the piece and myself. Now this is *our* project; I've stopped imagining what you are going to think.

In sisterhood,
Marcia Nowlan

I hoped that a newsletter would help provide a greater sense of connection with the overall project. In addition to the newsletters, published about eight months apart, we sent out what we called "love packets" containing recent articles or letters from me updating everyone on my activities and the progress of the project.

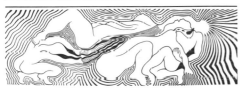

The Birth Project

Finishing work presented a whole new area of difficulty. Quite a number of needleworkers decided that they were "finished," not because the piece was done, but because they *wanted* to be through. This sometimes resulted in pieces not being as good as they could be, or, in some cases, being ruined by careless work at the end.

We tried to make finishing a positive experience and encouraged the stitchers to have a showing of their work for family and friends before sending it to Benicia. If the needleworker brought the finished piece to Through the Flower, we had a formal champagne celebration, which we also tried to have informally in Houston or at regional reviews.

Two needleworkers discuss the sense of loss associated with finishing:

"I look at my children and know that someday I will have to let them go. And the piece is the same way. I think there will be a void there for a while. I will feel restless because so much of my day for the last two years has been planned around, 'I am going to do this and then it is stitching time again.' "

Needleworker Merrily Whitaker
Clear Lake City, Texas

"When I realized today that I actually could be finished soon, I got such a rush of feeling—it was almost orgasmic in its intensity. Looking at my labor of the past twenty months, I can hardly believe it took so long, and yet I cannot imagine no longer working on it." Mary Ann Hickey

I used to quip at potlucks, "First there was starting and now there's finishing," which referred to difficulties many of the needleworkers had had at both these points. To help ease the transition after a *Birth Project* piece was done, we tried to have private celebrations as often as we could.

Lael Cohen and I shake hands upon the completion of *Creation of the World NP 3.*

Drinking champagne with Mary Ann Seamon and Dorothy Cavanaugh to celebrate the completion of *Birth Tear Q* in Houston.

There was a wonderful closing party and exhibition in Houston in early 1984.

In addition to the newsletter, love packets, phone calls, and postcards from me or Sally, and general correspondence and regular reviews, we tried to make the needleworkers feel important and recognized in other ways.

Lael Cohen celebrating her fiftieth birthday at Through the Flower.

The stitching area at Through the Flower, where we encouraged everyone to bring her piece to work on during reviews and vacations. It was wonderful to see women from all over gathered together stitching and sharing their experiences.

Whenever someone finished a piece, we sent them a "closure packet" consisting of a thank-you letter from me, a lifetime membership in Through the Flower, and a *Birth Project* T-shirt. Later they received slides and photographs of the work they had executed, showing the way it looked finished and prepared for exhibition, along with a copy of the documentation included in the exhibition unit.

In some cases, the needleworkers found a way to sustain themselves and to develop both dialogue and support. In the east, a number of the stitchers initiated a progressive letter.

"In December 1982, Judy held a review in North Jersey for the needleworkers living in the area. About twenty of us came, some from as far away as Boston and Pittsburgh. Previous to this, I had had very little contact with the other stitchers. When I came to an impasse, I usually reread Judy's books to bolster my spirits. I left the review with mixed emotions of exhilaration and sadness. I was elated at finally having met Judy and feeling first-hand her intense commitment, and I was saddened that it would be another year until we East Coast stitchers gathered again for an in-person review with Judy.

"Correspondence appeared a viable way to keep in touch: a progressive letter which would travel from stitcher to stitcher, each responding within a week to the previous letters by adding her own to the packet and mailing it to the next participant—a *continuous letter*. We did not include Judy in our letters, as we felt we needed a support group independent of her.

"A dialogue unfolded among us on a number of topics vital to ourselves as women. We also exchanged ideas on how to handle the comment: 'You're not getting *paid?*' As we discussed this issue, we all began to see that this comment arose out of a total lack of understanding of our volunteerism. Most of us had never gotten paid for our needlework, and no one had ever been concerned about that until we began doing needlework on behalf of women. And no one would think of questioning my community volunteer fire department or rescue squad, though we in *The Birth Project* were, in essence, involved for the same reason—caring. We all care about our sisters and hope that through Judy's images, women will reclaim and acknowledge parts of their lives previously belittled by society." Frannie Yablonsky

The participants in the progressive letter agreed to send me selected material to be considered for the book. I was very interested to read their dialogue about working with me, and I was pleased that they had a framework for dealing with some of their feelings. It was difficult for me to comprehend the way many of the people I worked with viewed me: they seemed to overreact to my responses. If I said something positive about the work, they were elated; if my comments were negative, they became extraordinarily depressed. And if I got upset and raised my voice, it was as if the world had come to an end. This was really baffling to me, as I was raised in a family where everyone yelled, and the expression of strong feeling was completely acceptable.

I had also observed this in *The Dinner Party*, but I had greater distance from the people I worked with then. It was as if, because they were working in my studio, I had to maintain a greater reserve. In *The Birth Project*, I really became much more involved with people personally, probably because the character and quality of their lives affected the outcome of the work.

Excerpts from the progressive letters

On feminism:

"Perhaps our greatest contribution to feminism is that we aren't strident. I like to think of us as transitionalists."

Jackie Moore

"I like your word 'transitionalist,' Jackie. Long before I applied the word 'feminist' to myself, I'd always considered myself and others in my generation as a transitional generation in that I could relate to my mother's generation and also to my daughters' generation. I still see myself in that role."

Dolly Kaminski

"Jackie, your comments on being a transitionalist were great. We need the vision-seekers and radicals to confront the status quo and imagine new worlds, but it is women like us, who can step between both worlds, who make feminism more than words and ideas."

Maria Lo Biondo

"We're all trying to introduce female values into our culture, and how difficult that is! We're at the very beginning, just trying to define what female values are."

Dolly Kaminski

"Now that we have more freedom to do and be more for ourselves, perhaps we are devaluing our own roles as nurturing mothers to our own children. The fact that we are able to do more than 'mothering' is due in no small part to the feminists, who demand more choices, yet I worry that 'mothering' is moving further and further down the list of life choices for women."

Jackie Moore

"My particular dilemma as a transitionalist is that ideologically my sympathies are with radical feminists, but practically I am a product of a traditional culture."

Dolly Kaminski

On working with Judy:

"Our fear of Judy's not liking our work was mentioned in almost every letter in this packet!! Don't misunderstand; I feel it too, and I was very anxious for Judy's assurance that she was pleased with my progress thus far."

Jackie Moore

"I know that Judy's approval is important to me, but I see her more as an overall artistic director, especially because her knowledge of needlepoint is limited. Judy is the orchestrator, but our work has a life of its own. She can approve or disapprove, but that's only part of the process."

Maria Lo Biondo

"When I asked some of the women in the project if they ever got angry with Judy, they were all emphatic about the fact that they did and that that was okay—but I don't know how many of them openly expressed it. Personally, I took Judy's criticism as an attack. I did not express how I felt, which did not exactly encourage productive communication."

Maria Lo Biondo

"I am definitely dependent upon Judy's approval. I have placed her on a pedestal. That's not good for her or me."

Jan Lo Biondo

"I'm not afraid of Judy's criticism, nor do I fear her. In fact, if I ever found myself experiencing fear in our relationship, I'd ship my canvas back to California in a second. For all of Judy's insight and vision, she does not fully comprehend the impact her images have on us. We are stitching with our souls—our deepest spiritual self is woven into our work."

Frannie Yablonsky

"Most of us are not professionals, and it's difficult for us to separate the personal from the artistic. Judy doesn't understand us or our lives completely; we don't understand her and her life as an artist either. But we keep trying, all of us."

Dolly Kaminski

It really bothered me when people tended to treat me like an "authority" rather than a human being. I always made an effort to break down any distance that arose as a result of people viewing me as a "famous person."

An unusual moment with Gerry Melot's baby in Houston.

Sally Babson and I caught off guard.

Myself, Sally Babson, Jane Dadey (in doorway), Pam Nesbit (seated), Pippa Davies (standing), and Franny Minervini-Zick relaxing during a review weekend.

Creation of the World Embroidery Project

Tuesday, July 15, 1981

I'm working on patterns to be silk-screened for a series of embroideries for people around the country. I have a lot of energy for work in the studio. In fact, that's all I really want to do. I just want to let my mind wander among the ideas that are bubbling up and then go into the studio and develop them in quiet and solitude.

For the *Creation of the World* embroidery project, I chose a series of six different color ranges, all in closely related tones, and wrote instructions about using the assigned colors in whatever way the stitcher desired as long as she worked the beige areas only. This meant that in some pieces the outlines and small figures would be stitched, while in others the body and background would be filled. Gold thread could be added for embellishment. We assigned the pieces based on the skills suggested in the samples—if someone demonstrated particular skill in filling stitches, that determined which version she would receive.

Each of the pieces turned out quite differently but they all celebrated the mythic power of female fecundity.

Franny and her daughter working at home.

"I looked up the myth of the goddess Gaia and was amazed that it seemed to be about the piece I was stitching. Now I call this work Gaia."   Franny Minervini-Zick

In the beginning, the Greeks said, there was only formless chaos: light and dark, sea and land, blended in a shapeless pudding. Then chaos settled into form, and that form was the huge Gaea, the deep-breasted one, the earth. In the timeless span before creation, she existed, to herself and of herself alone. (20)

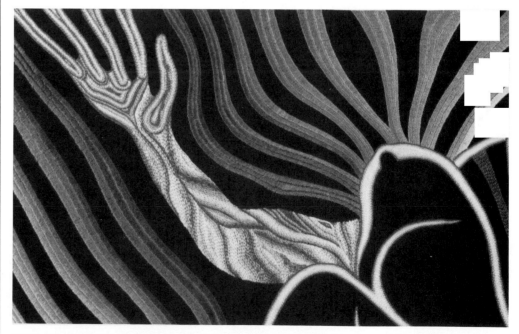

Detail, *Creation of the World E 8/9,* ©Judy Chicago, 1982. Embroidered by Franny Minervini-Zick, Sebastopol, California. DMC floss over silk-screened fabric. Overall size: 15'' x 32''.

"Most of the image is done in the chain stitch. The rays (aura) are done in the satin stitch. The split stitch (taught to me by Sally Babson) is the third stitch I used. The only other stitch I used is the French knot [not pictured]."

Needleworker Franny Minervini-Zick, Sebastopol, California

Jan Kinney, of Seattle, Washington, worked on the same base pattern as Franny Minervini-Zick, but the results were quite different. She recorded the process of working on the piece in her journals:

"The shading goes mathematically. I count the number of rows to find the next color combination in the sequence. I count in waltz time: *AAA, AAA, ABB, B*. The piece sings back to me in light. The right breast goes easily inside to out, darkness to light, round the dark contour. The left one will be harder. I avoid it. The inside shape is complicated and different from the outside shape. I work around it for weeks. I'm unemployed now, and I have a lot of time to stitch.

"One day I decide it's time to face the problem of the outside shape. I finally see the solution. Rivers flowing out of the breast—the beginning of the creation process. Go to the rivers; start with the inside, darkest one—figure the shifts out, from the outside in—counting darker and darker colors. I visualize this as an area of great darkness. But as it grows I see that it has its own ideas: It is not darkness, but waiting light, like glowing coals waiting to burst into flame.

"The contour of the innermost river becomes the basis for the outside contour of the breast. I adjust the shape with one or two stitches here and there—and when it's done, the light wheels around the curves the way I want it to. I've taped samples of the colors in the order they go, light to dark—I keep each color in a separate baggie now, and all the baggies are in a metal fruitcake box. So even in bad light I know where I am.

"I have torn out so *much* in the past couple of weeks—it feels like everything I do has to be done again. The stitches are too heavy for the little shapes—suddenly I feel like the split stitch doesn't fit the rest of the piece. I'm suddenly thinking *posterity*. I want people a hundred years from now to look at the piece and say, yes, that was it—she said what needed to be said here." Needleworker Jan Kinney, Seattle, Washington

Jan Kinney and I discuss the shading in the embroidery.

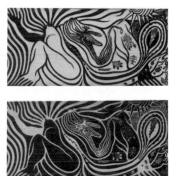

This is the way the two versions of the *Creation of the World* pattern looked after Shari Knapp and Laura Cavanaugh had silk-screened them and before they were embroidered.

Creation of the World, **the first image I developed for** *The Birth Project*, **was the basis for many works, some highly individualized and others based on a "multiples" concept. The** *Creation of the World* **embroidery project was conceived as a series of twelve works, six silk-screened in black on beige fabric, the other six in beige on black.**

Detail of primordial scene from *Creation of the World E 7/9*, ©Judy Chicago, 1982. Embroidered by Jan Kinney, Seattle, Washington. DMC floss over silk-screened fabric. Overall size: 20" x 37".

Although all the stitchers used DMC floss, some embroidered with the full six strands and a variety of stitches, while others, like Jan Kinney, used only a few strands and a single stitch. Jan concentrated on the shading, which she achieved entirely with the split stitch and a rigorous blending formula.

The issue of the size of the *Birth Project* work was always quite interesting to me; what appeared small to me seemed huge in the eyes of many of the needleworkers. The pieces that made up the *Creation of the World* embroidery project were small in scale, at least to me. But there was a difference between my view and that of the stitchers.

The other discrepancy between my point of view and theirs involved time. Almost every needleworker kept track of the hours she stitched and usually included them in the documentation of her work process. I tried to explain again and again that, in art, time is of no consequence. Who cares how long a painting takes? What matters is whether it's any good or not. Despite my insistence on this, I continued to receive lengthy records of hours spent. One group went so far as to list the respective quilting times of every member, down to the minute.

"When I first saw the piece, I was shocked by its size, although I realized that it was entirely appropriate to the importance of the work."
Needleworker Dina Broyde
New York, New York

Detail of sun from *Creation of the World E 2/9*, ©Judy Chicago, 1982. Executed by Dina Broyde, New York, New York. DMC floss over silk-screened fabric. Overall size: 22¼'' x 38½''.

"The sun was done with six strands of floss and two strands of gold thread. The hand was done in three strands of floss. Both were done in the outline stitch. Sometimes Judy didn't like the direction of the stitches or suggested more blending or disliked the way I broke up an area. At first, I felt terrible at having to rip things out—as the work progressed, I became more philosophical about it."   Dina Broyde

Dina Broyde with her daughter Sara, who seems to want to help her mother work.

Detail, *Creation of the World E 6/9*, ©Judy Chicago, 1982. Executed by Christine Hager, Raleigh, North Carolina. DMC floss over silk-screened fabric. Overall size: 15'' x 32''.

The main stitches used in this piece were the split, satin, and Roumanian, with some small details in the coral, closed feather, stem, and chain stitch. Some couching was used to outline forms. Most of the stitching was done with four strands of DMC and more delicate shading done with one strand.

"I believe the experience of being female is beginning to empower the imagination of women, and I am excited about the possibilities for the expression of our experience. Art provides a shape and form to what instincts, senses, and intuition say." Needleworker Christine Hager, Raleigh, North Carolina

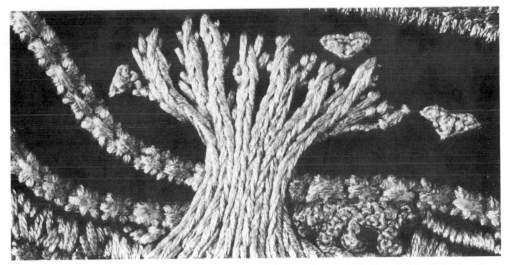

Detail, primordial scene from *Creation of the World E 9/9*, ©Judy Chicago, 1982. Executed by Catherine Russo, Houston, Texas. DMC floss and gold thread on silk-screened fabric. Overall size: 27½'' x 45''.

Catherine Russo and her family at the opening of the exhibition at the *Birth Project* space in Houston featuring her work.

''My main reason for becoming involved in *The Birth Project* was because of its emphasis on birth as an important and positive part of being a woman. For there can be nothing more wondrous than the miracle of life.'' Needleworker Catherine Russo, Houston, Texas

Detail, egg/fetus from *Creation of the World E 9/9*.

The egg is done in French knots with three strands of floss, and the outline is done with four strands in the padded outline stitch. The swirling form is in ten strands of gold thread couched with two strands. Other stitches used include the whipped running stitch, the satin stitch, and the long and short stitch.

''Stitches used in the primordial scene include the chain stitch, straight stitch, French knots, couching, and double cross stitch. They are all done in two to six strands of floss. Total hours: 367.''

Catherine Russo

109

Creation of the World E 3/9, ©Judy Chicago, 1984. Executed by Merrily Rush Whitaker, Clear Lake City, Texas. DMC floss and gold thread on silk-screened fabric, 24'' x 40''.

"I used a floor stand with special brackets to hold the piece. This enabled me to work with the piece flat or tilted. During the final months, I worked with the piece flat across my lap. I used an up/down needle motion rather than the traditional slant-needle technique, as I had better control that way. All the stitches are basic embroidery filling stitches—satin, split, stem, French knots, bullion knots, and long and short. The split stitch allowed me great control and was the best technique for blending. The long and short stitch added a nice contrast for the background. The French and bullion knots provided needed textural interest. The stem stitch just seemed natural for the 'flow' of the birth canal, while the satin stitch attracts the eye to the sun and womb area. The main body of the figure was worked with three strands of floss. The background used four strands, and the birth canal and womb were worked with five strands. Most of the creatures were worked with four strands, depending on the height of the

surrounding areas. The gold thread was always worked with two or more strands of floss; it was difficult to use, as it stretched and knotted and separated from the cotton backing. It was a pain, but the results were spectacular. I do not consider myself an artist and feel very fortunate to work in such talented company. It is so important that the world understand that a woman with a needle can do more than darn socks!''

Merrily Rush Whitaker

Merrily Rush Whitaker and I, with *Creation of the World E 3/9*, at Merrily's home in Clear Lake City, Texas.

Birth Trinity: One Image, Three Versions

Study for *Birth Trinity*, ©Judy Chicago, 1981. Prismacolor pencil and ink on paper, 16" x 24".

Tuesday, July 30, 1981

We are still getting a steady stream of letters of inquiry, despite an ever-tougher system of application and acceptance. At this point, after a sample has been reviewed and accepted, a letter goes out asking people a lot of questions and getting them to evaluate whether they really can put aside ten hours a week regularly for at least a year in order to complete a project.

I've just done a 10-foot-long pattern for a 6-mesh needlepoint project to be coordinated by a woman named Susan Bloomenstein, from New Jersey, who came out here to work on the Benicia canvas project for two weeks. She's gone back and organized another small group, and I've developed this project for them. I'm also working out two other large-scale versions of this image, one in batik and quilting and the other in reverse appliqué.

After this weekend of reviews in Benicia, I will spend a few days traveling around California to do reviews in situ, so to speak. I've decided that I want to see some of the women's work in the context of their lives, and this will be a first step in doing that.

I did this color study for the *Birth Trinity* needlepoint project. I had been very intrigued by Susan Bloomenstein's suggestion of doing a piece on 6-mesh canvas. Although I was a little dubious about the roughness of the stitching resulting from such a large mesh, I was willing to give it a try. I sent the drawing and a full-scale black and white pattern to Susan and the group she had formed. Soon thereafter, I did a review in the east and looked at the translation samples the group had done. Many of their ideas were completely inappropriate to the image, although the stitches themselves were beautiful.

This was not the first time I had encountered the problem of needleworkers not understanding that technique had to be at the service of the meaning of the image. In this case, the image depended upon a consistency of surface and a pictorial illusion. Many of the group's sample stitches were quite textural and, when put together, would have created a reliefed surface on the piece, distorting the nature of the forms. They were very attached to their ideas, however, and we had a somewhat tense review.

We managed to resolve our differences and arrive at a plan. I color-coded the piece and went back to Benicia with the hope that this feisty group would find a way to focus their energies on the challenges presented by the *Birth Trinity* rather than on struggling with me.

Working with this group was often difficult for me, though the way the piece turned out helped compensate for the strain.

Working with several of the Teaneck Seven in Benicia.

"The process of bringing this version of *Birth Trinity* to life has taken two years—quite a long gestation period. During that time, the members of our group met faithfully on Tuesdays, Tuesday evenings, and all day on Wednesdays. We all gained a sense of joy from the communal womanly experience we shared each week.

Six of the Teaneck Seven working on Susan Bloomenstein's dining-room table, which was occupied by the canvas for two years.

"We were sparked by Susan Bloomenstein, who had seen a notice in a needlework publication asking for stitchers. Susan thought it would be tremendously exciting to join a community of women working together. She went to Benicia in June 1981, and after her return to Teaneck she organized our group of seven.

"After Judy had sent us the full-scale black and white cartoon and color study, we transferred the pattern to 6-mesh canvas and did a number of translation samples to get her approval of the stitching quality before beginning on the real canvas.

"We did our samplers using the colors in Judy's drawing. We worried that she wouldn't like our kind of stitchery, as we knew she preferred needlepoint to be flat, fine, and untextured. But our argument, based on the needlework style Susan developed and we all admire, was that we should use a large variety of stitches to get as much texture as possible, so that the yarn itself would become a factor in the design.

"When Judy arrived for a meeting of the northeast section of stitchers, we had a very stormy session with her. We had wanted to use a tremendous variety of stitches to achieve different texture for the hair and other portions of the design. But we compromised and agreed to use only three stitches.

"After that review, our group had a lengthy discussion about whether it was more important to act on our individual feelings or to have the project carried to completion. We all feel that there's an element of exploitation involved in the project: there's no way for Judy to get it done without volunteers. No stitchers are paid, and many aren't even having their materials paid for.

"Ultimately, we determined that it was exploitation for a good cause. After a great deal of soul-searching, we decided that any personality differences we might have with the artist were less important than the artwork itself and the goal of bringing images of birth to the public."

Needleworkers "The Teaneck Seven":
Susan Bloomenstein, Elizabeth Colten, Karen Fogel, Helene Hirmes, Bernice Levitt, Linda Rothenberg, Miriam Vogelman
Teaneck, New Jersey

The issue of being paid for their work seemed to come up for all the needleworkers. Of course, no one was ever concerned about the fact that I don't get paid either.

"During the time I worked on the piece, the most consistent question from those who saw the work in progress was whether I was being paid for my work. I was baffled by this question, as I had never before done needlework for money. In fact, I've given most of my handwork away as gifts to some of the same people who asked if I was receiving payment for my work on *The Birth Project*."

Mary Ewanoski

"I know that my friends and family would have been very impressed at what I was doing had I been getting money for my efforts. Little did anyone consider (with the exception of my husband, Bud, and my artist friends) the fact that I was getting an incredible art education which was costing me no money at all! And to think of all the money I spent going to college, just to drop out feeling angry, disillusioned, and burned out!"

Pamella Nesbit

"What I liked least about *The Birth Project* was the question asked by other people: ARE YOU GETTING PAID? They seemed to be projecting themselves and their values on me, and they wouldn't let their ears hear what nonmonetary benefits I felt I was getting—art know-how, a feminist education, a reason to travel, and a way of meeting people."

Jane Dadey

When I was a young woman, full of enthusiasm for the "life of an artist" which I knew I was going to lead, money was the farthest thing from my mind. I always knew that artists made art because they had to, not because they got paid. I did not expect to get paid—not then, not now. I did expect to make my way in life through my work, and I have—by selling, by lecturing, and by writing about my work—never having the kind of financial security most people take for granted.

In our society, art is a free-enterprise activity. As of the 1978 census figures, there were 900,000 artists in America, and their median income was $7,900 a year. Only 6 percent of all artists made more than $25,000 a year. We have no pension plan, health insurance, or Social Security unless we pay for it ourselves. And yet, when a civilization is over, it is its art that endures and provides us with an understanding of the lives and dreams of that civilization.

Is it right that artists don't get paid? No. Should they get paid? Yes. Should I and everyone who worked on *The Birth Project* get paid? Yes. Should I be able to pay everyone who works for me? Yes. Can I? No. Should I stop doing this work because I can't pay for it? Are there other rewards for work besides money? Is this work of art which the needleworkers and I created together enough reason for us to have struggled through our differentness, our lack of communication, our mistrust—mine of them, theirs of me?

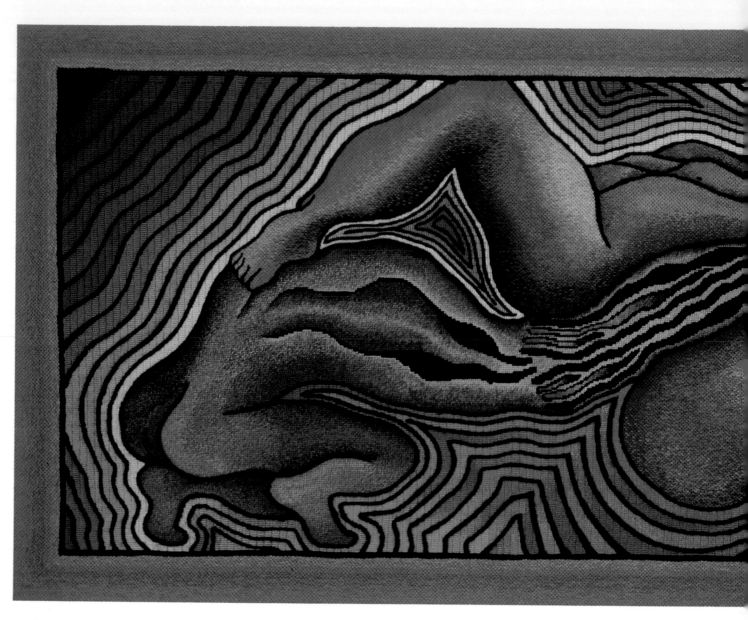

When the piece was finished—this piece that speaks of woman and nature and of the upheaval in the body and the earth that is necessary for life to begin—I and four of the seven in this group all drank champagne together and celebrated the fact that, despite our differences and our struggles, we had achieved this work of art together. And that is our reward.

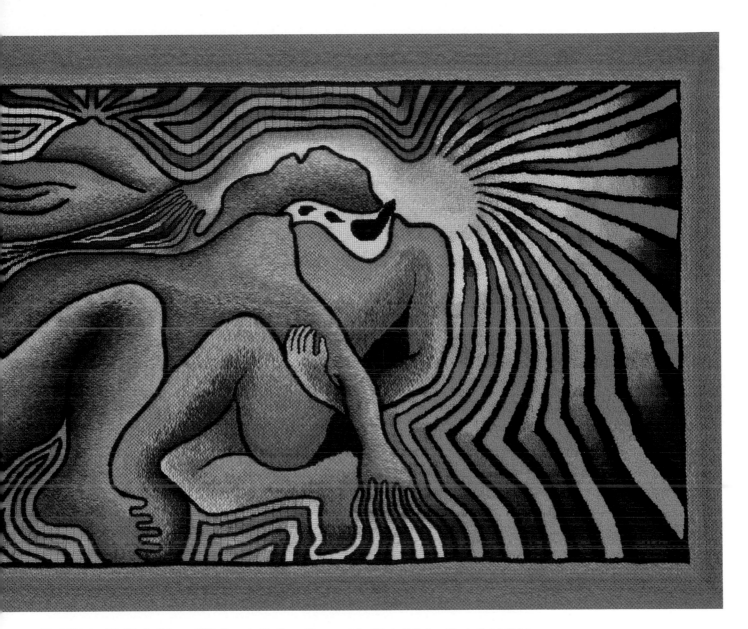

Birth Trinity NP, ©Judy Chicago, 1983. Executed by Susan Bloomenstein, Elizabeth Colten, Karen Fogel, Helene Hirmes, Bernice Levitt, Linda Rothenberg, and Miriam Vogelman. Paternayan yarn on 6-mesh canvas, 51½'' x 133''. Stitches used include: the wrap stitch, six plies in the grid background; the continental/basketweave stitch, six plies in the left figure and the birth canal; the brick stitch, eight plies in the other figures and on the border; French knots, six plies in the hair; and couching, with one ply over, as many plies as needed.

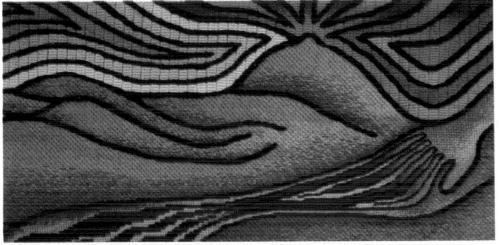

Detail from *Birth Trinity NP.*

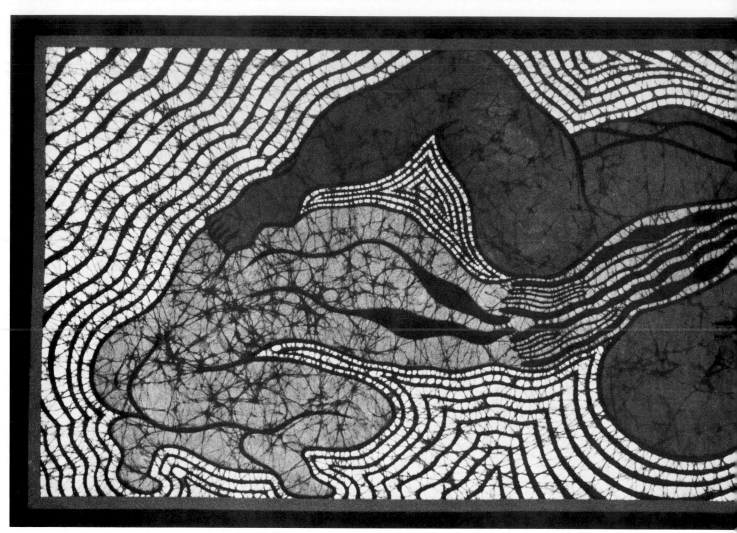

Birth Trinity Q Batik, © Judy Chicago, 1983. Batiking by Dianne Barber, Jenner, California; quilting by Judith Meyers, Greeley, Colorado. Size: 44'' x 124''.

The *Birth Trinity* image is derived from historical information we gathered on birthing postures. It was once traditional for the woman in labor to be supported from behind by another woman (or, in some cultures, by her husband) while the midwife knelt beneath her. In my version of this posture, the kneeling figure on the left is both the midwife (or "bringer of life") and the child pulling itself out of the birth canal. And the woman giving birth is both a human female and the Earth—an overlaid image that joins the personal to the universal aspect of the birth process.

This sculpture from Cyprus perfectly represents the historical reality of the image of *Birth Trinity.* (21)

This Greek relief demonstrates a birthing posture similar to that represented in the earlier sculpture. (15)

Dianne Barber batiked this version of *Birth Trinity* from my drawing. By the time she did it, she had developed a great mastery of the batiking process, and the pattern transferred to fabric without significant distortion of the form.

"*Birth Trinity* is my favorite image in the project. From the moment when I saw a tiny sketch of it, I wanted to batik this image. At first I couldn't imagine how I would be able to achieve such detailed work in batik, but I was willing to do whatever was necessary to make it work."

Dianne Barber

Judith Meyers at work.

Judith Meyers, of Greeley, Colorado, quilted the piece, using thread the same color as the dark outline of the forms.

"*Birth Trinity* is an image of a woman at the moment of delivery, with a figure supporting her and a figure receiving the 'flow.' It all flows together, around and through. It expresses perfectly the birth experience I had with my first child—especially the 'flow' coming from the mother's body. It felt just like this looks."

Needleworker Judith Meyers, Greeley, Colorado

Monday, September 14, 1981

I'm on the plane to Houston for reviews tomorrow. I must say, I'm beginning to question what is too often a supervisory role in the execution of the Birth Project work. On the other hand, I'm extending my art-making process and training women while they work on my images. But I need to work in the studio myself, and I hate having given any part of that process away.

117

Birth Trinity Quilt (in progress), ©Judy Chicago, 1984. Reverse appliqué by Barbara Velazquez, Lockport, New York; quilting by Ann Raschke, Lincoln Nebraska; body quilting by Jacquelyn Moore, Mendon, Massachusetts, 39'' x 122''.

I worry a little about whether I've gotten out of touch with the **Birth Project** *content. That's one reason I started a research section—in order to develop source material for more imagery. The Houston people have gathered a certain amount of information, but when people begin to do this research, they quickly get demoralized by the small amount of material they find. They don't realize that I only need little bits of information to stimulate an image.*

The third large-scale version of *Birth Trinity* was developed very differently from the other two. First, Barbara Velazquez, who lived in nearby Walnut Creek at the time, approached me about doing a *mola*, or complex reverse appliqué, involving the cutting through of multiple layers of fabric. This is a difficult process, and Barbara did many small samples of different images before we decided on a project. She was excited about my idea of trying a large piece, as, traditionally, *molas* are relatively small.

We picked out thirteen pieces of brightly colored fabrics, which Barbara basted together after having transferred my drawing to the top piece of fabric. (She is a skilled draftswoman, and her tracing was quite accurate.) She then cut through and turned under all the layers until the image was transformed into a veritable rainbow of hues. The only problem was that the fabrics became quite distorted by all the handwork, and the surface was terribly uneven, especially the large areas in the body.

By then, Barbara had moved to the east and couldn't continue working on the piece. Ann

Barbara Velazquez and her daughter in Lockport, New York.

118

Raschke, a quilter from Nebraska, applied to *The Birth Project*, and we offered her *Birth Trinity* to quilt, as we had no new work to give out. Ann worked all the edges of the forms in tiny, regular, almost invisible stitches, which helped even out the surface—but then the large areas of the body seemed to sag even more than they had before.

Finally, Jacquelyn Moore, whose needle skills had become known to us through the two pieces she had already executed, agreed to quilt the body shapes. I wanted them done in absolutely regular stitches that flowed with the forms. Unfortunately, the final quilting was not finished in time for this photograph, so the piece is presented "in progress" without the bodies done.

Thursday, September 24, 1981

Well, I've done reviews in Benicia and around California, and I think The Birth Project has actually taken hold after a year of struggle. There are certainly still a lot of problems, but people are working (sometimes not altogether successfully, but working nonetheless).

This series of reviews has shown me a lot about the process the women have been going through.

I'm finally beginning to see progress in the work and, finally, some finished work that is quite unique and probably could never have been made except through this process, as difficult as it may be.

Ann Raschke with her husband and son, Lincoln, Nebraska.

Jacquelyn Moore (center) at home in Mendon, Massachusetts, with her daughter and husband.

What Did Women Wear?
The History of Maternity Clothes

One day I began thinking about maternity clothes. I don't know why I started thinking about them; perhaps I had noticed them in the pattern sections of the fabric stores Sally and I were visiting, or maybe it was the pregnant women who stood looking so uncomfortable and slightly self-conscious as they flipped through the available patterns. I soon found myself looking through those patterns for maternity clothes. They all seemed so silly—little bows and collars, small checks and modest plaids, tent-like shapes that hid protruding stomachs and bulging breasts. There were never any low necks or exposed flesh in these patterns; everything was all covered up. It seemed so ironic and ridiculous to me—a pregnant woman is such a clear reminder of our connection to life, to our bodies, to our basic animality. But maternity clothes looked so hygienic; they seemed intended primarily for disguise or camouflage.

At the time I knew very little about the history of these clothes. For example, I had no idea that women had been ashamed to appear in public while pregnant less than a hundred years ago. I began to look at paintings to see if I could tell what women had worn in the past when they were pregnant. After all, if a woman gave birth ten or twelve times in her life—as many women did before the advent of birth control—she was pregnant a great deal of the time. What did she wear?

It is difficult to know what women wore long ago during what were often virtually continuous states of pregnancy, as there are few records of birthing garments. Consulting art history doesn't help because even when paintings seem to depict pregnant women (as in Van Eyck's famous portrait of the Arnolfini family), historians insist that it is not pregnancy that produced the protruding stomach, but the "fashionable style of the time."

The Marriage of Giovanni Arnolfini and Giovanna Cenami, by Jan Van Eyck (22). Original: London, The National Gallery.

The swelling abdomen was too conventional a female attribute to be useful for specific references to pregnancy. Giovanna Arnolfini in Van Eyck's famous double portrait, often thought to be pregnant, is in fact demonstrating how a young bride's fashionably slim shoulders and chest might be set off by an equally chic abdominal swell, exaggerated on purpose to display the fur-lined green excesses of her gown.
— Ann Hollander (23)

We know that the Spartans "prescribed loose garments for their women in pregnancy," but who wrote the "prescriptions" is unknown. In ancient Rome girdles were prohibited, while in later societies no decent pregnant woman would be seen uncorseted. For centuries, debates continued on the merits and/or negative consequences of wearing constricting garments during pregnancy.

During Marie Antoinette's first pregnancy, French fashion was revolutionized when she discarded "her bejewelled silks" and "put on cambrics," whereupon her court and the townswomen not only changed their style of dress accordingly, but padded their undershirts progressively to keep pace with their queen's expanding waistline.

A satiric illustration of the ladies of Marie Antoinette's court, who padded their stomachs to look like the pregnant queen. (15)

In the nineteenth century, French women camouflaged their pregnancies with ever tighter corsets and specially fashioned clothing. American women who were pregnant during the eighteenth and nineteenth centuries simply did not appear in public. Even into the twentieth century, women were expected to stay out of sight during pregnancy.

Pregnancy and maternity clothes as presented by the compassionate Käthe Kollwitz (24).

The body of a pregnant woman was thought to be hideous; it was the subject for obscene jokes when it could be observed. Thus we find pregnant women creeping about almost apologizing for their existence and for the fact that children could not be born without them. They would wear many stuffy clothes to conceal themselves, keep within doors and recline upon sofas, or hide in the kitchen.

— Dora Russell (25)

Lena Himmelstein Bryant was responsible for the early twentieth-century development of the maternity dress. She encouraged the mother-to-be to go about among people. To do this, the pregnant woman could wear one of Mrs. Bryant's maternity dresses designed for street wear, a revolutionary piece of clothing. The first maternity dress Lane Bryant created was a "tea gown for at-home entertaining, featuring accordion pleats from bust to ankle that allowed for expansion." This garment launched the fashion house of Lane Bryant and led to a complete line of maternity wear for all occasions.

Lane Bryant's off-Fifth Avenue address in New York City appealed to expectant mothers. They could enter and leave the shop in relative anonymity, often wearing veils to disguise themselves. The Lane Bryant mail-order business also boomed, and plain brown wrappers were frequently requested. Old social customs die slowly.

Pregnant women now appear in public and lead normal lives, but only personal determination saves a woman from being enveloped from neck to knee in the garments available in the marketplace. In the United States today, manufacturers of maternity clothes have a constant market of more than three million captive customers each year. The fashion designers' concept of the appropriate function of maternity garb continued to conceal the body and deny the power and sexuality of pregnant women, however. And the following quotes make it clear that the pregnant belly still made quite a few people uncomfortable. The first woman quoted is Jinx Falkenburg, a tennis player and TV personality. The second is Esther Williams, an Olympic swimmer and movie star who once described herself and then-husband Ben Gage as a "good baby factory."

Concentrate especially on how you look from the neck up by applying makeup carefully and keeping your hair clean and shiny.

—Jinx Falkenburg (26)

I made a point of choosing a maternity wardrobe and accessories that had above-the-shoulder interest.

Esther Williams (26)

Compiled and written by Michele Manning with Judy Chicago, ©Through the Flower, 1983.

Birth Garments: The Power of Pregnancy

I've had a week of evaluation and thinking about the Birth Project work. I've been so busy that I got sort of out of touch with myself, so I've been trying to take some space and see how I feel. I have a long list of work for people which I have not begun yet, particularly since I needed to do some thinking. On Monday, clothes designer Holly Harp worked with Sally and me. Thanks to her, I was able to see the contradiction between my intention and the completed work and also look at the work objectively in terms of quality.

First, some of the work is clumsy, and none of it is as good as I want it to be. Even though it is in the nature of fabric to sag, the pieces could be prepared better—worked on different fabrics and backed with a more stable material so they would hang better. But Sally and I never really thought things through thoroughly, so eager were we to get on with the work.

Just the admission of my dissatisfactions helped me see certain things, but it also plunged me into a pit of doubt as to the entire validity of The Birth Project. *One thing that helped was working in the studio yesterday. In order to begin sorting things out, I thought I would spend some time alone and work on something that would just give me some satisfaction and some sense of control over the process.*

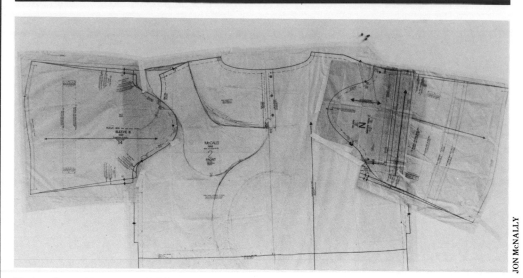

JON McNALLY

Maternity patterns overlaid one upon the other to create an oversized form.

I asked Sally to work with me on some ideas I wanted to develop about maternity clothes. Because Sally is a dressmaker, I figured that she'd be helpful in developing birth garments that had a certain grace to them but were nonetheless expressive of my feelings on the subject of maternity clothes. I had no intention of making anything wearable; rather, I wanted to create figures/forms—the *Birth Garments*—that speak of power and imprisonment simultaneously.

Sally Babson and I discussing the *Birth Garments.*

"Judy had bought a series of oversized patterns for the loose, short garments generally featured for pregnant women. We began by cutting all the pattern pieces apart. Judy disregarded the fact that the patterns had any particular way of being put together. She was only interested in the shapes of the patterns. She put them together in a marvelous way. Only an artist with no clothing construction skills could have such freedom and innocence."

Sally Babson

Sally and I working on *All Laced Up.*

After we'd arrived at a form I liked, Sally and I began to plan some garments. We wanted to do one with the lace collection that had been passed down from *The Dinner Party.* Susan Hill, the needlework supervisor, had purchased and tediously washed hundreds of pieces of lace that we had bought for $20 at a church bazaar. Sally and I supplemented this collection with some new purchases and set to work on a pieced lace top. The filet-crochet butterfly in the belly seemed a perfect touch, as the butterfly is a symbol of mine, both personally and esthetically.

Installation view, *All Laced Up* and *Golden Girl*, © Judy Chicago, 1983. Fabricated by Sally Babson with assistance from Pamella Nesbit. Appliqué and embroidery, 44'' x 42½'' each. Overall size of installation: 18'9'' long.

These *Birth Garments* are not garments in the literal sense, but rather represent a sort of combined figure and maternity smock. They strongly assert the fact of the pregnant body, unlike most garments for pregnant women, which downplay the fact of pregnancy. The design of most maternity clothes ignores or minimizes something that is worthy of attention and celebration. The *Birth Garments* project allowed me to express my sense of the reality of pregnancy and to explore some of the feelings I associated with maternity.

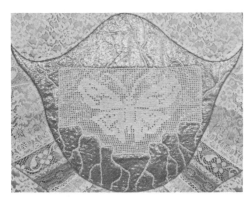

Detail of *All Laced Up.*

Detail of *Golden Girl.*

All the lace in *All Laced Up* was pieced together by Sally Babson and Pamella Nesbit. Then Pamella couched a series of thin cords around the filet-crochet insert to resemble veins. She couched a heavier cord around the body forms because I felt they needed a visual edge to distinguish the parts. The lace top is backed with heavy gold satin to create the "feeling" of flesh.

The bands around the arms in *Golden Girl*, though almost invisible in some lights, are there to remind us that, even though this figure/garment is glorious in color and surface, it is still constrained by the demands of pregnancy and the imminent needs of a new life.

I am about to start work on a "birth garment," an oversized maternity shirt to be put on the wall in a very formal structure, into which Sally and I will introduce various panels or sections of needle techniques. I hope that this will provide us with a form we can control while also allowing a wide range of techniques which—because of the technical structure—will not sag or be wonky.

I have been looking at maternity clothes and realizing that they're actually obscene. Their whole point is to neuter the form and reality of a pregnant woman. The materials used are so inappropriate—little flowers, chintz, small plaids and checks, nothing to bring attention to the miracle or power of birth. I've been thinking about this for a while. I bought a series of maternity patterns which I'm starting to play with in terms of forming a base for a series of birth garments.

Monday, October 19, 1981

I have worked out the pattern for the Birth Garments. *I used regular maternity patterns, in extra-large sizes, and modified them dramatically, creating garments that have a certain ungainly quality. Garment and body are both powerful and passive and will allow a variety of needlework translations. I am excited about them. There will be a series of* Birth Garments, *two that Sally and I are doing, two that will be quilted, and some others that will combine different techniques.*

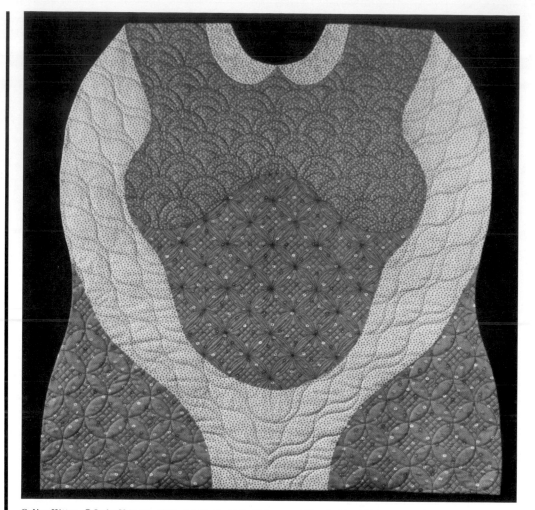

Calico Kitten, © Judy Chicago, 1983. Piecing by Sally Babson; quilting by Carol Strittmatter, Houston, Texas. Size: 42'' x 41½''.

Calico Kitten is both playful and somber. It is pieced with a series of brightly colored calico fabrics, then quilted in small, even stitches with DMC thread in colors that contrast with the fabric. Carol Strittmatter modified traditional quilting patterns by changing their scale in relationship to the form to be quilted. She plotted the patterns so they would meet at the edges of each shape. This produced an unbroken rhythm of quilting on the surface of the piece.

Detail, *Calico Kitten,* showing the way the quilting patterns meet perfectly at the seams.

Carol Strittmatter quilting *Calico Kitten* at home in Houston, Texas.

"When Judy visited my home, we talked about the obstacles created by my mothering responsibilities. I know where my talents lie, and I need to express them. Time and energy—setting priorities—these are the things I must control. These frustrations have been expressed in the lines of my quilting."

Needleworker Carol Strittmatter
Houston, Texas

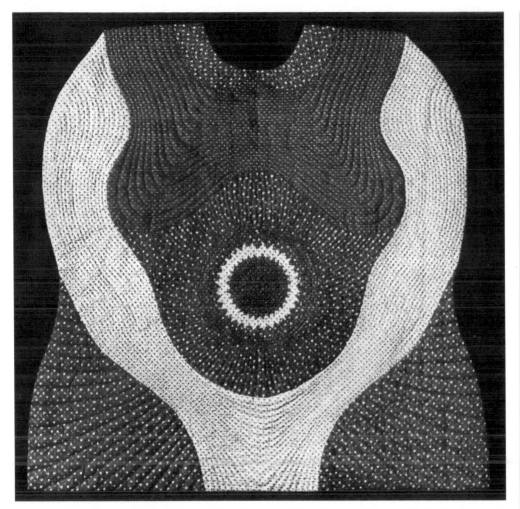

Great American Mother, ©Judy Chicago, 1984. Piecing by Sally Babson; quilting by Linda Gaughenbaugh, Sacramento, California. Size 42'' x 41½''.

Both the quilting and the colors on this piece are quite different from those on *Calico Kitten*. Linda Gaughenbaugh developed a quilting pattern that followed the forms of the body/garment, which was also pieced with calico fabrics. I chose colors that were suggestive of the American flag. The quilting was done in contrasting colors of DMC floss.

Linda Gaughenbaugh with *Great American Mother* (in progress) and the quilting pattern for the piece.

Detail, *Great American Mother*.

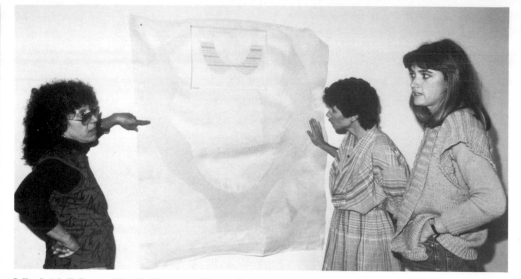

Sally, Leigh Heller, and I with *Whitework Wanda* (in progress).

There is one *Birth Garment* that we've been working on for some time. Based on three samples that were submitted, Sally and I planned a piece which would involve pulled threadwork, needlepoint, and crewel embroidery. The pulled threadwork was done by Leigh Heller of Littleton, Colorado. She used an 18-mesh, ecru-colored linen canvas and a #5 perle cotton. In pulled threadwork, each stitch pulls the fabric thread together to form the design—usually an open, lace-like pattern. Leigh used a single faggot stitch worked over three threads. The size of the piece was a real technical challenge.

The needlepoint collar and bottom band had to match the quality and color of the pulled work. We chose a limited color range for Tere Jensen, of Cardiff-by-the-Sea, California, who worked these pieces in a sequence of three tones close to white. The center has been a problem. I drew a fetal image on hymo to be embroidered in similar tones by a woman in Oregon. It moved along slowly and went downhill visually toward the end, and we scrapped it.

Then a weaver applied, sending a sample of very fine silk weaving. After her application had been accepted, I reconceived the center image for weaving; Deborah Carlson, of Whitmore Lake, Michigan, began work on it early in 1984. When her section is complete, Sally and I will put the whole piece together.

We looked at the pulled-work arms in relation to the needlepoint collar to see whether they worked together. The scale of the stitching, both in the collar and in the band needlepointed by Tere Jensen, matched the delicacy of the pulled work perfectly. It was heartening for Sally and me to see this, as we had had only our instincts to go on when we specified the work for the two stitchers, who were far apart geographically.

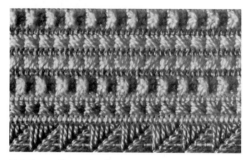

Detail, needlepoint collar.

Detail, arm from *Whitework Wanda*. Pulled threadwork on linen canvas by Leigh Heller, Littleton, Colorado. Overall size: 42'' x 41''.

"I was pregnant, for the second time. Here I was an accomplished adult, over thirty, involved in one of the most womanly functions possible, and everyone was trying to dress me like a little girl—as in frills, ruffles, cutesy stuff! I may be short, but I'm not a little girl, and I've never liked cutesy."

Needleworker Tere Jensen
Cardiff-by-the-Sea, California

This collar was needlepointed in DMC floss and perle cotton. The stitches include cubed cross, cashmere, and Scotch variation.

Detail, center of woven belly (in progress).

Deborah Carlson and I discuss her woven samples for the center of *Whitework Wanda*.

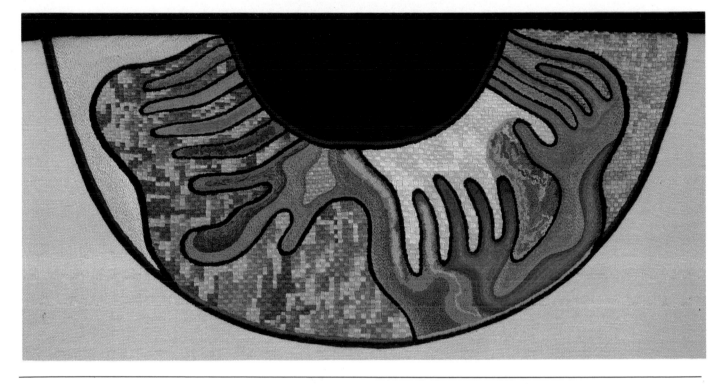

Detail of *Fingered by Nature*. Overall size 44'' x 42½''.

I first met Mary Burke in 1981 at a meeting for embroiderers interested in working on *The Birth Project*. She hung back until everyone else had shown their samples or examples of their work. Finally, she thrust a small, quite uninteresting sample at Sally and me. We were very disappointed with the careless stitching and ill-thought-out translation of my pattern. We rather tactfully told her that we didn't think it was "her best," and she visibly brightened. It was as if we had passed a test—had we accepted her shoddy sample, she would have known that we weren't people she'd want to work with. Almost triumphantly, she then produced an amazing embroidery—an image covered with countless stitches, intricately wrought and brightly colored, but esthetically naive. I took one look at it and knew she could carry out a *Birth Project* work if I could conceive something appropriate to her gorgeously personal style.

I designed some inserts for a *Birth Garment*—a yoke and two arm sections which I colored in prismacolor pencil on linen. I wanted the pieces to relate to Mary's life, so I made a series of reaching finger forms. I imagined that if I, like Mary, were a single mother struggling to raise a child while also trying to express my talent, I might feel "fingered" by the fact that, as an accident of nature, I had been born a female and therefore had to carry the species burdens of both birth and child-rearing.

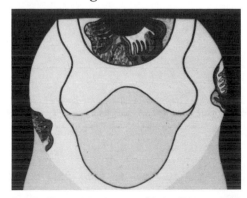

Detail, *Fingered by Nature*, ©Judy Chicago, 1983. Fabricated by Sally Babson; embroidery by Mary Burke, Hyannis, Massachusetts. Overall size: 44'' x 42½''.

Mary Burke and her daughter at home in Hyannis, Massachusetts.

birth (bûrth), *n. 1.* fact or act of being born or of bearing offspring. *2.* lineage or descent. *3.* supposedly natural heritage. *4.* any coming into being or existence. *v. 5.* give birth to, *a.* to bear, as an offspring. *b.* to originate. (27)

gar-ment (gär´ ment), *n.* any article of clothing. (27)

127

During the course of *The Birth Project,* I received many applications from weavers. Since most contemporary weaving is not pictorial in nature, it is, to my mind, not appropriate to my imagery. But I kept getting applications from weavers, and one day, while looking at slides sent by Dr. Helen Courvoisie, I suddenly realized that there was something familiar about them. As I thought about it, I remembered seeing hand-woven garments in almost every set of slides sent by weavers. Moreover, these garments were usually loose types of jackets or smocks. I started thinking immediately about whether I could develop some ''garments'' that would allow weavers to participate in the project.

The pieces executed by Dr. Helen (as I call her) and Penny Davidson were designed by me specifically for their particular skills. As participants, they met and became friends, and both became pregnant at the same time. It is interesting that of all the hundreds of women involved in the five years of *The Birth Project,* only four had babies during that time. Of these four, two worked on *Birth Garments.* Dr. Helen once commented about the ''magical'' properties of these images; perhaps she was right.

These birth garments were executed by two fiber artists on opposite coasts. While working on *The Birth Project,* they met and became friends. In addition, their processes were similar and combined a variety of textile techniques. Penny Davidson first sheared the family sheep, then spun the wool and dyed the yarn, and, finally, wove the fabric and needle-pointed the belly insert.

Penny Davidson and friend at home in Pacheco, California.

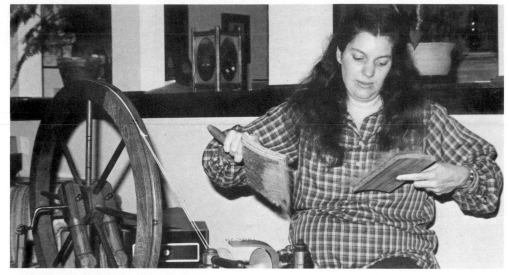

Penny Davidson carding wool.

Creation Drawing—Study for Birth Garment (Flowering Shrub), ©Judy Chicago, 1981. Prismacolor on rag paper, 15'' x 11''.

This is the drawing upon which the *Birth Garment* called *Flowering Shrub* is based. Following this, I did a full-scale painted mock-up from which Penny Davidson then worked.

Penny Davidson with my painted mock-up and needlepoint insert (in progress).

Penny wove the cloth, needlepointed the flowering belly shape in a long and short stitch, and embroidered the nipples after the piece had been put together.

Dr. Helen with her husband and colleague, Dr. Ritz C. Ray, Jr., in front of their joint office in Winston-Salem, North Carolina.

Dr. Helen at work in Benicia.

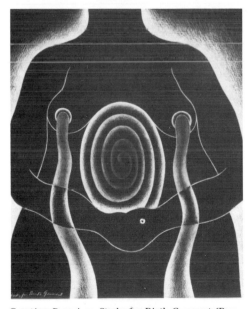

Creation Drawing—Study for Birth Garment (Pregnant Amazon), ©Judy Chicago, 1981. Prismacolor on rag paper, 15'' x 11''.

I called the Birth Garment based on this drawing Pregnant Amazon because its colors—red, black, and purple—were the colors associated with the ancient Amazon tribes.

Dr. Helen Courvoisie, like Penny Davidson, dyed the threads, wove the fabrics, and needlepointed the belly insert for Pregnant Amazon. She wove one piece of fabric from wool yarn and the other with a Lurex weft and a rayon warp. The needlepoint was stitched in yarn and DMC. Dr. Helen cut down her practice as a child psychologist in order to pursue her Birth Project work.

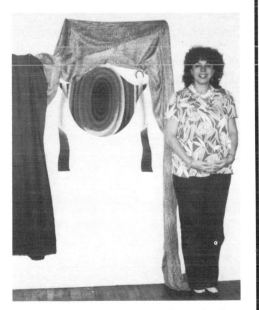

JON McNALLY

Dr. Helen and assorted patterns and parts for Pregnant Amazon.

Dr. Helen, her woven fabric, and the needlepoint insert (pictured here in progress), which was stitched in the long and short brick stitch in yarn and DMC directly on top of the 18-mesh canvas I had air-brushed.

There is also a similarity between these two women's technical processes; they both dyed their own yarns, wove the fabric for their pieces, and needlepointed the center sections. It is true that I had imagined these techniques when I painted the full-scale mock-ups from which they worked. But many projects began with my initial concepts, then changed dramatically as they developed. Even though both Dr. Helen and Penny wove much rougher types of fabric in their own work, both struggled to weave fine fabrics that had the quality of my painted fades. They both wove numerous samples. When Dr. Helen came to California on her first visit, we arranged for her to do some dye samples at Penny's house, which is how they happened to meet.

After all the sections of both pieces had been completed, Sally put them together, carefully manipulating the various weights of the fabric and the different heights of the stitched and woven sections to produce flat and consistent surfaces. I decided to present the two works together because somehow, as a result of the way they had been created, they were forever linked in my mind.

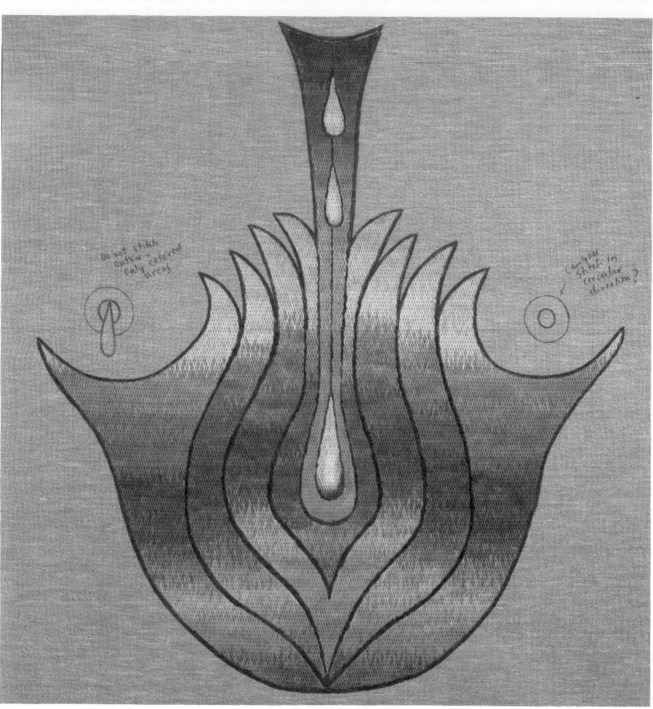

Detail, center of *Flowering Shrub* (in progress), ©Judy Chicago, 1984. Needlepoint by Penny Davidson, Pacheco, California. Hand-dyed yarn on 18-mesh canvas. Overall size: 30¼" x 27".

Maternity clothes. Those dreadfully "cute" or resignedly serviceable garments. Should I insist upon nonsexist maternity clothes? They have them! Denim coveralls, studded jeans, lumberjack shirts, mixed in with the little-girl pinafores, the sturdy shirtwaist dresses. Who can afford to buy a full season's worth of maternity clothes? You do eventually give birth, don't you, and then you can't wear these clothes anymore. . . .

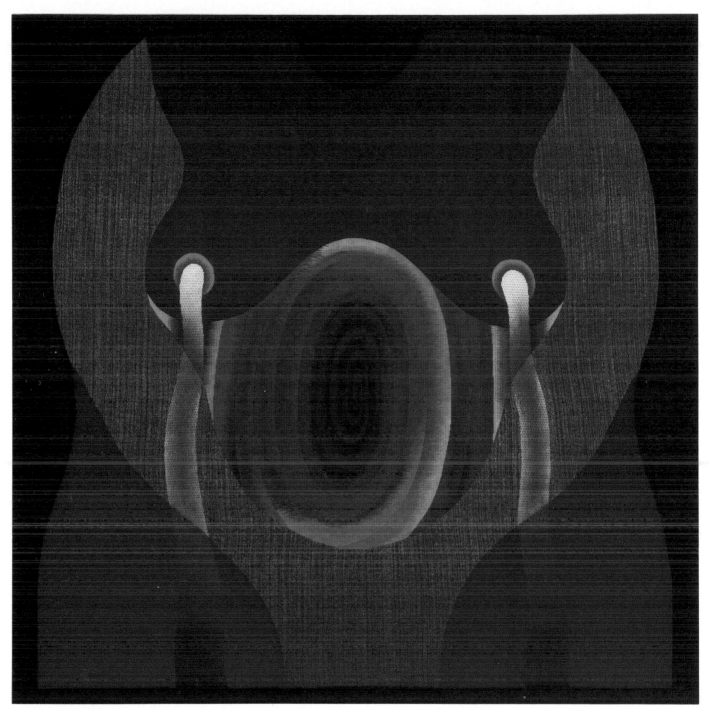

Detail, *Pregnant Amazon,* ©Judy Chicago, 1984. Weaving and needlepoint by Dr. Helen Courvoisie, Winston-Salem, North Carolina; fabricated by Sally Babson, 43½'' x 42''.

What I'd like to wear, my baby, is a hundred-breasted, thousand-jeweled garment of sapphire; a great coat of many colors; disposable gowns flecked with fake precious metals. Large, exotic clothes, to loudly and gorgeously proclaim your passage into being.

Where can I buy such clothes? Where can I wear such clothes?

—Phyllis Chesler (28)

About Sally Babson:
Our Technical Supervisor

Monday, November 30, 1981

Last night, Sally admitted that she felt resistant to making fabric lay flat and that I would have to lower my expectations. Beside that, what she really wanted was to be able to just stitch and not have to struggle with problems outside her area of expertise. Although I certainly sympathized with her, I insisted that our No. 1 priority was to complete all the work we started with the highest possible standards—and if that meant doing a lot of work that was boring and frustrating, that was just too bad. I had to do that, too. I didn't tell her what conflicts I was having myself.

Once we began to have completed work, we had to develop systems for the finishing, packing, and shipping of the pieces. Although I was involved in all aspects of the planning, it was primarily Sally who solved the technical problems about how the pieces were to be backed and packed.

"I did all the preparation for hanging and packaging the work for traveling. Generally, I had initially prepared the work for the stitchers after Judy designed or painted the images, and usually I had worked on the technical problems of the pieces in process. By the time we got them back, I would have already thought some about the proper way to finish each work.

"The first thing I did was to square the image. Considering the fact that I had never used a ruler and didn't even know what a T-square was before *The Birth Project,* the problem of making fabric perfectly symmetrical was a huge challenge. I had no teacher—only Judy's insistence that the work be done properly and look right. So I had to develop all the systems for squaring and finishing the pieces myself. It was trial and error all the way.

"After I had squared the image and cut away the excess fabric, I began to build up the backing. I usually started by applying a layer of either canvas or hymo (a hair canvas woven of goat hair and wool) on the back of the piece. Both of these fabrics have a minimum of stretch and distortion. Then I built up a border around the piece in order to establish a uniform surface. I literally connected the border layers to the layers of the piece, butting them up against each other and almost suturing them together.

"I then stitched the piece onto the hymo or canvas, tacking it both horizontally and vertically every few inches. I used long basting stitches or a tailor-tacking stitch. If I thought the surface or the shape of the piece was going to become distorted, I used a padded stitch, turning the piece over at intervals to see whether there was any sagging. If, as in some of the quilts, there were large unquilted areas, I literally pulled both the batting and the backing tightly down and tacked through all the layers, which seemed to decrease sagging of the fabric.

"After that, I turned the piece face up and applied the borders and any interior edging, hand-sewing the inside edges to the piece. I then squared the border and mitered the corners. Mitering was tedious; it has to be done on the bias, and you have to be careful not to stretch the fabric.

"I turned the piece face down again, cut the final backing fabric and the Velcro strips, and sewed the Velcro and the backing fabric together so they were on the same level. Using blind stitches, I tacked the backing to the hymo. Then I folded over the edges of the border strips and stitched them to the edges of the Velcro so that the entire back was flat and the Velcro basically inset in the backing fabric. I blind-stitched the border edge to the Velcro, catching the hymo with a double thread so the Velcro was holding the hymo securely, thereby ensuring that the piece would hang from the hymo and the Velcro rather than from itself.

"Then I constructed a special bag made out of Gore-Tex (a breathable fabric) and a waterproof plastic bag for the accompanying documentation. These were stenciled with identifying numbers and were both stored and transported in specially constructed crates."

Sally Babson

Sally and I worked closely together throughout the early years of the project. Later, our tasks diverged and we worked more independently. Sally told me that it was then very difficult for her to face the solitary task of becoming a professional and that she, like many of the needleworkers, had trouble working alone. Her journal entries describe some of the process she went through—one that was not too different from that described by other needleworkers.

Sally and I planning the border for a completed work.

"Judy thinks me more capable than I feel. I don't want to be organized! I don't even want to learn to be organized. Will it help? Will it *really really* help me become more—or better—or a different person?

"I have a feeling of great insecurity about my work. I don't know where it will take me or even where I want it to take me. I feel that I have so much to learn. Maybe the most important aspect is the direct effect on my personality in relation to my home life.

Sally working on backing and bordering.

"Judy would look down the line of the border of a piece and say 'It's all wonky.' I'd say 'That's the way fabric is. I like fabric wonky.' So she handed me a ruler and a square and said, 'Here, use these.' It took me a long time to be able to use them properly. Sometimes I had to do pieces over and over again before I got them right. It was always difficult for me to take something apart that had taken weeks to do. And sometimes pieces came back from shows with their borders wrecked because they had been rolled the wrong way. The first time that happened, I just cried and cried.

Sally packing *Birth Project* work.

"I told Judy that I miss not having much time for stitching anymore. She told me that some people do the hands-on work and some people have to do the hands-off work. I guess I am learning about the hands-off work.

Sally towards the end of *The Birth Project*.

"I feel, at last, that my personal struggle is over. I no longer feel myself resisting the process necessary for producing high-quality work. Work toward perfection has always been my goal. I am now aware that I am a capable woman and secure enough to handle whatever comes along. When I feel overwhelmed, I look back at all that I have accomplished. Perseverence furthers!"

Sally Babson

Monday, December 7

I'm on the plane to Chicago. I've been working very hard since Thanksgiving. I finished up all the Birth Project *pieces for pending needleworkers (as we refer to people whose samples have been accepted and are finishing our application process or waiting for work).*

I started reviewing work on Friday afternoon at Helen Eisenberg's in Berkeley. She coordinates a small group which is needlepointing one of the large canvases. The women in the group were still at an early stage in terms of their development in the project—afraid to take any responsibility and wanting strict guidelines and guaranteed success, as if being involved in The Birth Project *could be as safe as working on a needlework kit. Interestingly, this theme was repeated throughout the weekend reviews. It is interesting how, as the work develops, different problems seem to dominate each review—one time the problem had to do with work schedules and pace; this time it was taking personal responsibility for the work instead of thinking of it as mine.*

The reviews went very well. Susan Lynn and Mary Ross had it well set up. There was a warm and friendly atmosphere at the building and a spectacular potluck. People made a connection with each other, the building, and the project. I still have no idea whether the work will ever get exhibited or have an impact of any kind; we're just beginning to consider the exhibition process. I'm just working on the art and not thinking about that very much right now.

133

Buying Fabrics at Britex

Tuesday, December 22, 1981

It seems that there's a big problem about Helen Eisenberg. I was away and Susan was not going to tell me, but Sally blurted it out on the phone. After the last review, Helen called the office and announced that she and everyone in her group were quitting and she was returning the canvas. I immediately got Helen on the phone, only to be told how badly I had acted at their review, how she needed love all around her all the time, how intimidating I was, and on and on. The funny thing is, she was finally telling me what feelings she and the group had had at the review. Instead of responding at the time to my request that they express their feelings, they had all dissembled to me—and then later poured out their real feelings to each other. Since Helen had done the same thing, she was in no position to help them through their projections onto me, but rather got involved in the same process herself. Her announcement about quitting was more distressing than anything else. But I think the situation is salvageable. The one thing I learned was that I need to moderate my behavior with these middle-class women, at least until they become more confident and relaxed in the project. It was a painful but illuminating conversation.

Wednesday, January 13, 1982

Yesterday Sally and I reviewed all the in-process Birth Project work in slides

Sally and I regularly went on fabric-buying trips. The same thing would always happen as soon as we got in the car; it was like being in a time capsule. We would instantly start talking about ideas for pieces. Sally would present me with many things she'd been thinking about, which always surprised me, as I never could figure out when she had the time to think up all these ideas about trying this kind of technique or that type of fabric. By the time we got to Britex, we would have come up with a whole new series of work and dramatically expanded our fabric buy, which meant that we spent about twice as much money as we had planned.

We did most of our shopping for the fabrics we used in *The Birth Project* at Britex, in San Francisco. The array of fabrics on their four floors was dazzling and I always felt overwhelmed.

Somehow we were always drawn to the silks and satins downstairs, and we naturally liked those that cost $50 a yard. Still, in relation to painting, working in textiles was cheap.

At Britex we usually worked with a woman named Edith Lurie, who seemed to be able to solve any problem we presented her with. We'd bring the pieces with us and unwrap them one at a time. Edith would invite the other salespeople to look at the pieces she particularly liked. They'd ooh and aah and ask if the work was done by hand or on a machine. Then Edith would start hunting for a piece of fabric with the right color and texture for a border. After a while, she could anticipate our preferences—no synthetics, no patterns, appropriate colors. Sometimes I would settle on a fabric even though it wasn't exactly right. But Edith would say "Just a minute" and disappear. She always returned with the perfect thing.

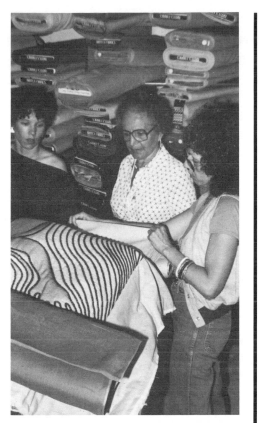
Sally and I usually worked with Edith Lurie (center) at Britex.

Inevitably, we left Britex loaded down with fabric and excited about what we'd bought.

and came to some conclusions about what is working, what's not working, and what kinds of additional pieces are needed to make presentable exhibitions. We blocked out a good deal of new work—quilts, embroideries, and needlepoints—which will occupy us both for some months to come.

Friday, February 2

It's 8:30 p.m. Yesterday morning, Jon McNally—our photographer—and I went to shoot one of the Birth Project people. (I'm beginning to work with him to get pictures of people in their own environments.) Then Sally and I went to the city on another fabric buy. In the car, she laid all this stuff on me about her struggles with her boyfriend. Last night I went to dinner with a composer friend who didn't want to do anything but gossip; it really wore me out.

Today, however, Sally and I worked well together and had a really good day, right on the heels of my starting to worry about my not working enough creatively. I'm nuts.

There were lots of people at the opening on Saturday, and my drawing show really looks quite good. It was very gratifying for me to see a body of work completed. It's quite difficult to work and see so few results, with everyone in The Birth Project working so slowly and the work so spread out around the country. Also, it's instructive to see the products of my own hand and be able to compare these to the work being produced cooperatively. There is definitely something missing in a lot of that cooperative work—visual skill and acuity, I think.

Myth Quilts: Art from Creation Images

Monday, February 8, 1982

Last Thursday, Sally and I finished preparing two large new quilts which contain creation images. One is a narrative with a sequence of images; the other one has a series of repeated images. Both have very strong colors, and Sally and I feel quite pleased with them.

Both pieces are conceived to be quilted. We had thought of one of them as a potential friendship quilt, with a different person quilting each section, but that won't work, as we want a high level of excellence and consistency in the quilting. Sally will probably end up quilting that one herself, which will give her some of the "hands-on" work she's yearning to do.

The myth quilts developed, in part, out of my desire to work more directly with fabric—to cut and position it much like Matisse's paper cut-outs. I wanted the color to be bold and the forms dramatic. I worked out a series of line drawings, and Sally and I transferred them to fabric, which we just pinned together until I was satisfied with the color and the form. The first one, *Myth Q 1*, contains a sequence of images that reads like a narrative from left to right, and the second one has a series of related images that are repeated. In both works, the forms relate to creation myths and are done in linen appliqué. In *Myth Q 2*, five images are repeated and appliquéd to two different-colored fabrics to make a strong positive/negative visual effect.

We sent *Myth Q 1* to Jane Dadey in Marquette, Nebraska. She finished the appliqué, which Sally had begun, and then quilted the background of this 11' x 5' piece. Then I realized that some of the interior shapes were sagging, and Jane and I agreed on interior quilting and, finally, a couched edge of DMC thread around all the forms to give them the crispness they had before the quilting, which had softened them.

The second piece was taken on by Sally after we realized that we wanted a consistency of quilting which is possible only with one stitcher's hand. Several times during the course of the development of this piece, I tried to get Sally to agree to let one of our other experienced quilters complete it. But she was resolute in her determination to finish it, and when I saw the quality of her quilting I could understand why.

Sally Babson and I approving the progress of *Myth Q 2.*

Line drawing for *Cracking the Mythical Egg* (one of the five images in *Myth Q 2*), ©Judy Chicago, 1980.

I adapted the imagery I'd been using for the series on *Hatching the Universal Egg* and made an egg/belly form that was simultaneously a womb and the Goddess holding the sun and the moon.

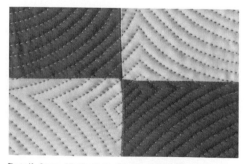

Detail from *Myth Q 2*, ©Judy Chicago, 1984. Executed by Sally Babson. Appliqué and quilting. Overall size: 90'' x 120''.

Section of *Myth Q 2*, ©Judy Chicago, 1984. Appliqué and quilting by Sally Babson. Overall size: 90'' x 120''.

The images seen here (clockwise) are: *Life Uncoiling from Chaos, Hatching the Universal Egg, Climbing the Tree of Life,* and *Cracking the Mythical Egg.* There are five images, each repeated three times in a different color configuration.

The Benicia reviews went very well. It seems that there is a point—about eight or ten months into a project—at which people get so invested that they can't go back, and the work reflects that. It begins to improve and to have a visual continuity as a result of regular stitching.

We're going to have a big review in June, one that I sense will be a point of culmination in the project. I'm encouraging all the needleworkers to come. Sally and I are pretty much agreed that I'll have to stop generating any more images by the end of the year, as the staff is staggering under the load of keeping track of all the work that's in progress now.

There was a big blow-up at the potluck around an "us-and-them" feeling, to which I have been very oblivious, between the needleworkers and the staff. Everybody got all upset, especially the staff members, who had already been feeling overworked, underpaid, and unappreciated. I was left with having to handle everyone's hurt feelings and confused emotions right in the middle of reviews, which are demanding enough as it is.

Jane Dadey, Sally, and I discuss the development of *Myth Q 1* at a review in Benicia.

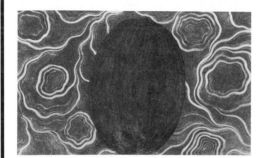

This ancient drawing was the basis for my design *Life Uncoiling from Chaos,* one of my favorite images in the myth quilts. (29)

There is an extraordinary visual rhythm possible with quilting stitches that are perfectly regular and evenly spaced. To achieve this, many of the quilters, including Sally, worked with small rulers. I decided on the width of the quilted rows based on the nature of the image. The only visual problem associated with quilting was that unquilted areas sagged, which disrupted the integrity of the forms.

Life Uncoiling from Chaos, ©Judy Chicago, 1980. Ink on vellum, 22'' x 18''.

Detail of *Life Uncoiling from Chaos,* from *Myth Q 2.* Quilted by Sally Babson.

Detail of *The Sun Birthing Twins*, from *Myth Q 1*, ©Judy Chicago, 1984. Executed by Jane Dadey. Appliqué, quilting, and embroidery. Overall size: 60'' x 132''.

Nana-Daho, the Mother-Creator, created the Primordial Twins —the Moon, who was female, and the Sun, who was male. These twins mated during a series of eclipses and were responsible for all further creation.

(30)

The linen was appliquéd and parts of it overlaid with metallic fabric; the quilting was done in DMC floss and the couching in DMC and metallic thread.

"Sally had basted the appliqué pieces in place on the background material and had begun some of the appliquéing. I completed the appliquéing by carefully clipping and turning the edges under and blind-stitching them. The appliqué work was done on my kitchen table, the largest flat surface I had. After the appliqué top was sandwiched together with polyester batting and muslin, I put it onto my quilting frame. The quilting was done in contour lines rippling out from and accentuating the shape of the appliqué pieces in two strands of DMC embroidery thread. The color of the quilting stitches next to an appliquéd piece matched the color of the appliqué. As the quilting stitches moved away from that piece, the color of the stitches gradually changed to the color of the next section of appliqué.

"I did the couching along each edge of the appliquéd pieces in a contrasting or complementary color in twelve strands of DMC floss. I controlled the visual width of the couching by changing the distance between the spaces used to hold the couching in place; the closer together the catch-threads, the thinner the line appeared. This was important because Judy wanted the couched lines to have the same visual consistency as the lines of quilting, which I had measured as I worked.

"To do the quilting, I found it necessary to use three thimbles on the hand working the needle . . . a metal thimble on the middle finger and two leather thimbles, one on the first finger and one on the thumb."
Jane Dadey

Jane worked with an unusual selection of thimbles.

Myth Q 1, ©Judy Chicago, 1984. Executed by Jane Dadey. Appliqué, quilting, and embroidery, 60'' x 132''.

Many of the needleworkers developed their own interpretations of my images. For me, the images in this piece read as follows: *Life Uncoiling from Chaos, Hatching the Universal Egg, The Sun Giving Birth to Twins, Climbing the Tree of Life, The Goddess Breathing Life Into the World While Holding the Sun and the Moon.* But I like Jane Dadey's impressions just as well, especially her description of the teardrop shapes.

"As I see Judy's images, beginning at the left, there is a large, dark image with many spirals; beside this are two flying bluebirds. In some myths, a bird laid the Universal Egg from which life hatched forth. Under the form depicting chaos, there is a chartreuse egg with a serpent coiled around to hatch it. On the other side of the birds is a vibrant yellow, orange, and gold sun/egg which is hatching or giving birth to red twins. These twins are being nurtured with blood-red milk flowing and spewing forth from a forest-green-nippled, light-blue breast. Behind the breast and rising upward are chartreuse twins taking in the breath of

life, which is represented in a large, dark-blue spiral coming from the mouth of a dark-green/black, Mother Earth/Universal Goddess figure who has blood-red, Medusa-like hair spiraling out around her. She is cradling the sun and the moon, a male and a female symbol. Under her arms are three teardrop shapes on a forest-green background—the first symbolizing the empty uterus; the second, the uterus with menstrual blood; and the third, the fertile uterus. Perhaps this area also symbolizes the idea of the Goddess dreaming dreams from her breast.''

Jane Dadey

Developing Our Exhibition Program

Thursday, December 15, 1982

I've been all over the country reviewing—Houston, New York, and Chicago. Most of the work I saw was pretty good. It has been wonderful for me to be able to connect names and faces and to see so much work and know that it is progressing. I still get waves of anxiety, but it does seem that the project is finally taking hold and moving along.

The next thing is to launch the exhibition part; it will require a lot of planning and really needs to get underway. My idea is to extend the "democratization" of art (which is what I've been involved in for some time) so that it not only allows more people to participate in the art-making process, but also brings work to communities that would not ordinarily have access to high-quality art, particularly art from a woman's point of view. I am structuring the Birth Project work so that different pieces are appropriate for different audiences. Some of the work is intended for a

When I began to think about the exhibition program for *The Birth Project*, I quickly realized that I needed help. Although I had a sense of what I wanted, I have no skills in exhibition design. I approached Michael Cronan, a graphic designer, whose child I had seen born. Afterward Michael had written and offered his help if I needed it. I also spoke with Stephen Hamilton, an exhibition designer whom I had met and become friends with through a show he had designed for Chevron, which included my work.

The three of us started to work together to establish a way of presenting contextual information with the needlework. I wanted a system that was straightforward, inexpensive to ship, and easy to install. Michael suggested using laminated panels which, we agreed, could be push-pinned to the wall. We did some samples and soon discovered that the problem with push-pins was that they could be as easily removed as installed—and so could the panels. So we decided to use brads. That was fine until we hung the panels with brads only on the top and noticed that a strong shadow was cast by the bottom of the panel. We then decided to use four brads in each panel—which definitely made for a more complicated installation. But still, lamination was cheaper than framing and a lot lighter to ship.

Michael set up a graphic format for the panels, and we chose the type. Of course we encountered millions of problems like the one with the push-pins. We had been spray-mounting photos to the photostats we used for the text.

When we shipped them by air, we found that all the laminates popped at the seams because of the glue. We then changed to a dry-mounting process, which was costlier and slower but more stable. We built canvas-wrapped panels for some of the documentation units, and they all warped because we had used such light wood in order to keep shipping costs down. When we used heavier wood, the shipping costs increased accordingly, but the warping stopped. Slowly, out of the nightmarish months of these continual problems, an exhibition system emerged for the design, production, lamination, packing, and crating of all the documentary materials. Although the system is not quite as simple as I would like, it is workable.

Once the graphic format was solved, Stephen took over the exhibition design, working with me to create each exhibition unit and then doing plans and drawings for the installation of each one. For a long time, he designed every exhibition we had, both in Benicia and around the country. But eventually, we included an exact installation drawing in the packing of each piece and allowed institutions to position the exhibition units as they desired.

Designers Stephen Hamilton, Michael Cronan, and I working on exhibition design.

DEBORAH LOHRKE

Stephen and I planning an exhibition unit.

I would go through the files we kept on each project and select the material that interested me, the "story" I wanted to tell. Then Stephen and I would look it over, and he would help me narrow the focus to the essential material. First we had too much documentation, then we had too little. The proper relationship between the art and documentation took us a long time to work out.

Stephen, Sally, and I.

It sounds ridiculous, but we spent hours trying to decide how to position framed pieces in relation to the laminated panels. The top edge of the laminates was one-half inch high, while the interior edge of the plastic frame was one-quarter inch. Should the inside top edge of the frame line up with the top edge of the paper, or should the top plastic edges of both pieces line up?

Trying out our installation procedures with our staff: Scott Lewis, our curator; Linda Moschell, who worked as our first exhibition coordinator; and Kathleen O'Connor, who was our first graphics production person.

When I began to conceive of the documentary materials that would surround and contextualize the *Birth Project* pieces, I had in mind educating viewers about the birth experience itself and the way it affects women as they look at the art. That way, viewers would be able to understand the context from which the images arose as well as their truth. I also wanted to use the graphic format developed by Michael and Stephen to reveal what women's lives are really like. The *Birth Project* work was done in the context of those lives, which reflect a wide spectrum of women's experience. Additionally, I wanted to raise some questions about the nature of art and what makes an artist—issues which are suggested by the photographs we include of the needleworkers stitching, not in a clean, white studio, alienated from the world, but in their own bedrooms or dens.

When one views art, one sees it—whether consciously or not—in the context of art history; however, there was almost no art-historical context for creating birth images. That was one of the problems I encountered when I approached the subject of birth. I had to go to direct experience for the source of the images—working directly with women, gathering testimony, hearing in their own voices what their experiences were like, reading, witnessing births. To really understand what the actual experience was and then translate and transform it, I had to work out of raw experience and build a whole iconography.

museum and gallery context, while other works are aimed at non-art contexts.

It is important to define the audience for each work, as different audiences bring different experiences and expectations to the viewing situation. For example, an art audience has knowledge of art but little understanding of women's history. A feminist audience, on the other hand, is familiar with the historical context from which my work emerges, but generally is unsophisticated about art. Both of these audiences see my work, and, in presenting it, I try to provide an appropriate framework. Now that my audience has broadened and diversified even further, the exhibition problems have become more complex.

Moreover, although the crowds at the Dinner Party *exhibitions were flattering, I still believe that the best viewing situation is one in which art can be contemplated in an intimate atmosphere. I want the* Birth Project *pieces to be exhibited in multiple showings, in different settings, for different audiences, while retaining a certain modesty in scale and format. The number of works that are in progress now, if finished, should make this possible. Now I have to establish a visual and philosophical context for each of the works so that they can be understood in terms of the experiences they reflect— experiences that are still outside the cultural mainstream.*

143

When there is no art context from which to make and then view the art, one comes to the subject matter unprepared. Viewers usually come to the *Birth Project* work with very little information about birth, about women, and, in many cases, about art, and therefore I felt that this contextual material was essential to the understanding of the images themselves.

Stephen brought a set of skills from exhibition design which are not usually applied to art. Because he had worked on many shows that were geared toward a sizable public audience, he was able to help me create a bridge between my work and an audience that is larger than the usual one for art.

"I became involved with Judy in 1978 on an exhibition project, 'Creativity: The Human Resource.' The show presented the creative processes of men and women in the arts as well as the sciences. The criteria for inclusion were that the individual was living, was an American, and had documented his or her process. Judy was one of the few women who met those criteria. Little did I know that six years later I would be involved with her in an effort to present and document a body of work as complex as *The Birth Project.*

"When Judy asked Michael Cronan and me to help her in getting the work prepared for exhibition, none of us fully appreciated the scope of the task we had undertaken. Usually an exhibition project has a client, a site, a budget, fabricators, and a deadline. *The Birth Project* had none of these from the outset.

"It was a tedious and frustrating process. Often, as Judy and I sat on the floor with the work and the needleworkers' lives spread around us, we were overwhelmed. It was difficult to shape each exhibition unit. Sometimes we agreed, and sometimes we literally fought. Judy is strong-willed. She can be relentless in her demands for clear thinking and attention to detail. Her memory astounds me.

"Much of Judy's staff, and all of the needleworkers, are volunteers. How demanding can one be of people who are donating their time? Very! I was amazed; she got results that no employer could draw from mere employees.

"At dinner one evening, a mutual friend commented: 'Judy, everyone thinks you're a bitch; why not be one?' Well, she can't, because she isn't. Being 'nice' didn't get *The Birth Project* into the world. Hard work did."

Exhibition designer, Stephen Hamilton
San Francisco, California

Stephen at work on installation drawing.

Linda Moschell and Kathleen O'Connor installing the laminated panels, which requires drawing a chalk line to establish the height of the top panel and then leveling the panels as they are positioned. Stephen's installation drawing (on the wall) specifies the exact position of every item to be installed.

Marj Moore, who worked both as our bookkeeper and as a gallery docent, enjoyed explaining the work to viewers, who never imagined the amount of time it had taken us to figure out how to get that work up on the wall.

Mary Ross took on the monumental task of developing and coordinating our exhibition program.

"We received a lot of exhibition inquiries that started out, 'You've probably never thought of coming to . . .', but our goal was to reach a diverse audience. The University of Texas Medical School at Galveston celebrated its tenth anniversary by showing art from *The Birth Project*. Many colleges and universities mounted exhibitions using student activity funds usually slated for rock concerts and sports events. Cities in Montana and Alaska wanted exhibitions which could go on to even smaller towns in their states.

"As our exhibition program grew, we heard that all kinds of people were standing in line at civic centers, community college galleries, libraries. The show organizers I worked with told me they'd never had such excitement about any show. It was exciting for me, too; I was seeing a huge audience emerge, just as I'd hoped and expected. I hope that some of those college students grow up to be museum directors!"

Mary Ross Taylor

Mary Ross discussing a prospective *Birth Project* exhibition.

This poster from the exhibition at Artisans gallery in Mill Valley, California, marked the beginning of our formal exhibition program. By the time *The Birth Project* was completed in the spring of 1985, we had held more than thirty-five exhibitions.

Our exhibition program, which has been coordinated by Mary Ross Taylor, is built on the same decentralized basis as *The Birth Project* itself. We have no plans to present all the work together, and, in fact, that would be neither practical nor desirable. Over the last few years, we have provided simultaneous shows to galleries, universities, conferences, and libraries. Once all the work is completed, we will offer a series of traveling exhibitions for different spaces, contexts, and audiences.

We both solicit exhibitions and respond to requests, and we have developed a procedure that allows us to match the exhibition space and situation with an appropriate grouping of *Birth Project* works. There will be eighty exhibition units ranging in size from 12 to 45 linear feet. Exhibitions consist of between one and twenty of these units and are available for rental fees based upon the size of the show. It is my hope that *Birth Project* work will travel widely and reach any audience that is interested in it. I have tried to structure the work so that both its form and its content make it extremely accessible. I am also interested in trying to place or donate the pieces for permanent location so that images of birth can become a part of our cultural heritage.

At Home with the Needleworkers

Undated journal entry

I just returned from another photo trip with Jon. I am wiped out after doing two photo sessions. I have long wanted to start this project of photographing and interviewing the needleworkers in their own homes. Last week I went to Helen Cohen's in Palo Alto. She is a returning graduate student in art and collects all sorts of wonderful objects. Her story is so typical—a woman who wanted to be an artist and struggled for years with the dual responsibility of five children, a marriage, and an ongoing need to paint and then finally went back to school when the children were grown. While we were there, I realized that I had gotten no real sense of her as a person during the whole time she worked on a Crowning batik quilt.

DEBORAH LOHRKE

When I visited Helen Cohen at home, she and I went through her scrapbooks and chose material for the documentation that accompanied the piece when it was exhibited at Through the Flower. Later we cut down the size of the exhibition unit for easier traveling. Unfortunately, our graphic format had changed, and we had to omit a lot of the material from the scrapbook.

In deciding how to present *Birth Project* work in a contextual framework, it seemed important that in our decentralized network, almost everyone had "worked at home." Women have always been identified with the home and domesticity, and this has been seen as personally limiting. Then why had so many of the needleworkers chosen to do their stitching at home? I could hope to answer this only after visiting them where they lived and worked.

JON McNALLY

Lael Cohen at work on *Creation of the World NP 3* in her basement room in Oakland, California.

JON McNALLY

Hope Wingert working on *The Crowning Q 2/9* at home in Benicia, California.

JON McNALLY

Lael worked as a housekeeper/domestic.

The first trip Jon and I made was not altogether satisfactory. Although the woman we photographed, Hope Wingert, is an old friend of Jon's, she had gotten all dressed up. But I want everyone to be seen in their natural situation—that's the whole point. We decided that we had better take more time with each visit and give the woman a chance to relax.

On another photo trip, we drove up to a large, rather elegant house in the Oakland hills. Lael Cohen, who was needlepointing *Creation of the World* on 24-mesh canvas, met us even before we got out of the car. She was obviously excited by our visit. She led us through the spacious house and down to her small, cramped apartment in the basement. She had prepared fruit, cheese, crackers, and strong coffee, which she knew I liked. I had already eaten a big breakfast, but I realized, and pointed out to Jon, that we could probably count on food at every woman's house

and should probably not eat before setting out on these trips so we could accept women's natural hospitality. Lael was working as a housekeeper/domestic for two lawyers and caring for their children. She worked from 7:30 a.m. to 7:00 p.m., then stitched until midnight. She told us her entire life story. I could have killed myself for not bringing a tape recorder.

After our visit to Lael's we went to the home of another woman, who was, like Lael, working on a *Creation of the World* needlepoint. But this one is on 18-mesh canvas, and the colors are altogether different. If our present screening procedure had been in place when the project started, she would never have received a work. In fact, when I saw the actual quality of her life and the apartment, which so clearly reflects her spirit, I was tempted to wrest the piece from her hands, but I'm afraid it was too late.

Jackie Moore working on *The Crowning Q 5* in Mendon, Massachusetts.

JON McNALLY

"The time I have spent on this work has been emotionally and spiritually the most satisfying thing I have ever done. My needlework is the one area I control and, when assaulted from all sides by the demands and needs of others, I've always found sanctuary in my work."

Jacquelyn Moore

A poem about stitching, 1982

I have a tiny magic wand
And I know its secrets in my fingers,
To move it to and fro,
Make loops and curves
Shining bright,
To appear for me, then disappear,
Turning its trail into silky smooth vapor
And leaving me
A canvas filled with visions and hues
Of a most magical texture
And tiny, most intricate details.
A vision of dreams
And mysteries of creation
Brought alive by my own fingers
Waving the tiny magic wand.

Kathy Lenhart

As a way of trying to get her to relax in front of the camera, I asked her to tell me about herself and about how she spent her days. I was curious because the progress on her piece had been so slow, although she didn't work full-time. She reported that she got up between 8:30 and 9:00, "got herself together," made business calls (about unspecified business matters), did paperwork (she said she was on so many mailing lists it was overwhelming), then ate, read, took a nap, and finally, at 2 p.m., went out to do errands or volunteer work until 6 p.m. Then she came home, got dressed, and went out for the evening. When she returned home after her evening out, she sat down in front of the TV and ate and stitched for several hours. The idea of my beautifully painted needlepoint canvas being worked on in front of the TV with food and stained hands totally undid me.

The worst part of the day, especially for Jon, was when this woman disappeared into her bedroom and then re-emerged dressed in an outlandish belly-dancing outfit—veils and chiffons, rayons and polyesters, all covered with sequins which she'd carefully sewn on when she was supposed to be needlepointing *Creation of the World* and contributing to the liberation of women on the planet. Jon and I finally stumbled out, leaving an uneaten plate of bagels and cream cheese. We got into the car, I trembled for twelve blocks, and, when we stopped for gas, Jon was so shaken that he couldn't get the gas to pump into the gas tank. I never imagined where this project would lead me or what lifestyles I'd be forced to confront. It made me wonder how women think they can do serious work while living a life that is so unfocused and fragmented.

147

These trips are really something for me; I'm learning a lot about women's real lives—and I hate a lot of what I'm learning. I'm discovering many of the reasons that women have so much difficulty in achieving their goals. They may "want" to do something, and they may have the talent, but so many women don't realize that their lives must be structured to accommodate their work. Moreover, so many of them have no idea what the world is really like, and thus they can't deal with what takes place when they try to achieve what they want.

So many times, when I work with the needleworkers and when I lecture, I am faced with the fact that most women seem totally confused about what power means. They see me as being powerful, and therefore they assume that I can change everything—make the world view needlework as art, arrange things so everyone can get paid for their work, ensure that my work force is racially and ethnically balanced—and it does no good to try to explain. When people are committed to a fantasy, it's hard to get them to change their views.

Almost all the stitchers worked on their *Birth Project* pieces at home, although the Lo Biondo family stitched at the needlepoint shop they own. Some of the needleworkers were homemakers, some were professional needleworkers, and others had full-time jobs in an array of fields. (We tried to capture something about each woman's life in the photographs we took.) The fact that most of the work was situated in people's homes all over the country for periods of one to three years did bring the art, the meaning and implications of the imagery, and the seriousness with which most of the stitchers took their work to the attention of their families, their friends, and their communities. No one could work on *The Birth Project* and then go back to her "real life" at nights as people did in *The Dinner Party*. However, everyone was certainly involved for a different reason.

There was, I must admit, something extremely touching about seeing all these women take the risk of bringing *Birth Project* works into their homes. For each one, it meant an inevitable confrontation with ignorance—ignorance about art and why one makes it, ignorance about birth and women's feelings about it, ignorance about women and how we really feel. This ignorance was often expressed in the question continually (and usually suspiciously) put to me: "Why do these women want to work with you?" As I mentioned, different people had different reasons. But one thing bound us all together— a belief in the art.

(Left to right) Marion, Sharon (with child), Maria, and Jan Lo Biondo at their shop with *The Crowning NP 5.*

The Lo Biondos, who worked as a family, executed their needlepoint of *The Crowning* at their needlecraft shop in Vineland, New Jersey. I thought it was wonderful for an image like mine to be in the middle of traditional needlework patterns and for the customers and students to have a chance to see that needlepoint can be a personally expressive medium.

Maria Lo Biondo at home in Vineland, New Jersey.

"It seems that being part of *The Birth Project* has unleashed our energies in many ways. Who would have dreamed that a 'sewing circle' would become so revolutionary!"
Maria Lo Biondo

DEBORAH LOHRKE

Carol Hill at work.

Although Carol Hill did not execute the piece she embroidered at her shop in Chico, California, she was another woman who, like the Lo Biondos, owned her own business. But unlike theirs, hers was not connected to needlework.

Rhonda Gerson working on a petit point of *Creation of the World.*

"When I first heard about *The Birth Project,* I wasn't sure what to expect. When I saw Judy's drawings, I was surprised; but it only took seconds for them to soak in: birth and creation are powerful and symbolic, as well as personal."

Rhonda Gerson

Jean Berens is a childbirth educator and nurse practitioner at Planned Parenthood in Milwaukee, Wisconsin.

"My two paternal great grandmothers were midwives. In addition to my heritage, I have long been personally involved in family planning and reproductive health, as both a nurse and a sexuality educator. *The Birth Project* has allowed me to express my beliefs, the thoughts I feel and teach every day, in an art form."

Needleworker Jean Berens
Milwaukee, Wisconsin

Jean Berens working on petit-point version of *Creation of the World.*

"You can't work on this without examining your own feelings about birth and women and motherhood."

Jean Berens

"An aspect of this project that I like a lot is getting exhibition credit for my work. I'm real proud that I did my best work for this project and that, when it is displayed, I will be given public credit in the documentation."

Kathy Lenhart

"Ignorance is the big enemy. It makes you powerless and keeps you afraid. Knowledge gives you power and courage. And you need courage to give birth, to believe in yourself as a part of nature, equipped with all the necessary natural processes."

Dee Thompson

"I would like to contribute to documenting the greatness of women and expose birth for the strong female experience it is."

Ann Raschke

"By donating my time and skill to a project that already has the resources to reach such a wide audience, it is possible for me to 'make a mark' more swiftly, and swift action is surely needed by the women's movement."

Kris Wetterlund

"I've been able to see myself as a more creative person since being a part of the project. I've always been practical, not allowing much time for extras. And art, in any form, was extra. But now I see art—and especially women's crafts—as a necessary part of living. I've always loved grandma's quilts and afghans, but they were presented to me as 'just something women did.' Now I see 'women's work' as art in the most real sense."

Tere Jensen

"The piece I worked on came to be synonymous with my personal growth and a formal statement of my refusal to accept the expectations imposed on me."

Needleworker Candis Duncan Pomykala
DeKalb, Illinois

"*The Birth Project* has provided the means for my renewed self-respect—trying to wrest some privacy and time away from family life to be myself and to be creative."

Dee Thompson

"By showing us as ordinary women working in ordinary homes, recognition is placed in the realm of the possible for other women. Our talents are validated."

Kathy Lenhart

On the other hand, many of the needle-workers have integrated their lives and their work to an extent that I can't help but envy a little, though I have no desire for the kind of lives most of them lead. At the same time that there is something suspect about the quality of work possible in a day that includes cooking, cleaning, stitching, taking care of kids, and then stitching some more, there is also the undeniable fact that the sense of despair which accompanies the isolation I've imposed upon myself in order to do concentrated work does not exist for these women.

I feel that all this is having a profound effect on me—more than I know yet, as it will be a while before I've seen as much of these lives as I need to see. If I continue to work as I'm doing, designing for a decentralized network, I will be much more realistic in my expectations. If I decide not to, that will be, at least in part, a result of my coming to the conclusion that this way of working is not something I want to do again.

Many of the needle-workers could never have been involved in *The Birth Project* if they had not been able to work at home. For some, being at home presented problems, but most felt good about it. These pages present different people and demonstrate a range of attitudes toward working at home, working with me, and becoming involved in *The Birth Project*.

Sally at work at Through the Flower after she stopped working at home.

Catherine Russo working at home in Houston, Texas, on *Creation of the World 9/9*.

"*The Birth Project* changed the focus of my work; it was probably the first time in my life that I ever worked outside the home. At first I came close to panicking, but then I found that I actually enjoyed it and realized that I didn't need to be home all the time. At home, I didn't have anybody to bump up against."

Sally Babson

"Although women in my position have come in for a great deal of criticism in the last few years, I feel good about staying home, and what I'm doing now is very important to me. For years before having a family, I was free to be my own woman. The decision to stay home and be with my children was a conscious one, made on purpose. I like being the pillar of the PTA and civic groups. I have learned not to be upset by the social criticism, although, in this time of liberation, it's too bad women like me can't be allowed to do our own thing without constantly being hassled."

Merrily Rush Whitaker

"One reason *The Birth Project* appealed to me was the fact that I would be able to work at home. Initially, I thought, I could work a few hours in the afternoon while my two-year-old, Jason, slept and again later in the evening when both children were asleep. (Working at night was not possible because the colors were so close that blending them the way I wanted to could only be done in natural light.)

"Before I started stitching each area, I would jot down the number of the thread color and the type of stitch I would be using. Then, when Jason woke up, I would know right where I was and where to pick up the next time.

"By the time I was nearing completion of the piece, Jason would no longer sleep in the afternoon. I didn't believe it, but he had outgrown his afternoon nap. Luckily, I was able to finish up satisfactorily, but it was to a chorus of 'Can I get up now? Is nap time over? I'm not tired. Do I have to stay in my room?' On April 2, 1982, Jason climbed out of his crib and I finished *Creation of the World*."

Catherine Russo

"This art is about women's experience, done in a medium that women can relate to. Even those women who don't do needlework understand it; they have a mother or grandmother or aunt somewhere in their lives who has done needlework, and they can understand that needlework is women's realm."

Mary Ewanoski

"When Judy was delayed by a snowstorm in Chicago, I called the airline to ask whether she was on the next flight from Chicago to Des Moines. 'What is the name of the passenger?' the information clerk asked. 'Judy Chicago,' I answered. 'Ma'am, *what* is the name of the passenger?' she barked. 'Ju-dy Chi-ca-go,' I replied, drawing out the name. 'Ma'am, I'm asking you the name of the person flying,' she said, very exasperated with me. 'Her name is Judy Chicago. She's a famous artist living in California,' I replied (know-it-all). 'I never heard of her,' she retorted. 'Will you remember her now?' 'I'll never forget,' she laughed. And I didn't either."

Mickey Lorber

Mickey Lorber, who worked on *Creation of the World NP 1*, at home in her "Mickey Mouse" room in Des Moines, Iowa.

BIANCA INDELICATO

The town of Port Alexander has a small number of inhabitants, all of whom have deliberately chosen to live with only rudimentary services in an unspoiled environment.

"The community I live in is unique; we are a bubble, separate from the technological world most Americans live in. We have no electricity (some people own their own private generators), no roads, cars, or TVs. We aren't connected to any other town via a road, nor do we have any commercial ferries. We have mail-plane service twice a week. We listen to the radio for our news; we use our feet, wheelbarrows, bikes, and skiffs with outboard motors for transportation around town. Our economy is almost totally based on fishing—which puts everyone in very direct (almost daily) contact with Mother Earth."

Judy Wallen

"I have been a feminist since the day I was born. Throughout childhood, I gritted my teeth and buried my feelings of anger and sadness and disgust when I saw how the women around me allowed themselves to be treated and how they just settled for limited lives, not trying to make any changes to better themselves. I recall at a very early age promising myself that I would never be that kind of woman; that I would make my own decisions, do my own creative work, stand my ground. It was a tough battle, and it still is. Sometimes I tend to allow myself to be completely powerless—and it's an easy trap to get into when I am at home most of the time with a child." Pamella Nesbit

Judy Wallen, who executed *The Crowning Q 5/9,* at home in Port Alexander, Alaska.

"I think it's interesting and positive that even though I live in a small, isolated Alaskan town I was able to participate in *The Birth Project* because I could work at home. Therefore, our community was exposed to Judy Chicago and her work on a first-hand basis." Judy Wallen

Franny Minervini-Zick, who embroidered *Creation of the World 8/9,* at home with her child in Sebastopol, California.

I am hopeful.
  Hopeful of a future...
  Hopeful of a future free of
    prejudices...
  Hopeful that my children's children's
    children's children's children will
    look back and say we were
    barbarians—we didn't really know
    any better. But some of us knew,
    and we did all we could to change
    the way things were.
I am hopeful that my great, great,
  great, great, grandchildren will know
  that about me. Franny Minervini-Zick

Pamella Nesbit, who executed six *Birth Project* works, in her studio at home in Sebastopol, California.

Pamella Nesbit at home with her son, Christopher.

The experiences and the quality of life of some of the needleworkers seemed to me to have a great deal of meaning. The fact that the work was being done "at home," in the context of each woman's life—rather than apart from her everyday existence—seemed to suggest that the idea of the "alienated artist" working alone in the studio might not be relevant to women. If, by the very nature of our childbearing function, women are not alienated, then the prevailing definition of an artist excludes most women's participation in "serious" art.

Moreover, it seemed to me that the very qualities necessary for successful family life—nurturance, patience, understanding and compassion—were those qualities that are so blatantly missing from the world. My trips to the needleworkers' homes were instrumental in my decision to show the *Birth Project* images in the context of the environments in which they were executed. Part of the very nature of *Birth Project* art arises from the unique way in which each work was created. In order to understand the art and the experiences the work embodies, I felt it was essential to include the stories of the needleworkers' lives. When we know *every* woman's story, then no Freud will ever have to ask again: What do women want?

My trips to needleworkers' houses became an important part of the process of *The Birth Project*. More and more, I began to incorporate the experiences of the needleworkers into the material we included in the documentation accompanying each work. Mary Ann Hickey's life was typical of many of the women's in *The Birth Project*, as was the way she related the image she worked on to her life.

Mary Ann Hickey's Home on Chicago's South Side.

Mary Ann Hickey received us warmly when we first visited her on the South Side of Chicago. Throughout the project, she always found time to help at the midwestern reviews, to put up staff and needleworkers, and to cook wonderful food for us.

Mary Ann Hickey, who embroidered *Hatching the Universal Egg E 2*, at work in her home in Chicago, Illinois.

Mary Ann Hickey wearing the magnifying glasses she used while stitching.

As a result of her involvement in *The Birth Project*, Mary Ann became the editor of a needlework magazine.

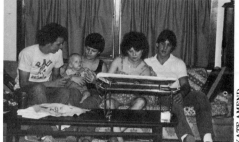

Mary Ann Hickey with her children.

Dear Judy,

I often recall what you said to me on the day you gave the piece to me—about sometimes thinking that my children were strangling me rather than hugging me. I began to see this ambivalence in the image itself—there is the nurturance/ entrapment dichotomy. The same form that is the child's alimentary tract becomes the umbilical cord which simultaneously nourishes the child and strangles the mother. This seems a powerful symbol of the symbiotic connections between mother and child, at least as I experienced it.

In addition to the visual associations of the piece, I experience physical sensations while I stitch; my lower back starts to ache. It reminds me of the labors I had—all back labor and down into the tops of my legs. It's like being back in that time again, only giving birth to our *Birth Project* baby this time.

Looking at the baby-embryo makes me think of the Universal baby, which includes my six children. I like the fact that you made the child featureless and did not include the mother's head. Even though I see her as myself, she is really Everywoman.

In sisterhood,
Mary Ann

152

From Home to Documentation

In 1982, I made a trip to Jane Gaddie Thompson's house in Houston with photographer Mary Margaret Hansen. While we were visiting, Jane told me that her husband, Ray, after an initial period of discomfort with the image, had become very supportive of her involvement in the project and had encouraged her to go to California with the finished piece. His only reservation, she said rather wickedly, was that he felt funny about having to pay for an extra ticket for "her," which is how they referred to the piece.

Jane, who has one child, lives in a nice suburban house with a lovely back yard. She stitched on a frame in a small room off the kitchen, which also contained her child's hobby horse and basket of toys. While her daughter napped in the afternoon or played with her father at night, Jane slowly added small, careful stitches to my anguished image of a woman being torn apart in childbirth. I had my usual reaction after being in the environment of one of the women who's working with me: My life is in such contrast to the tranquility of that calm, peaceful house and yard. It's as if all the struggle I'm used to were absent from Jane's life, and yet she was totally aware that the image she stitched, whose power and strength seemed so incongruous in that peaceful setting, is real and truthful.

"When Judy first asked me if she could come over with a photographer, I wondered why they were coming to my house. I supposed that it was expressly to photograph me, in my home, working on my stitching. Later I found that that was only a small reason for their coming. Judy asked me to please not get dressed up or put on a big spread of food. I hadn't even thought of doing either one. She said that some people she'd gone to visit were really decked out, and she wanted the opportunity to see us in our own surroundings, to see how we looked every day, not as we'd look if we were giving a party. 'How about lunch?' I asked, since Judy had said to expect them shortly after noon. I asked if a bologna sandwich would be too fancy. Judy laughed and said that would be fine, as long as I didn't go to any trouble.

"I remembered from the Saturday before that Judy liked mineral water and Diet 7-Up, and from reading the articles in a 'love packet,' I found out that one of her indulgences was cookies. So I made a quick trip to the grocery store, and Monday evening I baked a batch of Tollhouse cookies.

"Judy and Mary Margaret arrived about 12:30; they both started taking pictures the minute I opened the door. My daughter, Laura, was excited, as though she knew exactly who was paying us a visit. (She has told everyone all this week that Judy Chicago came to our house for lunch!) Judy went out the back door to see the yard and take pictures out there. I still don't see what on earth was so interesting about our house to deserve so many pictures.

"Judy wanted to go ahead and eat before they got down to the business of more formal picture-taking and question-asking. She really looked floored when I pulled out the cookies and exclaimed, 'You sure know a lot about me!' She said several times throughout the next few hours how touched she was that I'd done those special things just for her—the mineral water, the Diet 7-Up, and especially the cookies. To me, it just seemed the hospitable thing to do."

Jane Gaddie Thompson
Journal entry

Jane Gaddie Thompson's house in Houston, Texas.
MARY MARGARET HANSEN

Monday, March 29, 1982

I am working on something that I've had planned for some time now—a 5' x 30' drawing on black paper. I feel that it will give me a chance to take the original birth and creation material I've been working on and finally bring it to an end. It makes me feel better to go into the studio every morning with my colored pencils and see results at the end of the day—although the drawing is taking longer than I had anticipated. I have no idea how I'm going to handle it or what I'm going to do with it when I take it off the wall.

Working on *In the Beginning*, ©Judy Chicago, 1984. Prismacolor on Canzon paper, 62" x 30' 8¼".

JON McNALLY

153

Sunday, May 2, 1982

I woke up with a kind of startling revelation—I feel that I shouldn't have to do anything but work in the studio, and perhaps that is simply unrealistic. This is my project, my vision, my goals, and I just have to accept the responsibility and know that I can't give it away to anyone else. I hate it, but I guess I'll just have to muddle along and try to make the best of it.

There are some people waiting for work, but no new samples and not many letters of inquiry. My sense is that there will be another surge of interest in the project soon, and I will generate a whole new round of work between June and the end of September. Then the needlework will be over and the focus will be on finishing and exhibiting it. I wonder how I'll feel when my studio work is done.

Plans for the big June review are going well. People are coming from all over. It will be a chance for a lot of us to be together, as over half of the project people will be here. The last review in Houston went well; at the potluck, we discussed finances and our difficulties in raising the money this enterprise is costing (something which, as usual, I had not thought about when I began). I told people that they needed to think about generating money if they wanted to keep the Houston space we were using open, as we could not fund it forever, and that they also needed to think about what kind of exhibition they wanted. I just assumed that everyone would want their family and friends to see all the work that had been done in Houston. I've been

Enjoying the lunch Jane Gaddie Thompson made with Jane and her daughter Laura.

Jane showed me where she worked on *Birth Tear E 2,* and I took pictures sitting on Laura's hobby horse.

"I had my *Birth Project* folder and my two journal volumes piled up on the kitchen counter. Judy asked what these books were and whether she could look at them and read a little. I said sure, as long as she wouldn't be offended by anything she read. I was appalled when I saw her flip back to the date of the last review. She read quietly for a few minutes and then put it back on the counter. I didn't know whether to expect all hell to break loose or not. But then, in her own very emphatic way, Judy began to exclaim that this was exactly what she'd been trying to get people to do, to express their real feelings. She said that that was why she had asked us to keep journals, that knowing our true responses helped her to relate to us better.

"Judy asked if I might be willing to let someone edit my journal for use in the documentation and later in the book. I think I could do that without much hesitation, now that I know that what I've written will not be taken wrongly or with malice.

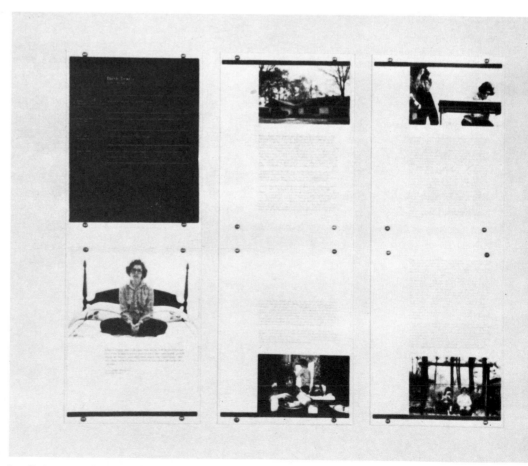

Installation view, *Birth Tear #2.*

Jane and I with Jane's daughter Laura in the backyard.

"Judy wanted to go outside for a while, to see the greenhouse and to sit outside and talk. . . . I turned around to see Judy and Laura swinging in the lawn swing and talking to each other. I couldn't resist; I had to run inside to get *my* camera. Some day, Laura will have great pride in being able to see herself with Judy, to know that she, too, was part of something very important. The whole day was such a nice experience."

Jane Gaddie Thompson
Journal entry 3/1/82

The first exhibition unit that Stephen, Michael, and I formatted contained the version of *Birth Tear* embroidered by Jane Gaddie Thompson. Jane had provided me with a great deal of documentation from her journal, and her description of my visit to her home was, I thought, quite representative of the transactions between me and the needleworkers. The exhibition unit contains, in addition to the work of art itself, stitching samples by Jane, excerpts from her journal chronicling the stitching process, photographs of and text about my visit to her home, and a portrait of Jane, which is captioned by a statement expressing her hopes for the work she executed and for *The Birth Project* generally. This is the type of installation we tried to design for each work of art.

encouraging all the needleworkers to think about informal exhibitions of the works they're stitching in their own communities. I want everyone to have the sense of completion that comes with showing the work they've done, but there is no way we can guarantee exhibitions of works everywhere they've been executed.

My comments were met by shock and resistance; obviously the needleworkers, just like me and so many other women, find it hard to take responsibility. They seemed perfectly content to keep their noses to the canvas or fabric, be provided with images, materials, and an organizational structure, and not have to think about generating anything themselves. One needleworker told Pat Morton, our Houston administrator, that when she returned home from the meeting and told her husband about the discussion, he said, "Welcome to the real world."

Big June Review

Wednesday, June 2, 1982

Well, the big June review weekend is here. Even before anyone arrived, it was hectic; the phone never stopped ringing, and there was tons of mail. I worked all week under the pressure of too much to do.

People started arriving today. I'm sure I'll be in so deep for the next few days, I won't have a chance to think, at least until Monday.

Tuesday, June 8

The review weekend officially began Thursday night, when we had a barbeque at Susan's house; her husband, Lynn Francom, prepared two delicious smoked turkeys. There seemed to be a million things to do Wednesday and Thursday, but mostly I tried to be loose and go with what was happening. There were so many pieces here that Sally and I reviewed all day Friday, Saturday, and Sunday.

Birth Project participants start the June review weekend with a barbeque.

KATE AMEND

Pat Morton and Hazel Hood Kiley arrive at the Benicia Inn.

JON McNALLY

The Benicia Inn welcomed the *Birth Project* women, who filled all the hotel's rooms.

JON McNALLY

Gathered at the Benicia Inn for conversation (left to right): Judy Wallen (with daughter Serenity), Hazel Hood Kiley, Jane Dadey, Kathy Lenhart, Pat Morton, and Joyce Gilbert.

JON McNALLY

In June 1982, almost seventy *Birth Project* members—needleworkers, researchers, and staff—assembled for a review of over fifty works. People came from all over the country, staying at a small, local inn or camping at staff members' houses. Some folks even sacked out at the building so they wouldn't miss a moment's excitement.

In addition to the reviews themselves, which went on for three days, there were events and activities, formal lectures and informal raps, and, of course, food everywhere.

There were really some great moments during the weekend. The owners of the Benicia Inn, where most of the people stayed, made these great welcoming signs and produced champagne to toast the needleworkers, who stayed up half the night talking. There was this incredible sense of women sharing in a way that, if it could extend out into the world, could be a model for a global community based on cooperation rather than competition.

"The five-day weekend was so many things: wonderful, hard, full, intense, joyous, perfect, beautiful, kind and loving—especially for the out-of-towners. A weekend of sisterhood, indulgence, and irresponsibility; what more could our needleworkers want? Five days free of work, home, and family. How different for those of us on the staff who made it all happen. Now that it's over, it's hard to believe it all happened. I feel like I've been away—to a world of *Birth Project* women, cooking, eating, singing, talking, being together—it's hard to give it up and come back to day-to-day life, routine work, decisions, conflicts, and demands."

Birth Project Administrator
Susan Lynn
Benicia, California

Even though their spelling left something to be desired, the owners of the Benicia Inn made everyone feel appreciated.

Jane Dunbar Johnson, from Huntington Beach, California, one of the *Birth Project* researchers, worked with Beth Rose throughout the weekend.

JON McNALLY

On Friday night, thirty people crowded into a tiny Mexican restaurant, almost driving the besieged husband-and-wife cook/waitress team out of their minds. Eventually everyone was served a spicy and abundant dinner, and we all trooped back for an evening talk on the findings of our research team.

Beth Rose, a nurse and the Benicia research coordinator, showed slides and shared information and myths regarding birth in various cultures. While she worked with us, she corresponded with people all over the world, giving them assignments or topics she and I had outlined and receiving and acknowledging information which, for a while, seemed to pour in from everywhere.

I was personally interested in using the material for image-making, but we received much more information than I could use. Then I decided that it would be important to try and develop a global picture of the birth experience, which proved to be very difficult. Many countries kept no records of maternal mortality, as the mothers' experience is not considered crucial, only the infants'. Moreover, many countries don't gather any statistics at all. But we put together enough material to see that, for large segments of the world's population, the birth experience is not what the alternative birth movement would describe as "ecstatic."

One thing that made me quite angry at discussions about our findings is the way some women would try to push away the information with the argument that "things are getting better." Or, if Beth or I recounted the facts of birth conditions in this or that country, we would be silenced by someone recounting her "wonderful" home birth experience, as if her personal good fortune somehow overshadowed the larger political, social, and medical implications of what we had learned about the rest of the world.

We fell far short of my goal to assemble a file that provided a worldwide view of women's birth experience. This was a much larger task than any of us had dreamed. Page Prescott, our most recent research coordinator, has organized the material we did gather in the hope that it will have some value, as rough as it is.

157

The "Big June Review," as we at Through the Flower refer to this momentous gathering, was a culminating moment in The Birth Project. Before this event, there was still a sense of doubt about whether the project would work. Afterwards, we all knew that The Birth Project had taken hold. Almost half of the project members were assembled for this review, which involved so many works that they occupied every available wall of Through the Flower.

It was incredible for Sally and me to be able to see so many of the works at one time—unfinished as they were—hanging together. It was clear to us that we had succeeded in generating both the images and a network to produce those images. It was also overwhelming to see so much work at once, and it made me more convinced than ever that the work should be exhibited in small groupings.

The weekend was absolutely fantastic—the energy, the commitment and the level of sharing. The work looks good, though not as good as many of the people seem to think. I might be imposing inappropriate standards, but I still have trouble with the way the fabric puckers. I want embroideries to be as flat as painted canvases, and the fact that they are not bothers me, though it doesn't seem to bother anyone else.

(Left to right) Pamella Nesbit, Ann Gibson, Maggie Eoyang, Jean Berens, Roxanna Rutter, Franny Minervini-Zick, and me.

Needleworkers sometimes came to Benicia around review time to pitch in on another piece or to spend a few weeks completing their own work in close cooperation with me. Also, while the needleworkers were waiting for their personal reviews, they'd often sit down together and stitch. It was always nice to see everyone working together at the building, although I certainly didn't want them there all the time. I'd had enough of that with *The Dinner Party*.

(Left to right) Susan MacMillan, Janis Wicks, Scott Lewis, Sally, and I at a somber review.

Linda Gaughenbaugh, Sally, and I during a review.

(Left to right) Debbie Lohrke, Susan Lynn, Linda Moschell, researcher Jane Dunbar Johnson, and Scott Lewis in our office.

The staff worked hard throughout the review weekend, and everyone felt a strong sense of connection and the satisfaction of being part of a well-functioning team.

Franny Minervini-Zick and I enjoying a humorous moment during a review.

JON McNALLY

There was always a group huddled around the "hospitality table" downstairs, where a continuous flow of food kept everyone well-nourished. Joyce Gilbert, Pat Morton, Kate Amend, and Mary Ross Taylor, along with everyone else, liked to hang around the overflowing table and—like Beth Rose and Linda Gaughenbaugh (in back)—look at the art.

Jane Dadey and Franny Minervini-Zick taking a break.

(Left to right) L.A. Hassing, Pamella Nesbit, and Sally let their hair down.

JON McNALLY

Mary Ross Taylor in her "traffic controller" beanie.

Mary Ross was "traffic controller" for the weekend, a job which consisted of organizing airport pickups, sleeping arrangements, and tours of the area and generally making sure that things ran smoothly.

(Left to right) Marcia Nowlan and friend, Maggie Eoyang, Penny Davidson, Page Prescott, Mary Ross Taylor, Roxanna Rutter, and others enjoy a relaxed moment during the intensity of Review Weekend.

(Left to right) Hazel Hood Kiley, Sally Babson, Ruth Posselt, Leigh Heller, Penny Davidson, and Debbie Lohrke listening to a needleworker discuss the piece she was working on. There were impromptu presentations throughout the weekend.

During all the years I've worked with women, the sharing of food has been a significant part of almost all the interactions among us. We had potlucks during *The Dinner Party* and we had potlucks during *The Birth Project,* and, in both cases, the preparation and eating of food together had a symbolic aspect. It was as if we were bringing to each other as women what we had provided for husbands and children for centuries—as if nourishing each other physically was a metaphor for giving to and affirming each other and our experience as women. Moreover, since most women know how to cook, the food was always divine.

At the June review, by the middle of Saturday afternoon, preparations were underway for the gala Saturday night potluck/feast where seventy people dined. Women started shopping, chopping, mixing, stirring, and cooking, and the building slowly filled with overpowering aromas. By dinner time, everyone was salivating as dish after fabulous dish was brought to the table. Succulent Texas ham, home-made Italian pasta, spicy Hungarian sausage, tangy guacamole, pungent cheese grits, authentic shoo-fly pie, and dozens of other delights filled the table until it overflowed—a fitting symbol for the overflowing feeling of warmth and connection that tied people together across the many miles that normally separate project members.

Judy Wallen arrived from Alaska with the *Crowning* batik quilt she was working on, accompanied by her baby and a whole salmon.

Judy Wallen preparing the salmon for cooking.

"I arrived at the San Francisco airport and was met by Michele Maier, who kept snapping pictures of me. She insisted that I take this twenty-pound king salmon I'd brought for the potluck out of its shipping box and hold it up for a picture! I considered this pretty funny—since the salmon was stiff from being iced. It seemed a pretty outrageous thing to do in a crowded airport, with an eleven-month-old baby on one arm—I was relieved when I managed to dissuade Michele from continuing with this idea—but it still strikes me as *funny!*"

Judy Wallen

(Left to right) Elisa Skarveland, Jan Lo Biondo, and Kathy Lenhart cooking in Through the Flower's kitchen.

(Left to right) Franny Minervini-Zick, Ann Gibson, and Janis Wicks preparing a sumptuous dish.

"Initially, I was intimidated by Judy's invitation to all of us to come to the June Review because I imagined it would be a 'hard-core women's lib' situation. What would I say? Who would I be? I was kind of relieved when I originally thought I wouldn't be able to go. But my husband and two daughters surprised me with a plane ticket at my birthday dinner, and I was on my way."

Jan Lo Biondo

160

Generally, at the potlucks, there were some people who couldn't wait to get their hands into the food.

(Left to right) Susan Lynn, Pamella Nesbit, and Leigh Heller "dishing up."

(Left to right) Franny Minervini-Zick, Sally, Susan, and Pamella.

After eating, discussions usually got quite heated.

(Left to right) Ann Gibson, Franny Minervini-Zick, Anne Stafford, Lael Cohen, and Susan MacMillan filling their plates.

Michele usually tried to avoid photographing me eating because my table manners are not the best. But after a long day of reviews, I was always starving.

I like to think of the potluck suppers as a kind of return to the original celebration of the Mass, when the community members all brought the food that was then consumed. Our "celebrations" were a coming together to share our feelings, a time when we became renewed through the assembling of our community. (31)

"I felt such a circle of warmth and love weaving us all together. I never went to camp or belonged to a sorority or had any other female group experiences, so this was really new and delightful and truly satisfying. I felt submerged in and attached to these beautiful women as if we had become one organism, laughing, sharing feelings, almost breathing as one."

Mary Ann Hickey

"The potlucks were really special, with all that excellent food and good fellowship. The communication at these dinners was very valuable to me and would provide topics for pondering during all the hours of stitching. Even more than the food, I enjoyed sharing and interacting with my fellow needleworkers."

Merrily Rush Whitaker

161

What Is a Review?

Undated journal entry

The June review was more than anyone could really take in at once, especially Sally and me. In some ways, we were responsible for it all, but not part of it. Everyone else was engaged in rather carefree dialogue, while we were struggling with the fact that we were succeeding beyond our wildest dreams, which brought us face to face with the number of pieces that would have to be backed and bordered and prepared for exhibition, the number of photographs that would have to be taken and printed, the research that would have to be collated, the money that would have to be raised—and the limits on our energy, our staff, and our resources. Without Mary Ross and our dedicated but overworked staff, we wouldn't have a chance. As it is, it will be a miracle if we can do it.

After the reviews on Sunday, we had a picnic at Benicia State Park and then a rap session at the Benicia Inn. It was there that I shared my excitement and my anxiety about seeing so much **Birth Project** *work together. On the one hand, as I mentioned, it was a thrill to see the work and to finally feel sure that* **The Birth Project** *had taken hold and that there would be some wonderful finished work. On the other hand, I suddenly felt the weight of the responsibility for preparing and getting all that work into the world.*

The spirit of community, the excitement, and the sharing of feelings and of food were an important aspect of the June reviews and of all *Birth Project* reviews. But the real reason everyone gathered together at the reviews was the art. From the beginning, the review process was fundamental to the project; without it, *The Birth Project* would never have succeeded.

What is a review? A review was a time when the needleworkers submitted for approval the work they had done, and the work they planned to do, on the piece they were executing. We reviewed work at two- or three-month intervals, or more frequently if necessary. Sometimes the stitcher brought or mailed the piece to Benicia, where reviews took place four or five times a year; sometimes she brought it to Houston or Chicago or New York, where I traveled in order to meet with the needleworkers in that area and review their work in person.

The first review was generally an occasion to look at translation samples, which demonstrated the stitcher's initial ideas about how to "translate" my design into needlework. In most cases, the needleworker tried out techniques she thought would work on a separate piece of fabric or canvas before any stitching began on the piece itself. Some brave souls worked on the piece right away, which was all right with me as long as they did not object to "reverse stitching," the euphemism we developed for taking work out.

Sally at June reviews with some of the work in progress, which, we suddenly realized, would have to be finished, prepared for exhibition, and cared for by us.

Some needleworkers resented doing samples and only learned their value after a considerable amount of reverse stitching. Working out ideas beforehand was not something the stitchers were used to doing, but by the time they were finished, most of them had learned to value the process of doing translation samples as a way of extending their techniques beyond anything they had imagined possible.

After I had approved the initial translation samples—based on whether they "worked with the image" and were technically feasible and excellent—the needleworker began work on the actual piece. It was quite common for additional translation samples to be done every time a new area of the piece was approached. Thus, one might do a translation sample for the stitching on the body, the background, the outline, and, finally, the border. If Sally or I didn't like one of these, new samples would be done until all of us felt satisfied. We didn't always wait until formal reviews to look at translation samples but, rather, reviewed them whenever they were submitted, which ended up taking a considerable amount of time.

Once the needleworker began work on those areas of the piece for which her translation samples had been approved, she brought or sent the work in for review at a specified time. Sally and I would check to see that she had done the amount of work we had agreed upon and that it looked good. (Sometimes it did not; an idea that worked on a small scrap of fabric might look terrible on the piece, and it would then have to be reverse-stitched.) If it looked all right, the needleworker would finish that section, and then go on to the next area approved through a translation sample. This process, which normally lasted anywhere from one to three years and sometimes longer, continued until the piece was done. Imagine doing this four to six times a year for each of more than a hundred works in progress, and you will get a sense of what the review process meant for us.

If the work did not look good, it could be for a multitude of reasons. The pace of the work might be too slow because the needleworker was not honoring her time commitment of a minimum of ten hours a week. This did not seem like very much time to me—it was the same number of hours I normally work in one day—but, for some of the women, it was a nearly impossible pace to maintain. If the piece was not developing at a consistent rate, and if the stitcher could not change her schedule, Sally and I stopped the project. At first we had been reluctant to do that; we tried everything we knew to help the person succeed. But, as the project developed, we realized that we had to have a time frame and that those who couldn't meet it would just have to go.

Other problems came up, often with the quality of the work itself. Sometimes it was shoddy; sometimes the stitcher got anxious and tried to go too fast, with devastating results; sometimes the problem was a lack of art training and a subsequent inability to "see" the visual needs of the piece.

Some of the needleworkers thought that I knew what I wanted from the start and that I had a sense of how the piece should look, which was not at all true. Rather, I had a lot of ideas about what could be done with a piece and definite ideas about what I liked and didn't like once I saw the work. But I tried to remain quite flexible about possible "translations," as there are many ways to make something work. What I expected was a sense of commitment to the piece itself and an understanding that the ultimate criterion was whether a solution worked according to a set of standards that I share with the entire professional art community in this country and abroad. Sometimes the stitchers seemed to think that I had arbitrarily made up these standards, but that just indicated that many of them did not understand that there are established, historical standards in art.

One might say that, despite the existence of historical standards, I was still the one who determined what "worked"—and that is true. But in most cases, I was the one with the most visual experience, which is what qualified me to make the decision. Moreover, it was precisely my level of esthetic development, as well as my connection to the larger world of art, that made the needleworkers want to work with me. And what of the old feminist argument about "male standards"? Was I just falling back on these instead of replacing them with something new?

The issue here, it seems to me, is not one of standards but of content. My struggle has been both to transform my own subject matter as a woman into art and to make it possible for that subject matter to be accepted in the world. There is nothing wrong with the standards of excellence we have inherited from men, as long as those standards do not carry with them—as, unfortunately, they usually do— the idea that the experience of women is inherently inappropriate to art, no matter what the level of excellence of the art may be.

Needless to say, all these issues came up in reviews and in discussions afterwards. But as difficult as the reviews often were—ego struggles, disappointments, and tears were not unusual—most of the stitchers found them both meaningful and illuminating.

I always tried to explain my reasons for not liking something, and I guess that, in some ways, I taught a lot. What I did was to take the same process I use in my studio and go through it out loud. For a long time, it was very difficult for me to remember what actually took place at a review—I just "did it," and somehow it worked. Now I understand that what I did was what I always do when I make art; it's just that during reviews, I shared a process that most artists usually go through alone.

Birth Project reviews were not like traditional art-school critiques, however, where a "teacher" criticizes someone else's work; this was *my* work, as well as the stitchers', and I brought all my critical faculties to bear on it. Thus, even though most of the stitchers didn't realize it, I was just as vulnerable as they were because it was as much my work as theirs.

The process of bringing the *Birth Project* work to fruition required a profound level of cooperation between the stitchers and me. I often quipped, when confronted by some needleworker saying, "I tried to figure out what *you* wanted," that if I wanted robots, I'd get some from Japan. What I wanted, and what I often—but not always—got, was what Frannie Yablonsky was referring to once when she said, "We are creating within Judy's creation." I provided the image, the framework, and the guidance, but for the two to three months between reviews, the stitchers were on their own.

The needleworkers and I did not always experience the reviews the same way. It was difficult for me to see myself as the "authority" they viewed me as. I certainly accepted the fact that I had, and in fact had earned, a certain amount of esthetic authority. But I found it difficult to accept that many of them felt nervous around me, especially those who, like Pamella, had worked with me a lot.

Pamella, Sally, and I discussing the outlining of the figure in *Egg/Her*.

"Over the years the reviews were always intense and very threatening, at least to me. I was always nervous and scared that Judy would hate what I had done. The worst fears came into my mind in those few minutes before the review: did I blow it? have I ruined the piece? I tried to remind myself that I couldn't ruin it—a little reverse stitching and a lot of thought could usually rectify any problem that arose. But my doubts continued: were my months of stitching for nothing? would the work have to be ripped out? More often than not, Judy and Sally liked what I'd done. My main problem was not taking the stitching far enough; I always seemed to stop short. During reviews, all of this was solved as we discussed ideas and I always felt very elated and very relieved!"
Pamella Nesbit

"The couple of weeks preceding a review were always awful for me. I'd work myself into a nervous frenzy— screaming at my family, sleeping badly, and hardly eating. As the work progressed, I managed to keep a lid on my nervous energy by cleaning house madly and stitching longer hours to alleviate the tension. But during the last year, I got to the point where my confidence had grown so strong that I hardly even dreaded the reviews."
Merrily Rush Whitaker

Hazel and I at June reviews.

The reviews were not over after Sally and I had looked at the pieces. The review forms still had to be typed, filed, and copies sent to the needleworkers. These forms specified the agreements made during the review process, outlined the work to be done, and established the next review date. We kept elaborate files on each project, a task that threatened to overwhelm us until Hazel Hood Kiley, an experienced office manager, quit her long-term job in Houston, Texas, and moved to Benicia to take over our rudimentary but disorganized system.

In addition to the in-person reviews, other pieces were sent in for review if the needleworker couldn't personally attend. The work from these mail-in reviews (which often dovetailed with the in-person reviews in Benicia) had to be repacked and returned to the stitchers after it had been documented and photographed like all the other work had been. (We tried to visually chronicle the development of each work through slides.) Mail-in reviews were consistently more trouble than the in-person ones. I don't know why the needleworkers had so much difficulty getting their work in on time, as they had plenty of notice beforehand, but some were invariably late. We tried all kinds of things—giving them a due date that was actually five days before our scheduled review date, sending out written reminder notices, following up with phone calls—but nothing worked. No matter what we did, a few days after the mail-in review, two or three more pieces would always straggle in.

Many of the needleworkers reported a series of funny incidents in relation to sending the pieces back and forth by UPS and the Postal Service.

"I had been sending the quilt back and forth to Benicia for almost a year. Every time I sent it, the same postal worker would help me. One day he asked me what exactly I had in the tube, and I told him. He asked to see it, so I showed it to him—and therefore to everyone standing in line behind me as well. Most of the men shook their heads, but the women ooh-ed and ah-ed."
Joanne Lanciotti

Some needleworkers, like Jane Dadey, decorated their mailing tubes; however, as Joanne pointed out, they seemed to attract attention even if they were plain and unadorned.

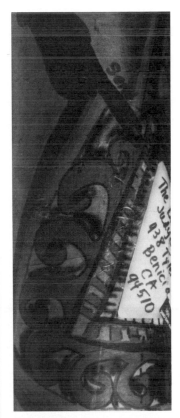

Jane Dadey's uniquely embellished mailing tube.

Wednesday, July 7, 1982

We're beginning to make progress in the planning of exhibitions; we're having four shows in the fall. I'm feeling more resolved now about working on the exhibition process, especially since Stephen told me that he spends 80 percent of his time implementing his designs and only 20 percent actually drawing.

We had a money crisis this week. They turned off our Sprint line, as it seems we had not been paying the bills. No one had informed me that our phone bills were $1,000 a month! I freaked.

Thursday, July 22

We're already beginning to run into certain problems with our exhibition program—people don't want to pay to show Birth Project *work. It's amazing how people pay for everything else but think art is supposed to be free. We really have to have rental fees for the work, particularly since it's one of the few ways we can recoup some of our costs. Mostly I've been working on exhibiting and going through a lot of feelings about being almost done with generating* Birth Project *images. I've started over a hundred and fifty* Birth Project *works in the last three years. Out of that we'll probably get seventy-five or eighty that are all right.*

The simple-mindedness with which a man may pursue his . . . goals is . . . alien to the feminine values and emotional traits that women are expected to show . . . Pursuit of achievement in literature, science and the arts is a single-minded ambition that will never be restructured . . . and men are right when they say that the required expenditure of time and effort leaves little room for life's other rewards.

—Susan Brownmiller (32)

"My lack of formal art training has definitely affected my work on the project. I'd say that this lack of training didn't discourage me, but it did slow my progress considerably."

Mary Ann Hickey

I am a single-minded, formally trained professional artist with twenty-five years of art-making behind me. I have been working with women who generally have little art training, are not professionals, and live lives that are totally different from mine. I suppose it was inevitable that the needleworkers would be put off by my directness and lack of social graces; that I would be driven mad by the fragmentation of their lives, their lack of focus, and all their excuses for not working; that they would react personally to my criticisms and become defensive and hurt; that I would become frustrated and exasperated by their undeveloped visual perception; and that they would be frightened of my general expressiveness, particularly my tendency to yell when I'm upset.

I spent a great deal of time at reviews being alternately reassuring and furious. But most of the time I spent trying to teach the stitchers to "see."

At a review, I explain how the blending of the thread colors has to follow the forms of the body and have a visual logic. (I have already color-coded the piece, done a diagram on the black and white pattern, and explained this before.)

(Left to right) Susan MacMillan, Sally Babson, Janis Wicks, and Maggie Eoyang watch as I draw a diagram for the blending of the threads while Hazel records the proceedings. This group had very different levels of visual skill, and they all struggled against accepting the leadership of their most visually trained member, Janis.

I always diagram the body forms so the stitchers can see how to keep the blending consistent with the overall shapes in the image. Despite this, the blending is often done wrong as one or another stitcher decides to disregard the diagram or just plain doesn't understand it.

(Left to right) Maggie Eoyang, Jeanette Russell, Janis Wicks, and Susan Mac-Millan watch me as I try to teach them to "see" the image as I do so they can all stitch and blend in a consistent manner.

Janis and Susan think about what I have said. Janis, the most visually sophisticated, eventually took over as the group's leader. But still, until everyone was able to "see," the problems continued.

Susan, Janis, and Jeanette listen intently. Shortly afterward, another area was "ruined" and took weeks to correct.

Maggie and Jeanette aren't always sure they understand, but they keep trying to learn to "see" in ways that are, I'm sure, totally new to them. Because of the discrepancy in their visions, a lot of group processing has gone on, facilitated by Sally and Susan Lynn.

"What was this review about? I already knew what Judy told Jeanette that day: 'The beginning is NOT the toughest part, continuing and finishing are the hard parts.' We are a group working for different reasons, looking for different things from the project, from the piece, from Judy, from one another. Judy right ly returns us to the point in hand—the art. She and this project are finitely involved in time, and our group consciousness-raising must be secondary." Maggie Eoyang

Yesterday, when I was working in the studio, I thought to myself: this process of working brings me such joy, why have I given it away? That's what I'm feeling now, terrible regret at having given the pleasure of working on my images to others who get to experience that joy, leaving me with this terrible emptiness and tons of work I don't want to do. I wondered how I got myself into this mess. I was so eager to prove that The Dinner Party *was not a fluke and that I could do it again (as if anyone cared), that I just plunged headlong into this project without really thinking it through.*

And now I have the responsibility of not only finishing all this work, but also struggling to get it out into the world. On one hand, my only hope—at least as I have seen it so far—seems to lie in awakening consciousness about art and expanding the support system I've already built. But support for what? For other people to have the joy of bringing my forms to life? On the other hand, I can't sit there and stitch all those pieces myself.

167

When I was preparing to work on this book, I asked the participants to answer a series of questions and to submit material reflecting their experiences. I was flooded with journals, poems, personal statements, and stitching records that demonstrated the exacting nature of the needlework, the personal investment of so many of the stitchers, and their struggle to achieve a balanced relationship with me.

Like many women, a number of the needleworkers had conflicts about authority. They often tended to react overly strongly to my every response: if I was pleased with their work, they were elated; if I was critical, they were devastated. Learning to accept my esthetic authority without being overwhelmed by my "authority" and learning to separate criticism of their work from criticism of them was hard for many of the stitchers. This 1983 excerpt from Jane Gaddie Thompson's journal about a review session aptly demonstrates the sensitivity of the needleworker and my own sometimes insensitive behavior.

"After I unwrapped the piece I was working on, Judy was uncharacteristically subdued. She was fairly quiet and deep in thought for a while and then said, 'Well, it is gorgeous and spectacular' and told me that my stitching was perfect, as usual. 'The only problem,' she continued, 'is that the embroidery is *too* spectacular and therefore doesn't work with the rest of the piece.' Judy tried and tried to explain it to me, to make me see what I was not able to see, probably because I have no art training.

"It was so clear to her; it was pea soup to me. I am detail-oriented, personally and professionally. Our training is worlds apart—how could she expect me to grasp so quickly something that was so new and so foreign? She said that my stitching was *too* good, *too* detailed, that it stood out too much on the piece, thus overpowering the image as a whole instead of working within the framework of the image and thereby making the whole piece stronger.

"Judy was trying to be patient and kind, but she was also being very hard on me as she got more and more exasperated with my inability to understand what she meant. In the meantime, I was becoming more and more confused. 'Stand up and

Jane Gaddie Thompson and I during a review.

168

JON McNALLY

look at it,' she demanded. 'Can't you see what I am talking about, how there are three distinct parts to the piece now—the painting, the quilting, and the embroidery? They all have to work together—and it's up to you to make that happen and to fit your embroidery into the overall nature of the piece.'

" 'Please give me a place to hide,' I thought. 'How can my work be *too* good? I thought I had to worry about its not being good enough. This doesn't make any sense.' Judy's voice rose as she tried to get me to 'open up,' widen my vision, and see the image as a whole. My focus is too narrow, she said. 'When will this stop, God?' I wondered.

"My prayers were answered as Judy went back to a state of concentration, thinking aloud about what could be done to make the piece work. I think that she must have seen how upset and confused and bewildered I was. Calmly now, Judy explained that my 'spectacular' embroidery on the piece had created certain visual problems. 'You just forgot,' she said, 'to make all the parts of the piece work together,' to which I replied that I could not forget that which I never knew to begin with. I thought that my job was to make my embroidery as fantastic and perfect as I could. It was Judy's job, I felt, to make the parts work together.

"I told her I was sorry I had screwed up. Her reply startled me. She said that I hadn't screwed up, that it was her fault, not mine. She went on to say that she should have known what I would do with a piece like the one she gave me, because she knew what my talent was, based on the first piece I'd stitched. She said that she had made the mistake of giving me this piece instead of one that was more appropriate to my skill.

"I told Judy that I dearly loved this piece, and then we talked about specific things I might do to make it work better. She gave me very detailed suggestions, but I could hardly concentrate on what she was saying because I was so overwhelmed by her criticisms. Judy said she wanted to see the piece again before the next Houston review and asked if there was any chance that I could bring it to Benicia and work with her there for a few days. 'Wouldn't that be nice,' I thought, 'and who would take care of my daughter and take her to school while I'm in California stitching?' But I didn't say anything. I put all my things away; I was so depressed I just wanted to go home and cry."

Jane Gaddie Thompson
Journal entry, June 1983

Ann Gibson, Sally, and I during a review.

"I had a problem with Judy's response to 'things going wrong.' She yelled a lot. Yelling in itself is no big deal, but with Judy there were two distinct phases of the explosion. It was the first phase that bothered me, wherein the person responsible for the mistake, rather than the deed itself, was subjected to a very hard 'calling down.' More often than not, the mistake seemed to have been committed out of ignorance rather than negligence or sloppiness. The second phase was directed at the problem to be rectified and quickly passed into constructive and positive instruction."

Ann Gibson

Despite Ann's criticism of my behavior at reviews, she got a great deal out of her sessions.

"I feel that I've been led by the hand through a process which I needed to experience but couldn't seem to initiate for myself. It seems to involve addressing and facing up to the questions:

"Who am I, really?

"What can I do, really?

"What do I want, really?

"Have I the courage to reach for what I want, take responsibility for what I can do?"

Ann Gibson

Thursday, September 9

Tonight the Mill Valley show opens—our first exhibition out of our own building. I'm not going. Instead, I'm going to go next week with Stephen and Michael so that we can evaluate how we did in terms of designing the installation. Since we will have to design most of our exhibitions from floor plans and photographs, we wanted to practice and see how well we could work with the space without actually having seen it.

Friday, September 17

Stephen, Michael, and I had lots of criticisms of the Mill Valley show; there are many problems still to be worked out.

From time to time, I get this flash—that I'm knee deep in work that has to do with showing, not making, art—and then I get upset, but what can I do? There's no existing support system for my work, and there's nothing to do but try and create one, so that's what I'm doing—building a way to support and show the work as well as creating it. It just doesn't seem fair.

The only other regular, formal in-person reviews were held at our space in Houston, where I went at least three times a year. It would have been wonderful to have the same kind of spaces in other regional centers around the country. Mary Ross thought that the same groups which had brought *The Dinner Party* to their cities would want to follow through with another opportunity for community involvement in my work. But that didn't happen, and we could barely afford to maintain the two spaces we had, much less open any more.

I don't know whether the quality of the work was better in California and Texas, where there were formal *Birth Project* spaces, but the quality of connection felt by the needleworkers was certainly greater in those areas. There was a terrific sense of camaraderie among the Houston stitchers, and I believe their potlucks were, by far, the best.

"I was always struck during reviews by how much Judy respected the talents and ideas of the needleworkers. I think the 'unpleasant' reviews I witnessed all occurred because the needleworker had not thought out her work—either by not having any rationale for the work already done or by not having any plans for the future of the piece.

"Before our first review, I felt as if I were going out on a first date—not knowing what to expect, full of anticipation. As the group 'coordinator,' I always felt somewhat in charge—or at least I projected that image—so I wouldn't let everyone know how nervous I was. Our group had agreed to meet for a drink before our review (not only were we nervous about our first review, but it was to be televised by Channel 8), so I personally was nervous about Judy Chicago *and* about looking thin for television!"

Joyce Gilbert

(Left to right) Joyce Gilbert, Jo Chester, Karin Telfer, Carol Strittmatter, Peggy Patton, and I during a review of the large needlepoint they executed. In background: installation of *Fingered by Nature* in the *Birth Project* gallery space (adjacent to the room where the Gilbert group stitched).

Gerry Melot and I during a review of *Creation of the World NP 2*.

"The very best thing about working on *The Birth Project* was my conviction that, for once in my life, I was working on something that held some meaning for me and had potential importance to a great many other people."

Gerry Melot

"My biggest complaint about the reviews was the short time allotted to each one. I was usually scheduled for the end of the day, and, by that time, Judy was often tired and sometimes angry or frustrated over what had transpired earlier. I would have liked to see the reviews spread out more, giving Judy time to rest in between and gather her thoughts and energy for the next one.

"A review is a very draining experience for everyone involved, and I think Judy always tried to give more than she actually could. I sometimes wished there could be more reviews, but I realize it is a miracle that the pieces were ever finished at all, given the geographical distance between us."

Gerry Melot

Wednesday, September 22, 1982

There are some good things happening—two women are moving here to work, one from Indiana, the other from Texas. The former, Kathleen O'Connor, has a graphics background, while the latter, Debbie Lohrke, is a whiz in the darkroom, both of which are skills we desperately need for exhibition. My whole staff is in tilt about the next phase of work, as I was myself. Everyone feels so unprepared.

I am over my initial freak-out about the work involved in exhibition, and I realize it won't be so terrible if I have to work less in the studio for a while—God knows, I've made an awful lot of art in the last twenty years. Also, I think I'd like to have a chance to see how this art affects people. If I'm going to expand my audience still further, it will be good to have more understanding of audience response.

There were other types of reviews that were less formal. Sometimes I visited needleworkers at home, photographed and interviewed them, and then reviewed their work. At other times, all the stitchers in the area gathered at one of the needleworkers' homes, and I spent the whole day reviewing.

I did a number of reviews in hotel suites, which I liked but the needleworkers didn't. These were crowded and usually a little noisy, and I would have to keep reminding everyone that I was "working." The trouble with hotel rooms, from the needleworkers' point of view, was that the reviews were more public than many of them would have liked. But I enjoyed the slightly chaotic energy and excitement that resulted from all of us being crowded into a small space.

Elizabeth Fleming's house in Occidental, California.

Sometimes I traveled to needleworkers' homes to review their work.

Working with Elizabeth Fleming during an individual review at her house.

The owners of the Mayfair-Regent Hotel in Chicago, Sally and Miles Berger, graciously extended the use of one of their hotel suites for *Birth Project* reviews.

MICHAEL WEINSTEIN

Reviewing inside our crowded suite in the hotel.

KATE AMEND

Mary Ann Hickey and I discuss blending problems while Jean Berens and Sally watch.

Elaine Coorens, former editor of *Needlework Times*, lent me her lovely Victorian house for reviews on several occasions.

KATE AMEND

(Left to right) Mary Ann Hickey, Jean Berens, Susan Fisher, Diane Duncan Rasmussen, at Elaine Coorens' house in Chicago.

Mary Ann Hickey's dancing prowess allowed her to work in many positions.

Sometimes we had to resort to unusual methods to be able to review *Birth Project* work. This crochet was too long to be stretched out in the apartment. The picture on the left was taken on the roof of a New York apartment lent to us by Lois Lindauer and Bill Seltz for reviews.

DR. RITZ C. RAY

Dr. Helen Courvoisie and her child outside their home.

Dr. Helen Courvoisie provided a place for reviewing with my Southeast participants.

Reviewing at Dr. Helen's house in Winston-Salem, North Carolina (left to right): Dr. Helen; Marguerite Crosby, from Ft. Lauderdale, Florida; Rebecca Hanner, from Pilot Mountain, North Carolina; Christine Hager, from Raleigh, North Carolina; me; and Sally.

Over the years, a number of people around the country repeatedly lent their houses and apartments for *Birth Project* reviews. The needleworkers liked these better, I think, as there was more room to spread out and greater privacy during the reviews themselves.

My favorite informal review was held at the home of my cousins, Arleen and Howard Rosen. Arleen, an avid collector of needlework, had attended several reviews, but it was not until I held one at their house that Howard began to understand what *The Birth Project* was all about.

Once, shortly after having surgery, I did a review in a hotel suite at the Chateau Marmont, where I was recuperating. Even though I was somewhat disabled, I could still see.

L.A. Hassing, Kate Amend, and I trying to achieve the proper lighting for a review in the hotel.

Candis Duncan Pomykala and I during a review at my cousins' apartment.

(Left to right) Mary Ann Hickey, Jean Berens, and I relaxing during a review at my cousins' home.

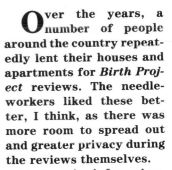

Howard and Arleen Rosen, my cousins in Chicago.

"The best part about working with Judy was watching how she dealt with people. Her role often put her in the awkward position of having to tell people they weren't working up to their potential. Because my work progressed so slowly, often I was one of the people she pressed. She insisted that if I wanted to keep the level of quality in needlework up to my standards and hers, I could not continue to do everything at once, as I was trying to do—I would have to set priorities. That one idea started me thinking and helped me to whittle down my activities to only the most important ones, thereby cutting out a lot of frustration and increasing my chances for success.

"Here I was, the youngest in a room of women, each of whom was an expert in her own field, and they were talking to me as if I were an expert too—quite an ego trip for a 21-year-old. After a while, the age difference disappeared, and I found myself conversing and sharing freely with all these women. I learned a lot about women's lives and began to see us all as very much alike despite age differences, life-style differences, and occupational and educational differences."

Candis Duncan Pomykala

Goddess Imagery

The goddess images in *The Birth Project* celebrate an aspect of the birth process I have heard many women express: feeling like a goddess when—right after the child is born—she stares at the face of her mother as if gazing at the divine.

This untitled poem by Gerry Melot seems quite appropriate to these images:

i am the goddess
the cave in which you live
i am the goddess
absorbing the pain
to ease your way
i am the goddess
the mysterious passage
through which you must
leave
i am the goddess
and it is my blood
that you ride to freedom
i am the goddess

Gerry Melot

Birth Goddess E 4 (in progress), ©Judy Chicago, 1984. Embroidered by Candis Duncan Pomykala, DeKalb, Illinois. DMC floss, yarn, and hand-spun silk, 19'' x 23''.

I designed this piece specifically for the unusual embroidery technique demonstrated by Candis Duncan Pomykala. Because it was unfinished at the time of the photograph, it is possible to see both my painting and the embroidery.

The background is done entirely in French knots. At one review, I asked Candis to try needle punch, which goes much faster than knots. She did try, but hated it, and went back to the slower, more tedious process of filling the large areas of the background with tiny French knots. The way the color blending and the surface of the knots look went a long way toward compensating for the slow pace of the piece.

"The knots give depth to the piece by causing small shadows or 'ditches' to catch and reflect light. The body stitches are a twisted chain laid down in a haphazard way so as to create no seams, to repeat the idea of the rough background, and to give the impression of mottled skin reminiscent of that of the early Paleolithic fertility goddesses.

"The stitch used for the hair and the babies is a type of Romanian stitch; I used it to give the impression of flowing hair. The outline is done in a couched stitch and the milk in a similar couched technique. For the milk, I spun silk into thread; plied it with a single, colored cotton thread; and then couched it with another colored cotton thread. I used silk to produce the glossier texture of milk and to reinforce the impression of a glowing life force." Candis Duncan Pomykala

I was working in the studio one day during a time when I was having a lot of doubts about whether I really wanted my paintings and drawings translated into needlework. I decided to do a drawing; I

Detail, *Birth Goddess E 4,* showing the field of French knots.

Detail, *Birth Goddess E 3.*

reached into a drawer, but instead of pulling out a sheet of paper, I picked up some pieces of silk which Sally had prepared for me in case I wanted to design some new embroideries.

I began to paint directly on the silk. I did three pieces, each one an image of a goddess giving life to the human race. The first one was conceived to be a line drawing in thread; the second, a stitched line drawing against my painted background; and the third, a fusion of painting and stitching. After I finished them, I called Pam Nesbit and asked if she would embroider them.

Birth Goddess E 3, ©Judy Chicago, 1982. Embroidered by Pamella Nesbit, Sebastopol, California. Acrylic, silk, and metallic thread on silk, 23"x 30".

"When I saw the three birth goddesses Judy had painted, I felt very overwhelmed by them. I was still nursing my little boy; it had been almost two years, and I was feeling tired, as if I'd been nursing my entire life. I related deeply to the images, particularly because of an experience I had at Mt. Shasta a few years ago. It was a vision that took place in a cloud. Toward the end of the vision, I saw myself bending over a large wave—as if I were floating in the air, or even just over the ocean. As the wave crashed down to earth very slowly, my arms were outstretched to the earth as in giving.

"The piece is stitched with a stem or outline stitch in silk thread. The shading is just lots of little stitches feathering out into nothing over Judy's painted shading. I like the softness of it, and I relate my vision at Shasta to it." Pamella Nesbit

Lucina—Early Italian goddess of light, invoked during childbirth because she is seen for the first time at birth.

Mami—the Sumerian goddess who mixed clay over the cosmic abyss and created women and men in her own image.

Mawu—the Dahomey goddess who created the Earth and the human race.

Nammu—Early creation goddess of Sumeria, who gave birth to the other gods and goddesses and, with their help, created human beings from clay.

Naicomis—the Algonquin "grandmother" and creator of food, who fed herself to her people—a symbol for the Algonquins' belief that life continues only if it consumes other life.

Neith—the Egyptian goddess called "The Great Weaver," who wove the world on her loom.

Nut—the Egyptian goddess who gave birth each morning to the Sun and every evening to the sky.

Omecinutl—a Meso-American goddess, considered the creator of human life and all nourishment.

In the fall of 1982, I went on a long trip across the country, visiting, photographing, and interviewing needleworkers and doing reviews. My old friend and former *Dinner Party* colleague, Kate Amend, traveled with me as far as Chicago, and then Sally and Michele met me and the three of us continued the trip East. By this time, *The Birth Project* had truly become a decentralized national network.

One of the highlights of the trip was our stop at Jane Dadey's house out in the open plains of Nebraska. She and her husband, Ed, a soft-spoken and witty mechanical genius who makes sculpture and furniture, moved five barns onto a section of his family's land and created an absolutely amazing personal environment. They live in two congested rooms, with the kitchen crowded into a section of one of the rooms and the toilet in plain view. Integrated into the middle of this half-finished, overcrowded, absolutely charming living space are a microwave oven, two television sets, and a superb stereo system which blares Philip Glass' most recent recording. Jane's quilt was mounted on a home-built frame which she lowered to work on when she came home from teaching school every day. Behind it, Ed ingeniously installed a darkroom, where, somehow, he is able to process both black and white and color film in a space no bigger than the one under most people's kitchen sink.

Jane and Ed Dadey greet us from the top of their home in Marquette, Nebraska.

Jane Dadey at home.

Jane with quilting-frame/darkroom combination built by her husband, Ed Dadey.

"Living in a rural area, on an unmarked, graveled road, I found myself listening to Judy, on the phone, calmly stating that she was in North Platte, Nebraska—a town 175 miles away—a little behind schedule for arriving at my house. Then, in something of a panic, her city voice demanded to know the name of the street I lived on."
Jane Dadey

176

Marjorie and Neil Smith's house in Solon, Ohio.

Marj Smith at work.

Sally, Neil and Marj Smith, and I toast Marj's having almost completed the pulled threadwork for *Guided by the Goddess.*

I have never been particularly interested in the goddess rituals that developed in feminist culture. After all, I never believed in a male god or God; why should a change in gender alter my fundamentally anti-religious stance? What I have been interested in, however, is all the imagery historically associated with the goddesses.

It is perfectly clear to me that the ancient statues of goddesses represent a time when women enjoyed social and political equality. The replacement of those wonderful, powerful female icons with male deities was a disastrous event for women, one that robbed us of the chance to see our value reflected in positive images. Reestablishment of reverence for the feminine and for some of the qualities associated with women —such as vulnerability and compassion—seems to be an essential goal for everyone if the human race is to survive. I have endeavored for many years to "make the feminine holy," and one way I have expressed that is by making images of a female god.

Monday, September 28, 1982

It's almost 10 p.m. After driving since 9 a.m. we've arrived in Rawlins, Wyoming. On the way stopped at the Mormon Hobbycraft Center in Salt Lake City, which features quilts and pillows and all kinds of crafts—some wonderful, others totally kitschy. Many of the needlework kits there reinforce the stereotyped female role, offering for stitching such phrases as "Be nice," "Accept God's will," "Be loving," and my favorite, "Anger makes you and everybody near you feel bad." The whole shop is a perfect example of how needlework is used as a means of oppressing women rather than as a medium for personal expression.

Monday, October 5

I'm in Solon, Ohio, at Marjorie Smith's house; Sally and Michele are with me. Kate went home after the Chicago reviews. There were a lot of people at the reviews, including some "pending" needleworkers and some friends of participants. I don't usually allow people to bring spouses or friends unless we have a potluck to which guests are invited. Some of the uninvolved or new people made me uncomfortable by treating me like a "star."

It made me feel much better when I got here and saw the piece Marj is working on, Guided by the Goddess, *which combines my sprayed painting and hand-drawing with her pulled threadwork and embroidery; it is a real fusion of painting and needlework. Moreover, I felt quite at home with the Smiths.*

Guided by the Goddess, ©Judy Chicago, 1983. Executed by Marjorie Smith, Solon, Ohio. Painting, pulled thread-work, appliqué, and embroidery, 54'' x 107''.

In this image, the goddess is giving birth to and providing nourishment for the human race. The creatures being born have emerged from both the body of the goddess and the body of the female Earth. I spray-painted the image with Versatex on a counted-thread cotton fabric and then hand-outlined the forms. After embroidering with a button-hole stitch around each area to be pulled, Marge did the pulled threadwork in a grid pattern and scale we had decided upon through a series of translation samples. She appliquéd the lavender satin onto the nipples and the tear/milk drop, then embroidered over my drawn outline with DMC floss in the satin stitch.

Mother India

One of the stops on this trip was in Greeley, Colorado, where I reviewed the quilt Judith Meyers is working on. Judith first became involved with **The Birth Project** by doing a research project on India in which she discovered some horrifying material on women's birth experiences, documented in a book by Katherine Mayo in 1927 (33).

I have been thinking about a piece that deals with this information. I want to try to make a series of images that combine painting and needlework and to convey these experiences, not from their point of view—because I can't do that—but from as enlightened and compassionate a view as I can. After all, there are more women on the planet whose experience is like theirs in India than like ours in America.

It's so overwhelmingly sad to confront the consequences for women and for men (but women are in worse shape) of the profound economic inequities in the world and the resulting ignorance and desperation. I'm looking forward to working on this, and I only hope I can do it justice. Judith is coming to Benicia to work with me early next year.

In *Mother India* (33), Katherine Mayo described the conditions under which most Indian women traditionally gave birth. Her frankness produced an outpouring of other books refuting her findings, and even I, when I read Mayo's book, found it hard to believe. In preparation for Judith's arrival and the beginning of work on the *Mother India* project, I spent considerable time in the library. Recent scholarship confirmed most of Mayo's information, although some change has occurred in India since 1927.

The conditions Mayo observed—child marriage, horrible birth environments and procedures, purdah, suttee, dowries, arranged marriages, widespread illiteracy among women, and terrible malnutrition (as a result of women eating last and least)—have been altered, but not abolished. The illiteracy rate among women is still 80 percent. Education is available to the upper and middle classes, whereas it was barely available to anyone when Mayo did her research. Women are "equal" under the law, but they are still a long way from *de facto* equality. Child marriage is not as widespread; suttee and female infanticide are illegal, though still certainly not wiped out; purdah has moved from India to Pakistan with the partitioning of India; more births take place in hospitals—a questionable gain—and there are more trained health attendants. Arranged marriages are still the norm, and women's lives are certainly still terribly painful and difficult. Hinduism generally oppresses women, of course, although Hindu laws are more progressive than those of the Moslems.

It is these truths that I tried to express in *Mother India* by creating a series of scenes depicting different aspects of the position of women in India. These scenes, in the style of Indian miniature paintings, surround a large image of Shiva, who has two colors associated with him/her—blue for male and yellow for female. I created a Shiva whose color is blue, but whose plight is that of a female, burdened by pregnancy, lactation, and demanding children.

Judith Meyers and I worked together for several weeks developing ideas for *Mother India*. I wanted to do a series of scenes that would be visually based on Indian miniatures.

Taping the outline before spray-painting the *Pregnant Shiva* panel.

I never cared for Oriental art, except for painted miniatures and illuminated books. The sculptures all seemed so stylized to me, and I intuitively knew that they revealed nothing about the lives of women in Eastern cultures. However, when I was looking at these sculptures for inspiration for *Mother India*, I got the idea of creating a Shiva figure who would reflect, rather than disguise, the condition of women in India.

Center panel of *Pregnant Shiva*, from *Mother India*, ©Judy Chicago, 1984. Sprayed Versatex and acrylic on fabric, 78" x 48".

When Judith Meyers sent me the results of her research on birth in India and, particularly, her discovery of the Katherine Mayo book, she wrote:

"This was, of course, written in 1927—over fifty years ago—but so far as I can tell from other readings, things have been very slow to change because the ideas underlying birth practices are very deeply rooted in the Hindu religion. There has been some change among the educated classes in the cities, but among the great bulk of the population—the poor and those in the villages—birth goes on as it has for centuries, and it is as Ms. Mayo describes in the passages I've enclosed."

Judith Meyers

According to the Hindu code, a woman in childbirth . . . is ceremonially unclean, contaminating all that she touches. Therefore, only those become midwives or "dhais" who are themselves of the unclean, "untouchable" class. . . . Further, no sort of training is held necessary for the work. . . The expectant mother makes no preparation for the baby's coming . . . she does toss into a shed or into a small, dark chamber . . . soiled and disreputable rags . . . and it is into this evil-smelling rubbish-hole that the young wife creeps when her hour is come upon her. "Unclean" she is, in her pain—unclean whatever she touches, and (therefore) . . . give her the unclean and the worthless . . . if there be a broken-legged, ragged string-cot, let her have that to lie upon . . . . When the pains begin, send for the "dhai" . . . who changes into rags she keeps for this purpose, infected and re-infected . . .

she makes a small charcoal fire in a pan beneath the bed.... If the delivery is at all delayed, the "dhai" ... thrusts her long-unwashed hand, loaded with dirty rings and bracelets...into the patient's body....

A . . . labor may last three, four, five, even six days. During all this period the woman is given no nourishment whatever ... to save the family utensils from pollution . . . meanwhile, the "dhai" resorts to all her traditions . . . she makes balls of strange substances, such as hollyhock roots . . . and thrusts them into the uterus, to hasten the event. (33).

—Katherine Mayo

These facts were reported in a contemporary collection of essays, published in the seventies:

A woman is considered impure during her menstrual periods and her confinement. During these times she is isolated and is not expected to touch anything or anyone, or to sleep near her husband. She is barred from the kitchen and can eat only what is given to her.... After delivery, confinement may last from ten to forty days. The impure woman often stays within a small, poorly lit and ventilated area in the house, reserved for such occasions. She is considered to be dirty and defiling.... The Indian female has a difficult time. She is underfed, overworked, and her body is constantly supporting a fetus or breastfeeding infant . . . her life expectancy is forty to fifty years....(34)

—Juliet Katona-Apte

The design for *Mother India* combines painting, appliqué, and embroidery. Because I felt very strongly about this piece, I did not want to take any chances on the project's falling apart. Therefore, Sally and I decided it would be done in such a way that, if all else failed, she and I could put it together ourselves. As of the writing of this book, the final form of *Mother India* is not finally determined, but I will describe it as it is now planned.

The painted sections will be put together with two-inch-wide, appliquéd, white cotton bands, a reference to "homespun" linen and to Gandhi's fight for Indian economic independence. Judith Meyers formed a group in Greeley, Colorado, to mirror and embroider these bands. It took a long time to work out the method of doing them; they contain round mirrors, positioned at regular intervals in the center of the bands and embroidered in a scroll pattern. These relate directly to the mirrored garments so typical of Indian textiles, which both Judith and I love.

In the four corners of the piece (which is 12 feet high by 7 feet wide), a lotus form and an image of the Taj Mahal, flanked by peacocks, is repeated in appliqué and embroidery. The lotus is a common reference in Indian art, and in *Mother India* the corner lotuses echo the form on which the figure of Shiva stands. The Taj Mahal was built in memory of a princess who died in childbirth and therefore seemed a fitting motif for this work.

The appliqué was done by Jackie Moore, of Mendon, Massachusetts, whose skill and reliability were already known to us. I had not originally intended that these corner pieces be embroidered, but when Judy Kendall, of Mt. Shasta, California—another project

member whose abilities we knew—wrote and asked for more work, Sally and I were thrilled at the prospect of enriching this ambitious piece. When it is all done, Sally will put it together, and it will be a nice example of the product of our decentralized working community.

Sally, Judy Kendall, and I planning the embroidery on the appliquéd corner motifs. It was a pleasure to have Judy's skill with a needle in the development of these pieces. She embroidered the appliquéd corner images with white perle cotton and silver metallic thread, combining the chain, outline, and herringbone stitches with couching.

The group in Greeley, Colorado, which was formed and coordinated by Judith Meyers to execute the mirrored strips connecting the sections of *Mother India*. Clockwise from lower left: Ruth Savig, Lydia Ruyle, Susan Herold (holding Elizabeth Herold), Norma Cordiner, Peggy Kennedy, Linda Lockyer, and Judith Meyers. (Not pictured: Sharon Fuller.)

"We are using white #8 perle cotton on white cotton fabric. The stitch is in two parts, a buttonhole stitch alternating with a chain stitch, creating a lip all the way around the perimeter of the mirrors, which are made of Mylar. The mirrors are two inches apart and connected with a scroll line of double chain stitch."

Judith Meyers

The Taj Mahal (35).

The origin of the Taj Mahal is recounted in this story:

Shajahan, at twenty and already the father of two children, was given Arjumand Bana Begum as a wife . . . who bore him six sons and eight daughters in eighteen years . . . followed him on his campaigns and excursions . . . and was called ''Mumtaz Mahat'' (ornament of the palace).

When she was in labor with their fifteenth child . . . the labor lasted thirty hours. . . legend had it that if the child cried out from her womb, she would know that she must die, as she did in June 1631 at the age of thirty-nine. Shajahan built the Taj Mahal as a tomb for her. (36)

As of the early seventies, 48.9% of rural births and 33.4% of urban births were still attended by untrained ''dhais.'' (37)

Detail from *Mother India*, showing the Taj Mahal, peacocks, and a lotus. Appliqué by Jacquelyn Moore, Mendon, Massachusetts; embroidery by Judy Kendall, Mt. Shasta, California; mirrored and embroidered band by Judith Meyers' group, Greeley, Colorado. Overall size: 127'' x 89.''

Mother India (in progress), ©Judy Chicago, 1984. Painting, appliqué, and embroidery, 127'' x 89''.

184

Detail from *Mother India*, showing scene of purdah. Spray and hand-painting on fabric. Size: 24'' x 17½''.

Purdah, the system of secluding and covering women, was introduced into India by the Muslims and then, with the partitioning of India, transferred into Pakistan. When Katherine Mayo and, later, the photographer Margaret Bourke-White traveled to India, the practice was still in force.

For this image, I adapted Margaret Bourke-White's photograph. I placed the women in front of a building whose facade is covered with a purdah screen, through which women peered at the world they could never enter unveiled.

This photograph (38) was the basis for my image of women in purdah.

In this photograph of *Mother India* (on the left), the mirrored strips are not included. When completed and appliquéd, they will act as a visual grid that both enhances and contains the various images. Moreover, the corner pieces (which are all the same) were not finished when this photograph was taken. The repeated motifs of the Taj Mahal and the lotus will visually lock the different sections together. The scenes that surround *Pregnant Shiva* include *Birth Scene* (bottom panel), *Arranged Marriage* (top panel), *Female Infanticide* and *Child Marriage* (left), and, on the right, the two images *Suttee* (top) and *Purdah* (bottom), which is shown in full (above.)

Detail of birth scene from *Mother India*. Sprayed and hand-painted acrylic on fabric. Overall size: 24'' x 48''.

This scene depicts a woman giving birth, attended by two dhais who are inserting hollyhock roots into the mother's uterus. In the background, a dung fire and a string bed, or ''charpoy,'' can be seen; the newborn infant is on a heap of bloody rags. Outside, the husband and other children attempt to avoid seeing the situation or hearing the cries of the weeping mother, who is, of course, ''untouchable'' during her period of confinement. While I was spraying these images, I began to cry; it was almost as if I had suddenly realized what the images were about—as if I hadn't drawn them, but rather had unexpectedly come upon them for the first time. And they were so sad.

Spraying the images for *Mother India*.

Spray-painting *Female Infanticide.*

Hand-painting the sprayed image—*Arranged Marriage.*

Forbidden in India by Imperial law, the ancient practice [of female infanticide]...still seems to persist in many parts of the country....

An old Hindu landowner said to me: "I have had twelve children. Ten girls, which, naturally, did not live. Who, indeed, could have borne that burden! The two boys, of course, I preserved."

—Katherine Mayo (33)

Though education of women has tended to raise the age at marriage and lower the birth rate, it has not brought about any radical change in the traditional pattern of arranged marriage with dowry.

—Alfred de Souza (39)

This song is sung when a Muslim bride leaves her father's home for that of her husband:

We are your cows, O Father; Whichever stake you tie us to, There we shall remain bound.

(40)

187

Difficult Truths

Dealing with subject matter as difficult as that contained in *Mother India* and transforming it into art was a challenging problem. Other information uncovered in our research presented even more formidable problems, most notably the scandalous practices of genital mutilation in Africa and the Middle East.

The birth experience of a circumcised and, particularly, an infibulated woman defy description. Although I was interested in dealing with this, as it affects millions of women, I didn't know if it was possible to create images that anyone would even be willing to stitch, much less view. Nonetheless, I wanted to try. I did this drawing when I was studying some of the African research we had gathered.

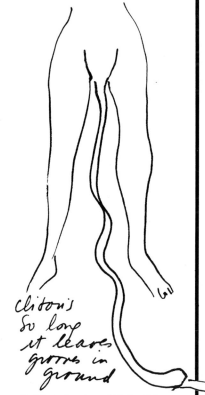

Untitled drawing, ©Judy Chicago, 1983. Pencil on paper, 5¼" x 3¾".

I was planning a project called *Father Africa,* in which I wanted to do what I had done in *Mother India*—present the experiences of African women, particularly their birth experiences—through art that incorporated some of the traditional imagery of African art. A combination of factors prevented this: First, by that time the project was quite far along, and my staff was staggering under the load of coordinating more than a hundred works of art and nearly two hundred people around the country; they were not enthused by the prospect of another major work. Secondly, I was really daunted by the question of visually representing genital mutilation—I frankly didn't know how I could present the African birth experience without confronting it. The third reason is harder to admit; I had been severely trashed, both in person and in print, for my representation of the black feminist and abolitionist Sojourner Truth in *The Dinner Party,* and I was somewhat afraid to deal with an issue that was so fraught with political ramifications. However, if it had not been for the limitations on our support resources, I probably would have tried anyway.

Here is some of the material we gathered, beginning with a series of letters from Mark Overmeyer, a college student from Colorado who became involved in the research project and was assigned, along with a number of other people, the task of investigating birth in Africa.

Dear Ms. Chicago,

I wanted to send a few excerpts from a journal I kept while doing research on Africa, along with some information. I hope that the projects you have initiated will help women become more free in our generation and in generations to come—for as women become free, we will all become a stronger, more healthy race. As I learned in one of my women's studies courses, "Freedom—not happiness—is the goal we must all strive for." And freedom comes from confronting the truth.

Thank you for allowing me to be a small part of *The Birth Project.*

Mark Overmeyer

"I am very excited about my research assignment: birth and the status of women in Africa. So far, what I have learned is very disturbing—the topic of genital mutilation of females is inevitable when studying women in Africa. I find it sickening when I read accounts of the operations that are conveniently labeled 'female circumcision,' male circumcision cannot be compared in any way to what women are forced to endure. The worst part is the attitude of certain authors (mostly men), who consider the operations 'harmless.' I find it impossible to understand how anyone can ignore the obvious torture of another person's body. Even ignorance of basic human anatomy is no excuse for not understanding the pain and degradation that millions of women continue to suffer around the world, and particularly in Africa."

Mark Overmeyer
Journal entry, 1/4/83

The following quotes from Fran Hosken and Mary Daly clearly describe the circumstances of genitally mutilated women.

I learned about mutilations quite by chance in 1973. Basically, I feel that my own personal sense of dignity and worth as a woman and human being is under attack by these mutilations, inflicted on helpless children for no other reason than that they are female. I cannot tolerate this. I find it impossible, indeed absurd, to work for the feminist goals, for human rights, for justice and equality, while ignoring the senseless attacks on the essence of the female personality. These operations represent more than sexual assault, more than physical torture and abuse. They represent a deliberate means to enslave women and a systematic attempt by men to subjugate women absolutely and life-long, to physically control women's bodies, reproduction, and sexuality. Whether performed in the bush or in the hospital, the basic purpose is the same. One can travel all over Africa today, and many people have lived in Africa for years, without ever learning the truth: that tens of millions of women are mutilated and many thousands of young children—even babies—continue to be operated on each year.

Midwifery training is, of course, of special importance, as infibulated women cannot give birth without assistance—that is, they have to be cut open to prevent extensive injury of the mother or death of the child, or both. Traditionally, an infibulated woman gave birth by hanging from a rope from the rafters by her arms while a midwife sat under her and "helped" by making repeated incisions and cuts in the infibulation. Alternatively, the woman tore apart in labor, or often, she and the baby died. Predictably, births took a frightful toll. The usual equipment of a traditional birth attendant consisted in a razor blade, generally wrapped round with a dirty piece of rag.

—Fran P. Hosken (41)

Line drawing (15) of woman "hanging from rafters" during labor.

It should be not be imagined that the horror of the life of an infibulated child/woman ends with this operation. Her legs are tied together, immobilizing her for weeks, during which time excrement remains within the bandage. Sometimes accidents occur during the operation: the bladder may be pierced or the rectum cut open. Sometimes in a spasm of agony the child bites off her own tongue. Infections are, needless to say, common. Scholars such as Lantier claim that death is not a very common immediate effect of the operation, but often there are complications which leave the women debilitated for the rest of their lives. No statistics are available on this point. What is certain is that the infibulated girl is mutilated and that she can look forward to a life of repeated encounters with "the little knife"—the instrument of her perpetual torture. For women who are infibulated have to be cut open—either by the husband or by another woman—to permit intercourse. They have to be cut open further for delivery of a child. Often they are sewn up again after delivery.

—Mary Daly (42)

Before he was finished with his research assignment, Mark discovered that needless suffering during birth was not restricted to Africa, although genitally mutilated women surely suffer at a level unimaginable to most of us.

"When my mother found out that I was doing research on birth, she seemed interested and pleased. When I received my assignment, a newsletter was inside the packet of information. It included a photo of a recently completed *Birth Tear* embroidery. Although it was in black and white, it was still graphic, and I wasn't sure how my mother would react.

"When she saw it, she stared for a few seconds and then told me for the first time about my oldest brother's birth. During my brother's birth, the doctor stood in the corner of the delivery room and watched my mother have the baby. He offered no assistance, and a nurse wiped my mother's forehead as my six-and-a-half-pound brother ripped from my mother's womb."

Mark Overmeyer
Journal entry, 1/26/83

I was interested to know if there was any relationship between the reality of genital mutilation and the mythology of Africa. This myth demonstrates how the symbols created by a culture sometimes mirror the practices common to that society.

The Dogon people of Western Sudan and Mali (Africa) believe that Amma (God) created Earth (Woman) from a lump of clay. God tried to mate with Earth but had trouble penetrating her because her clitoris (in the form of a termite hill) got in the way. God cut out the termite hill (clitoris) and mated with the earth. (43)

Friday, October 8

We're in Winston-Salem, North Carolina, at the home of Dr. Helen Courvoisie and her husband, Ritz C. Ray (what a Southern name!). I gave a lecture on The Birth Project *last night; it was packed with about 750 people, some of whom became hostile and unpleasant during the question-and-answer period. I got upset and confronted them, asking why they were attacking me. The bulk of the audience stood up and gave me a standing ovation; I cried.*

Childbirth in America

One approach we took to the historical material we uncovered was to use a more didactic format. We created a series of panels that combine pictures and text on the history of childbirth in America. Compiled and written by a feminist historian, Barbara Baldwin (in collaboration with me), this exhibition unit was specifically aimed at libraries, hospitals, and short conferences. We made three sets; each one included a *Crowning* batik quilt and documentation about the woman who executed it. I wanted these images to be seen in relation to the history they grew out of.

For nearly all of human history, childbirth and delivery have been the exclusive province of women. Giving birth was the natural and inevitable lot of women, who accomplished it in the company of other women. While in some instances the husband might be present as a helper, the cultural setting was clearly a female one.

White women living in Puritan New England or on Southern plantations, black slave women, and Native American women all participated in the birth process within this feminine cultural context.

In the New England colonies, women followed traditions of childbirth which they had brought from their original home and modified for the frontier environment. They depended on the community of women for companionship and assistance. Women who had moved away at marriage often returned to their parents' home for delivery; others summoned mothers, sisters, aunts, and female friends to attend them. Above all, they relied on the experience of midwives to guide them.

Midwives were the recognized authorities in matters of childbirth, giving advice on prenatal difficulties and supervising the birth itself. The woman in labor was seen as requiring only kindness, patience, and the natural wisdom of women experienced in the birthing process. The chief duty of a midwife was to comfort the woman as both waited for nature to take its course. She also cut and tied the umbilical cord and received the afterbirth.

There was very little attempt to license midwives in the colonies, and their training and skills varied enormously. Some were ignorant and untrained, others highly skilled and competent, with established reputations for expertise. There is evidence that some midwives were able to perform version—that is, turning the fetus in the womb by manipulating it, either externally or internally. Since breech or other abnormal presentations were a serious crisis, this skill was an extremely important one. Because of their importance, midwives achieved some status in the colonial community, and many records of their practice remain intact today.

Until the late 1700s, childbirth, especially the birth of a first child, was seen as an important rite of passage. Women were secluded, and their activities restricted, both before and after the birth. They re-emerged into the community only after the entire process had been completed.

Following delivery, the new mother was covered snugly and confined to her bed—ideally for three to four weeks, though some got up earlier, which occasioned much criticism. Whenever possible, family members and others relieved the mother of her household responsibilities. In addition to the midwife, a number of women would be present as helpers, visitors, and well-wishers. Women came together to be convivial as well as supportive, and one of the tasks for a woman approaching her confinement was to prepare refreshments for the women who would come to attend her during labor.

In this labor scene in early Virginia (15), the husband participated in the birth.

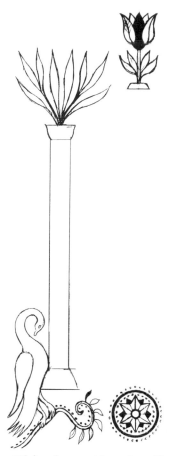

This is a thumbnail sketch for *Birth Certificate,* incorporating a tulip, an urn with leaves, a bird, and a six-pointed star. Later I changed the bird to a parrot.

Barbara Amelia Nace working at home.

"The demystification of the art-making process has been a profound experience for me. While I've been excited by learning how the process works, I've felt a loss at having the mystery dispelled. Yet intellectually I know that, like most other things, art-making is in large measure mostly hard work."

Barbara Amelia Nace

I did a full-scale drawing, then transferred it to the linen and began to paint the images in the colors Barbara had described as typical of baptismal certificates. These were completely different from the kinds of colors I customarily use, and I found it interesting to work with them. Moreover, there would be none of the airbrushed fades I am prone to use. Instead, the color was to be flat, as in the traditional Taufscheine.

By this point in the project, I had decided that some of the pieces I liked the best fused, rather than obscured, my painting with needlework. In *Birth Certificate,* my painting was to be visible—outlined, embellished, and balanced by the embroidery.

After I finished the painting, I called Barbara and told her about it. When I said that I planned to call it *Birth Certificate,* she was a bit put off. Barbara has a more rigorous academic training than I and tends to be quite literal, so she was somewhat taken aback by the liberties I had taken with the title—but I felt that that was its rightful name.

Originally Barbara had planned just to do the research, but when she actually saw the piece, she admitted that she had some needlework skills, which, though somewhat rusty, would be sufficient, she believed, to do the embroidery.

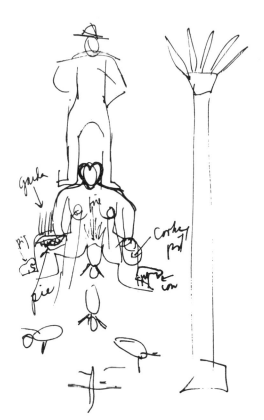

My initial sketch for *Birth Certificate.*

Although Barbara got off to a slow start and was anxious about her lack of art background and her long-unused needle skills, once she got going, she stitched like an angel. But the tension of her stitches caused puckering around the leaves, which were originally intended to be filled with embroidery. Sally and I decided to reverse-stitch what Barbara had put in, and Sally appliquéd a beautiful green silk, which Barbara then outlined. The appliqué had to be repeated somewhere else in the piece in order to make it work, and I decided to put red silk in the heart/head and center of the woman's body. Originally I wanted these to be done in pulled threadwork, which was often used in show towels.

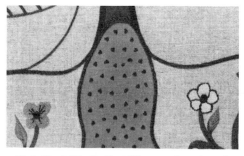

Detail of *Birth Certificate,* showing the appliqué on the woman's body, the painted potato baby with French knots, and the outlining stitching with #8 perle cotton in the whipped stem stitch.

Granny midwife Gussie Jackson was born in 1899 in Plains, Georgia. In addition to her own ten children, she delivered six hundred babies in her thirty-two years of practice as a midwife. (46)

I was the first midwife in my family. And I loved the job; you always need to get somebody to help when you have a baby, and I was always the woman they could get—I could stand it. I had a better nerve. You know you can't deliver a baby if you ain't got no nerve. (46)

A man midwife (15).

The tradition of the midwife lasted longest in the south, where "granny midwives" continued to practice until very recently. Virtually all the granny midwives were black, and, like their ancestors, they learned their skills in apprenticeship to older midwives. Most did not attend deliveries alone until they had borne a child of their own, although very often they began watching and assisting at an earlier age. Granny midwives delivered 70 percent of all black babies in the south in the 1930s and 1940s, at a much lower cost than physician-managed births. When the Public Health Service began supervising midwives, it was found that the quality of their care equaled that of the medical profession.

After the Revolutionary War, American doctors traveled to Europe for instruction. Near the end of the eighteenth century, formal training began in the United States, and, by 1807, five American medical schools offered courses in midwifery. Some professors of midwifery began to call themselves obstetricians, or professors of obstetrics, shunning the term "midwife" because of its feminine connotation. At first, training in midwifery was offered to men and women alike; but because women were excluded from the developing medical schools, they were discredited as the most desirable childbirth attendants.

By 1825 childbirth for most women was no longer the open social event it had

been up to that time. It had lost its identification as a sphere which was natural to the expertise of women—as a time when women gathered together for support. Although birth still took place at home, it became a formalized and private affair in which the role of the doctor grew in importance and the role of the mother, now a patient, declined. Because midwives resented this effort to exclude them from their means of livelihood, there ensued a bitter struggle between midwives, who argued that the modesty of women was endangered by male practitioners, and doctors, who argued that midwives were ignorant, intellectually inferior to men, and thus untrainable.

A doctor conducting an examination while "protecting the modesty of the patient." (47)

In addition to resistance from midwives, obstetricians met opposition from others who believed that natural female modesty would be violated by the presence of male obstetricians during labor. "Decent women" would never submit to such a violation of their privacy, it was argued, as to allow a man in their birth chambers.

Male doctors, therefore, assuming that their patients would regard any familiarity of manner as improper, behaved with formal reserve and coolness. In medical schools, students were taught that the importance of this demeanor was equal to the importance of their skills. To protect the modesty of the patient, vaginal examinations were discouraged, and babies were delivered by touch only, since the patient was draped to protect her from the eyes of the physician. The lights were, of course, dimmed. One male writer even pointed out, in justification of modesty, that one of the greatest obstetricians had been blind.

Throughout much of the Victorian era the female condition itself was seen as pathological, at least for upper- and middle-class women. It was generally assumed that "ladies of refinement" would respond with fainting or "hysteria" (from the Greek word *hyster,* meaning womb) to the slightest shock. Thus the stress of pregnancy was feared to be dangerous and totally debilitating.

By the mid-nineteenth century, it was thought that women were inherently delicate and frail and that their naturally weak constitutions had been further weakened by fashion and—as one doctor wrote—"indolence" until they could not survive "the crisis of confinement" without expert medical intervention. (48)

However, working women, domestic servants, slaves, and former peasant women were regarded as having much stronger constitutions, since their strength had not been attenuated by luxurious living, idleness, and corsets. It seems to have been no accident that these were also the women who were unable to afford the services of an obstetrician.

Childbirth was the second highest killer of women of childbearing age, after tuberculosis. Despite the development of "scientific childbirth," infant and maternal mortality rates remained virtually unchanged from 1850 through 1920. In the twenties the rates began to drop, and they continued to drop during the thirties. Medical care in hospitals became more routinized, and obstetrical skills were improved. Antibiotic drugs were developed. Society as a whole became more concerned with sanitation as the role of microorganisms became more widely understood, and hospitals seemed much more sanitary and germ-free than homes. As live-in nurses became less available, hospitals also began to provide postnatal care for women which could not be offered in their homes. Although this care was a poor substitute for the female support network of earlier times, it was an essential part of the hospitals' appeal.

The incidence of childbed fever, a result of infection contracted during childbirth, increased significantly with the development of obstetrics. While childbed fever had existed before, Oliver Wendell Holmes, Senior Dean of the Harvard Medical School, observed in 1844 that it was many times more prevalent among mothers in hospital wards than among mothers treated by midwives. Since students and doctors went directly from the dissecting rooms—where they performed post-mortems—to the delivery rooms, Holmes concluded that they carried the disease with them. He suggested that contagion could be prevented if doctors would wash their hands before attending obstetrical cases, and the same suggestion was made in 1847 by the Viennese doctor Semmelweiss. Fellow doctors greeted this suggestion with indignation, declaring that doctors were gentlemen and thus had clean hands, so they could not possibly carry the disease among women. It was several decades before the cleanliness requirement gained any credence with the medical profession, which continued to criticize midwives as dirty and ignorant.

As there were so many hazards attached to the use of male physicians, it seems surprising that upper- and middle-class women called on them in increasing numbers, despite their fears. One explanation may be that the physicians promised, through use of instruments and drugs, to make childbirth safe and even painless.

The rumor has gone out, from mouth to mouth, among women to the ends of the earth, that at last modern science has abolished that primal sentence of the Scriptures upon womankind: "In sorrow thou shalt bring forth child." (49)

Chloroform was first used in childbirth in 1847. It had been shown that contractions of the uterus would continue even if the woman were unconscious, and thus an anesthetic could be used against the pain of childbirth. At first there was some objection to the elimination of pain; a clergyman attacked anesthesia as "a decoy of Satan" which would "rob God of the deep, earnest cries which arise in time of trouble." One doctor said of the administration of ether, "In place of a woman bearing her pains with dignity and fortitude, it presents a creature only clamoring for ease." After Queen Victoria used chloroform successfully at a birth in 1848 and again in 1853, women did indeed clamor for ease in increasing numbers.

The development of anesthesia reinforced the interventionist attitude of modern obstetrics. One medical technique led to another: anesthesia increased the need to use forceps; tearing led to the development of the episiotomy (cutting the perineal area at the moment of tearing), a technique which had not been used in the past. All this intervention led to more deaths from infection. This, in turn, heightened the fear women felt about childbirth and increased their desire to be relieved of consciousness.

Fear and dread of childbirth was one theme openly expressed in female diaries and in correspondence among women friends or between husbands and wives. One can only guess at the effect upon the psychology of women exerted by the inevitable connection between sexual activity and consequent pregnancy at a time when it was much more likely for a woman to die in childbirth than it was for a man to die in war. (50)

By the late nineteenth century, as a consequence of the professionalization of medicine, midwives had lost nearly all their social status. Unlike doctors, they were not organized and did not succeed in developing criteria for certifi-

cation in their occupation. The costs of having a doctor in attendance explain the large proportion of births attended by midwives through the nineteenth and well into the twentieth century—particularly for immigrant women and black women. As late as 1910, about half of all births in the United States were attended by midwives, and the percentage was even higher in the cities because of the large poor populations. Most of the midwives who attended these births were themselves poor and had very little training. For immigrant women, however, having a birth attendant who spoke their language and understood their cultural traditions was very important. In the frontier regions many of the women who served as midwives were untrained or had only their own experience with birth to guide them. In some areas there were no midwives at all, and women often faced childbirth alone or with the inexpert help of their families or neighbors.

Labor scene, early Virginia (51).

Some women, confronted with having to deliver their own babies, devised clever contraptions to help them. Mary Richardson Walker, living in the Oregon territory in 1838, had her first child while her husband was away. She anticipated the event fearfully, writing in her journal, "If I were to yield to inclination, I should cry half the time without knowing why. So much danger attends me . . . without mother or sister to attend me, can I survive it all?" A nearby missionary woman helped her through the birth. By her third birth, she had become more adept at preparation and anticipated the event. She got up at 5 a.m., had an early breakfast, and finished her housework by 9 o'clock. "At nine that evening she was delivered of a son." (52)

In the 1940s, Grantly Dick-Read, the British obstetrician whose book *Childbirth Without Fear* (53) launched the natural childbirth movement, observed that "Pain in childbirth arises out of fear and tension." He began to train prospec-

tive mothers to relax by breathing correctly and understanding the birth process, urging that attending physicians be a calm, sure source of security rather than intervening surgeons, and that anesthesia be available but never used as a routine measure. While his view that childbirth was natural did serve as a counter to the medical interventionist model, he was extremely patriarchal in his view of women.

In 1951 Fernand Lamaze, a French physician, began to train women in breathing exercises and to include the husband as a trained helper in the breathing process during birth. Hundreds of thousands of women have used Dr. Lamaze's techniques, and although this undoubtedly relieved much of their suffering in childbirth, his outlook still viewed the birth process as a medical problem.

After World War II, women began expressing their desire for natural childbirth and breastfeeding; the response of doctors was largely negative. For one thing, the birth rate jumped dramatically in the decade following the war, and the strain on available maternity facilities in hospitals made the slower process of natural childbirth seem an inefficient as well as unscientific self-indulgence. The ideology of women as helpless, emotional, and incapable of understanding the technology or physiology of birth led to increased efforts to separate the mother from the birth process and to leave control with the obstetrician.

As a result of growing distrust of modern obstetrical procedures, there has recently been a move toward family-centered or woman-centered childbirth. The most important aspect of this movement is that the mother or both parents are seen as the essential actors in the birth, rather than the mother being simply the mechanical carrier of the infant and the father being an extraneous nuisance. Family-centered or woman-centered childbirth can take place in a birth center attached to a regular hospital. The woman may move around easily, have family and friends in attendance, and exercise more control over what is still an essentially medical procedure. Or it may be the increasingly common practice of home birth, with attendance by a trained nurse-midwife, a lay midwife, or, in some cases, a cooperative physician.

It is certainly true that for an increasing number of women, the birth experience is ecstatic. But it's very important to keep in mind that, from a global perspective, the birth experience is still not a positive one for millions of women.

Then on the next contraction I started to pull and was suddenly swept away with primitive strength. Everything went blank and lightning-like streaks flashed, it seemed. It was ecstatic, wonderfully thrilling! I heard myself moaning—in triumph, not in pain! There was no pain whatsoever, only a primitive and sexual elation. (47)

My child nearly killed me as he tore his way into life. (54)

My first daughter and I were both abused physically and emotionally at her birth in an English hospital. Fear reduced my pain threshold to such an extent that technology eventually intervened, and my baby was yanked from my body . . . .

My second daughter was born at home . . . in my own bed, welcomed by a gentle midwife and a few loving friends. (55)

Those who support home birth find the atmosphere of hospital births dehumanizing, pathological, and unnecessary for the great majority of births. The medical profession as a whole has tended to see home births as dangerous. The one study done on comparable populations who chose prepared home birth as opposed to hospital birth found that the infant death rates were about the same for both groups, but that the hospital babies suffered thirty times the number of birth injuries (primarily from the use of forceps), four times as many infections, and 3.7 times as many resuscitations (primarily because of the large proportion of hospital births during which the mother is sedated).

At this time, woman-centered birth is used primarily by well-educated middle- and upper-class women who are able to prepare themselves with information and assert their right to control their own experience. In addition, a smaller population of those who have rejected many major cultural institutions use lay midwives as part of their process of developing an alternative culture. The fact remains, however, that a humanized birth process is still unavailable to most people—despite the fact that birth is a universal experience and one that is central to women's lives.

We translated this historical information into a 25-foot exhibition unit intended for showing in libraries, hospitals, and birthing centers and at childbirth conferences. It has turned out to be a very successful installation, engendering tears, outrage, and, most of all, dialogue.

Mary Ross Taylor checking the installation of *Childbirth in America* at its exhibition in the Moody Medical Library of The University of Texas in Galveston.

Viewing *Childbirth in America*.

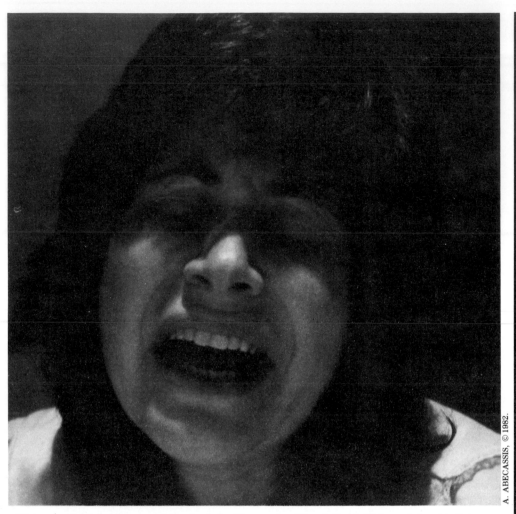

A. ABECASSIS, © 1982.

This wonderful photograph by Andrée Abecassis of Leah Potts Fisher giving birth to son Mischa seemed to relate to the following statement by another woman:

The miraculous moment was when I started singing as a continuation of the breathing. I sing to earn my living, and I sang to bring about this baby like I have never sung before. Imagine a labor room with singing women, what a chorus it would be! Singing was a great outlet for my emotions during pregnancy and at birth. It took the place of self-pity. So, when you are in doubt, keep on singing.

—Caterine Milinaire (56)

The preceding material also appears in *Childbirth in America*, a multi-media installation chronicling the history of childbirth through art, photographs, text, and personal testimony (Through the Flower, 1983).

Wouldn't it be wonderful if the birth experience could be joyful for every woman on the planet?

Judy Chicago

Birth Certificate: From Research to Art

Button sent by Barbara Amelia Nace indicating her feelings about her heritage.

"I'm a Pennsylvania German woman very much interested in celebrating my femaleness as well as in preserving my heritage, excited by life and the changes its passing brings, curious and wanting to learn and experience, eager to share."
Needleworker
Barbara Amelia Nace
Lansdale, Pennsylvania

Barbara Amelia Nace's home in Lansdale, Pennsylvania.

Barbara Amelia Nace wrote to *The Birth Project* saying that she was a Pennsylvania German woman interested in her heritage and wondered if I would be, too. I encouraged her to investigate both Pennsylvania German and Dutch traditions in relation to birth, birth-related imagery, needlework, and the status of women. She assembled a considerable amount of information:

Dear Judy,

Decorated hand towels, also known as "show towels," are the only form of needlework that is exclusively Pennsylvania German. In a culture that wastes nothing and subscribes to a form-follows-function philosophy, these towels are something of an oddity, as they seem to be purely decorative.

The only other type of needlework was not unique to us, but has traditionally been done by young girls of many cultures—samplers. Those common to Pennsylvania Dutch and German societies were typically embroidered on a homespun linen surface.

What I've learned from my research is that, except for some folklore revolving around medicinal herbs and superstitions concerning babies, information is scanty, and written information on the birth process is virtually nonexistent. The outstanding exception is the striking *Frakturschriften Taufscheine*, illuminated birth and baptismal records, which really represent my heritage and also refer to birth. All the symbols used on the Taufscheine are typical of Pennsylvania Dutch artifacts, and most of them have a religious orientation. Colors vary, but yellows, red, greens, browns, and blues are most often used. Originally, the Taufscheine honored only the child's baptism, but later they included birth information as well. Here is a list of symbols commonly used and their popular meanings:

Six-pointed stars—symbolize prosperity and fertility and stand for Christ: they indicate a perfectly balanced universe.

Hearts—represent God's love.

Birds—symbolize Christ.

Flowers—represent man's searching for god and the promise of hope. Tulips are often used and are shown with three petals to represent the Trinity.

Birth and baptismal record (Taufschein), circa 1810. Probably from Berks County, Pennsylvania. Hand drawing, hand lettering, and watercolor on laid paper. Artist unknown. Collection of Rare Book Department, Free Library of Philadelphia, Pennsylvania. (57)

All of life in a Pennsylvania Dutch or German community was structured by an unwritten set of rules of conduct. For example, no Pennsylvania Dutch housewife ever wondered what to make for dinner, as there was an ordered menu for each meal of the day for every day of the week.

A woman's day was similarly ordered; she rose first to tend to the household chores and prepare breakfast. Before breakfast, she would do the morning milking, which was considered "women's work." She also fed the pigs and carried the milk to the cellar for later production of butter and cheese.

Fried potatoes were almost indispensible for breakfast; in fact, potatoes were one of the staples of this culture's food, as was reflected in this prayer:

Potatoes in the morning for breakfast
 I see,
Potatoes for dinner, cooked in broth,
Potatoes at evening my supper will be,
Yes, potatoes into all eternity.   (58)

Breakfast was always topped off with some variety of pie, which was, like potatoes, eaten at every meal. In addition to doing all the cooking and baking pies of all varieties, women did the washing, cleaning, gardening, cultivation of flowers and ornamental plants, spinning, sewing and making clothing, and, of course, needlework. The times for these activities were strictly ordered by the season of the year and the day of the week.

One of the most important aspects of women's work was the "kitchen garden," with four beds and four paths meeting in the center to form a Greek cross. This garden was the chief source of sustenance on the farm; it produced vegetables, culinary and healing herbs, flowers to beautify the house, and holy plants to protect the homestead.

The Pennsylvania Dutch and Germans were patriarchal societies, and, though women were more esteemed than in other fundamentalist religions, the cultures were Biblical in their way of life, and therefore Father was always the head of the household; there are few records that testify to how the women felt about this.

I hope you find this information as interesting as I did, although I'm disappointed that there isn't more.

Sincerely,
Barbara Amelia Nace

Not only did I find the material fascinating, but I was eager to develop a piece based on everything Barbara had sent. I decided to design a piece on natural linen which had the proportions of a "show towel." I made a rough sketch of a man standing on a woman's shoulders—an image of patriarchy. Later, I added a cross/phallus, which the man holds in his hands, as a symbol of religious identification and also as a menacing weapon, guaranteed to keep the woman in her place.

The woman, who has a heart-shaped face, holds a cooking/milking pot in one hand. In my sketch, I had her holding a small garden in her other hand, which I later changed to a pie. The garden was transmuted into a tree of life, which refers to the kitchen gardens, to the female as provider, and to ancient images of the goddess as the tree of life.

I also included some potato-shaped babies emerging from the woman's body. When I was painting the piece, I turned to Sally, who was working at the other end of the studio, and asked, "Do you think I can get away with potato-babies? It's so bizarre." "Sure," Sally replied, "that's a great idea"—whereupon she promptly went downstairs and announced to everyone in the office, "Can you believe what she's doing up there? Painting potato babies!"

My sketch also included a tulip (which eventually became a tulip/hat on the man's head) and two tall urns filled with leaves. The only other thing I added later was two parrots, each clutching one of the woman's feet.

Show towel, 1860, Pennsylvania German; cotton and embroidery. The Titus C. Geesey Collection, Philadelphia Museum of Art. (59)

When I read about these hand or "show" towels, as they are called, and realized that they were generally embroidered in red, I wondered whether there was any unconscious connection in the minds of the needleworkers between these towels and what is called "bloody show," which is the blood-tinged mucous discharged from the vagina before or during labor.

Birth practices among Native American women varied widely from one tribe to another. In some tribes, special birthing areas were constructed. The mother was attended by other village women and a midwife, who had carpeted the floor of the hut with soft ferns or grasses. She would give birth while kneeling and clutching a pole in the center of the hut. A drumbeat was used to regulate her breathing, and herbal remedies were used to speed the process or to rectify problems during labor and delivery. There are many beautiful stories and legends describing Native American births.

A fire was burning, and my mother had made my bed, a soft buffalo robe folded with the hair side out. This bed was not to lie down on. Crow women do not lie down when their babies are born, nor even afterward, excepting to sleep when night comes, as others do. Two stakes had been driven into the ground for me to take hold of, and robes had been rolled up and piled against them, so that when I knelt on the bed-robe and took hold of the two stakes, my elbows would rest upon the pile of rolled robes.

While I stood by the door, Left-hand took four live coals from the lodge-fire. One of these she placed on the ground at the door, then one to the left, halfway to the head (center of back), one at the head, and one in front of the bed-robe, which was on the right of the door, halfway between it and the head of the lodge. Then she dropped a little of the-grass-that-the-buffalo-do-not-eat upon each of these coals, telling me to walk to the left, to go around my bed (as the sun goes), stepping over the coals. "Walk as though you are busy," she said, brushing my back with the tail of her buffalo robe, and grunting as a buffalo-cow grunts.

I had stepped over the second coal when I saw that I should have to *run* if I reached my bed-robe in time. I *jumped* the third coal, and the *fourth*, knelt down on the robe, took hold of the two stakes; and my first child, Pinefire, was there with us. (44)

Rose Emerson, a young Yuma mother, and her baby (45). Original: American of Museum Natural History.

Although midwifery continued to be a predominantly female occupation, the man-midwife, or accoucheur, began to appear in Europe in the seventeenth century and in the United States around 1720. His specialty was surgical intervention in births that could not be accomplished naturally. He was the direct predecessor of the obstetrician, and his origins lay in the barber-surgeon guilds of the thirteenth century. Along with barbering, these guild members practiced tooth extraction, bleeding, and other forms of surgery. Since forceps were not in general use until the eighteenth century, surgical intervention in childbirth consisted of extracting the fetus piecemeal, after crushing its skull to make removal from the birth canal possible, or performing a Caesarian section on the dead mother in order to save the infant. Women were excluded from the practice of barber-surgery and were prohibited from using surgical instruments.

Forceps for the removal of the live fetus were invented by a French family of doctors in the seventeenth century and kept secret for nearly a hundred years. The use of forceps was surrounded with a great deal of mystery, which included blindfolding the laboring woman so that she could not reveal the secret of the successful delivery.

The obstetricians of the seventeenth century were possessed with an incredible ardor for inventing instruments (15)—sometimes dangerous, often useless, but always ingenious. They were determined to replace the natural methods of the midwife with the surgical procedures they had invented.

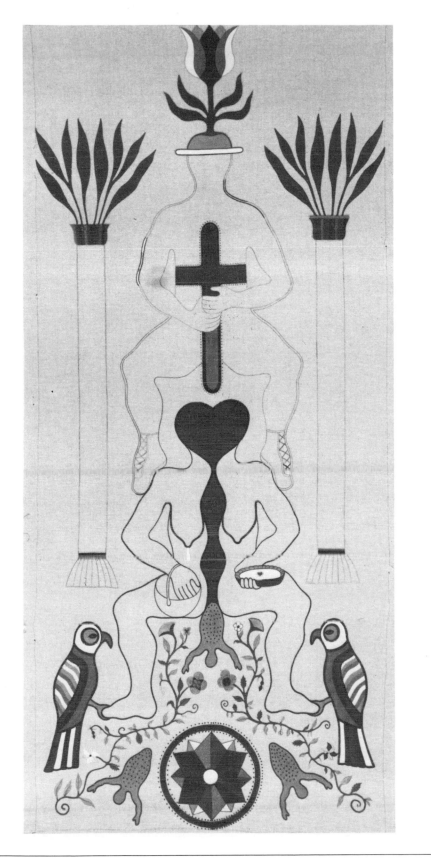

Birth Certificate (in progress), ©Judy Chicago, 1984. Embroidery by Barbara Amelia Nace, Lansdale, Pennsylvania. Painting, appliqué, and embroidery on linen, 39" x 90".

Barbara Amelia Nace
Journal entries:

June 10, 1983

Sometimes stitching mesmerizes me; it was doing that today while I was working on the vine of the tree of life. It's exciting to see the colors juxtaposed.

June 13

While I'm working, I'm smelling sweet flowers and herbs—appropriate when stitching the tree of life.

June 16

Sometimes I feel as though I'm consumed by *Birth Certificate*. It demands a good portion of my day; I wake thinking of it, sometimes dream about it, always worry about it.

August 1

As I was stitching today, I realized that I'm stitching secrets into *Birth Certificate*. Nowhere have I documented my putting in three two-knot clusters in each potato baby. The typical configuration is a three-knot cluster, so the lesser knots I've included are in memory of the women who deliberately added flaws to their needlework, believing that only God was perfect.

September 9

I've written little about the imagery in *Birth Certificate;* I'm intimately linked to the signs and symbols in this art, particularly the image of the woman. Joy, love, frustration, sadness, and anger are all parts of the link between me and this art. The *Birth Certificate* is really about *me*.

Barbara Amelia Nace

Only the bottom half of the piece was completed at the time of this photograph. The top section will all be outlined in embroidery, and the double line around the man will be filled with solid yellow thread.

This section of the *Birth Certificate* shows the feet of the woman, the two parrots that flank her, the three potato babies, the tree of life or flowering garden, and the six-pointed star.

"The embroidery is all done in DMC floss or in perle cotton, Nos. 3, 5, and 8. The outline of the woman's body is done in the whipped stem stitch; the potato babies are outlined in the stem stitch, and their bodies are filled with French knots; the birds are outlined with rows of stem stitches of different colors, and their eyes are solid stem; for the star, I combined French knots, the whipped stem, and the stem stitch.

"The most intricately embroidered area, the tree of life, contains five stitches: the leaves and vines are worked in a fishbone stitch; the aqua flowers combine the stem stitch and French knots; the small flowers at the top are made up of many, many small knots, while the pinwheel flowers combine knots and the fishbone stitch; and the large, morning-glory-like flowers combine the fishbone, the buttonhole, and the long and short stitch.

"I wanted to use the simple but expressive stitches my foremothers used in their needlework. I varied five basic stitches in relation to the imagery."

Barbara Amelia Nace

Detail, bottom half of *Birth Certificate*.

Transforming Filet Crochet

Monday, October 18, 1982

After visiting Barbara, we went to Dolly Kaminski's house in Bethlehem, Pennsylvania. She is doing what is probably the most mind-boggling piece in the project—an 8' x 21' filet crochet.

Dolly Kaminski's house in Bethlehem, Pennsylvania.

The first sample I received in filet crochet was from Dolly Kaminski, and I was intrigued by it. I had done some designing for crochet in *The Dinner Party* and I thought that some of the *Birth Project* patterns would lend themselves to this technique.

After Dolly had completed the application procedure, I called her to ask whether she was willing to try a large piece. What primarily interested me was the idea of dramatically enlarging the scale of crochet and thereby pushing it out of its visual associations with tablecloths and curtains, which is what filet crochet is most typically used for. Dolly asked, "How large?" I said, "At least four feet by eight feet." "No problem," she replied.

We decided on an image, and she began doing small translation samples. Every few weeks, an envelope would arrive, and out would tumble tiny pieces of crochet in different scales and dif-ferent colors, weights, and types of thread. I finally liked one of the samples, and, because crochet thread came in a limited color range, I decided to use black.

Dolly then began to grid out the image, which turned out to be quite a chore. When Dolly was about halfway through with the gridding, she called me and said calmly, "Judy, I think this piece is going to be much larger than we originally thought." "Really," I replied, "how large?" "About twenty feet long," she stated. "Well," I asked, "how do you feel about that, Dolly?"

"Fine," she replied.

I have to say that I was taken aback. My experience with most of the needleworkers was that they always thought my idea of small was not small, and my idea of large was gigantic. I had wanted to push the scale of crochet, but even I had not imagined doing such a big piece.

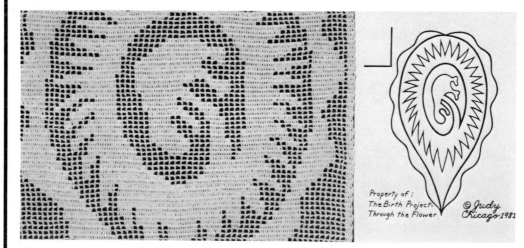

Filet-crochet sample submitted by Dolly Kaminski.

This sample demonstrated how the gridding process enlarged the scale and altered the image of my original design. It was crocheted with Coats & Clark "South Maid" crochet thread, with a #8 steel crochet hook. Each solid square consisted of three double crochet stitches and each open square of one double crochet and two chain stitches. One double crochet stitch was added at the end of each row. The foundation chain consisted of 178 stitches.

204

Tuesday, March 11, 1983

I am profoundly depressed; I'm sure that the only thing that will make me feel better is being at it again in the studio—and that can't happen for a while. I'm working, of course, but Birth Project work doesn't really "count" for me now, as it is mostly finish work.

Saturday, April 2

Last Sunday I did reviews in New York. It was wonderful to see that so much of the work is really coming along. Most of the needleworkers who were there had been involved for a long time, and there was a terrific sense of camaraderie between us. Doris Lessing once said that she thought one of the fundamental problems on the planet was that people had lost their "sense of we-ness." It is startling to realize that it is precisely that "sense of we-ness" which is the glue that holds The Birth Project together. Though geographically separate, we are all united by being engaged in work aimed at affirming our female experience—and because that work is so much larger than ourselves, we are able to transcend our personal differences and cooperate despite the vast differences between us.

Monday, April 11

The Birth Project received a bequest of $40,000 from a woman named Nanette Bruckner in Texas. I stayed with her when The Dinner Party was there. I can't believe it; enough money for six more months.

Drawing for *Beaded Birth Tear,* ©Judy Chicago, 1983. Ink and acrylic on rag paper, 26" x 15¾".

Upper right quarter, drawing for *Beaded Birth Tear.*

I sent Dee a drawing that contained both a color study (on the right) and a black and white pattern from which she could make a grid for the beading. She had provided me with a selection of bead colors, and I had painted the image to match the beads. Once she began beading, the piece became elongated, which I didn't mind, since it worked well with the image.

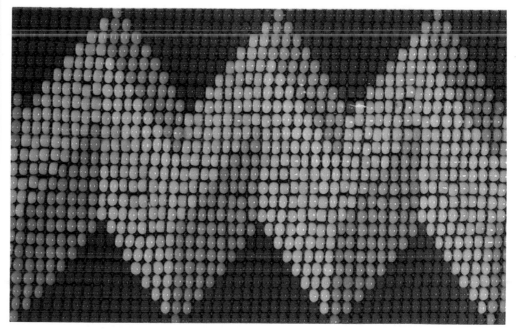

Detail of border of *Beaded Birth Tear.*

"I was carried away by the beauty of Judy's drawing and felt that she had, consciously or not, captured the essence of the spirituality of birth and the intensity that radiates from a birthing woman. The geometric image is split in two by the powerful creative energy involved in giving birth. Energy radiates from around it in the form of rainbows, and a dynamic border encloses the image."

Dee Thompson

Beaded Birth Tear

One of my most exciting visits to needleworkers' homes took place when I went to Hawaii to visit Dee Thompson, who executed the only beaded piece in the project. It was really wonderful to have an excuse to go to Hawaii. Dee Thompson wrote and told me that her loom was so big she couldn't ship it and obviously she couldn't cut the beading off before it was done so she couldn't send it for a review. As they say, if the mountain couldn't come to Mohammed, Judy could fly to Hawaii.

Tuesday, February 8, 1983

When I planned The Birth Project *in terms of building a creative and distributing network that would make art more accessible to people, I really didn't think about what that would mean. We get a lot of requests from people who are not familiar with hanging art, and therefore we decided it was necessary to provide simple, clear instructions so that anyone could hang a beautiful show. It took hours and hours to write installation instructions, as it's really difficult to break down all the steps we do automatically and explain everything to someone who's never installed an exhibition. And even if they're experienced, very few people know how to*

Early in 1983, I began to work on ideas for a beaded project. By that time, I was starting new pieces only if I was presented with an unusual sample or with either a technique which I had never designed for or one which was unrepresented in the project.

Dee Thompson asked if I would be interested in designing a beaded piece for her to execute. She did a sample and also sent examples of her beadwork, which I liked. I had designed beadwork in *The Dinner Party*—and had liked the results. I encouraged Dee, who had three children, to supply me with information about her life, her birth experiences, and historical designs she particularly liked. She sent me a considerable amount of material, including vivid descriptions of her birth experiences.

"I went into labor the first time in the morning. Around 9 a.m., the doctor came by to check my progress. He said that labor would probably continue for most of the day, that he would be out of town, and that his 'assistants' would be on call.

"I got through the day in a dreamy state. I was going to meet my child at last—whom I had been so close to all these months, whom I had already sung to and stroked and loved. Around 8 p.m. I was in heavy labor, but in control. My husband Jim called the office, but no one would come; they said it was too soon. Jim insisted, and after about an hour an older man and his wife, dressed in hospital-type garb, appeared. They were stern and unsmiling and demanded that I get up on the table they had brought. I had been hoping to deliver in bed and refused, but they bullied me into it . . .

"Pretty soon I was screaming, and the man was telling me to start pushing. I had taken a prepared childbirth class, and they had said the urge to push was unmistakable. No way did I feel this urge—but I pushed for an hour. I was really in pain and out of control. Jim finally kicked the

'doctor' out, and off we went to the hospital. As soon as we got there, someone said: 'Another fucked-up home birth we have to clean up after.'

"They wheeled me off to a labor room, and I had to say goodbye to Jim. They administered a pudendal block to deaden the vaginal nerves for the delivery: I couldn't feel anything as my baby was born; I couldn't hear her cry, and they didn't show her to me. Later they said, 'You had a third-degree tear,' meaning, 'We cut too far and went through your rectum.' I passed out, crying: 'My baby, please show me my baby.'

"My last birth was altogether different. No more hospitals for us. I woke up and knew I was in labor. Walking out to the morning sunshine, the sweet desert smell made my spirits soar, and I knew that my child would be born that day. I sat outside in a soft chair and breathed with Jim; in what seemed like no time, I was going through 'transition.' We sang—'Come out little baby, we love you,' with crazy tunes and a few coyote howls thrown in. I wasn't pushing and it was working—no breath-holding or gut-straining—the baby was coming out by itself, with my body's natural expulsion . . . the baby's body slithered out, and I lifted him onto my stomach. He opened his eyes and looked at me—his skin was so soft—and Jim and I were ecstatic, crying, holding our son and each other."

Dee Thompson

Dee Thompson with her three children.

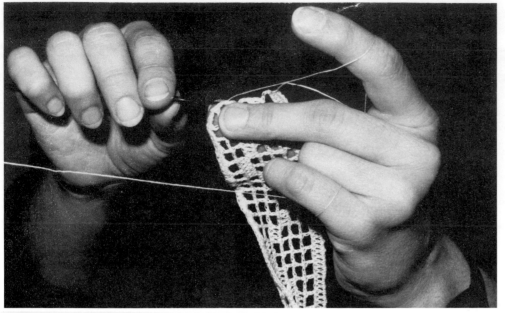

Martha Waterman crocheting.

"It is fascinating to me how crochet is created from a single strand of thread, worked one loop at a time on a hook, freely held in the air. Crochet can be made in hundreds of textures and patterns; anything your mind can invent for a line to do, crochet can follow."

Martha Waterman

The process of taking a traditional needle technique like filet crochet and transforming it into an expressive art-making tool required that I transcend my prejudices as a "fine artist." Instead of disregarding the technique as "craft," I tried to examine its inherent nature—the way it is basically based on an interplay of positive and negative patterns—and stop imagining it rippling like a curtain or covered with dishes at a holiday dinner. I hope that my investigation of filet crochet and the achievements of the needleworkers who worked with me will demonstrate how old ways can become the basis for new ideas if one has an open mind and an imagination unencumbered by intellectual categories or assumptions.

Section of grid and crochet for *Birth Trinity ST.*

Wednesday, January 19, 1983

I just have to force myself to put my shoulder under The Birth Project *and move it forward. I started on exhibition preparation yesterday and realized that I still have some things to say about women's lives and experiences, which I think can be best said through the documentation. But what a struggle to maintain my interest when I really want to be in my studio alone working on new ideas.*

Monday, January 24

I'm struggling with the feeling that every work of art I make imprisons me further in the problems of caring for and protecting it after I'm done with it. I hate it so much, and it's so unfair; I keep wondering whether I could live with just doing the work, even if it never goes anywhere. And maybe I could—for a while—because I so love the act of making art. But what would happen after ten or fifteen years?

Both Martha Waterman and I have a fascination with crochet and its implications in terms of women's history. It pleases me greatly that we have been able to take a technique that is so unappreciated and demonstrate what incredible visual beauty it has. As I said in *Embroidering Our Heritage: The Dinner Party Needlework:* ". . . Crochet is the [technique] most directly linked to the most devalued part of the domestic needlework tradition. It is difficult even to look at a crocheted piece without thinking of afghans, dresser scarves, table mats, or ruffled dolls' dresses. Even within the context of the home, where women's needlework is at least appreciated by her family, crocheted objects are overlooked and easily lost. Why, then, would we choose to include this technique . . . ?" (31)

"Women have always been artists; the things women have created to change or beautify their home environments require as much talent, hard work, time, skill, and learning as art created in the forms we see hanging in museums and galleries—and yet women have never received our society's recognition for their work."

Kris Wetterlund

Martha Waterman crocheting at home in Janesville, Iowa.

"In high school, I crocheted through boring study halls, sometimes while reading a magazine. However, I taught myself filet crochet just last summer while on a car trip. It was the best part of the trip! I was motivated by receiving an armload of crocheted doilies, chair sets, runners, and dresser scarves from my mother. They had been made by her, my grandmother, and my great-grandmother. I want this heritage of my foremothers to be passed on and respected."

Martha Waterman

Crochet by, and photographs of, Martha's foremothers.

LIZ STULL

Pattern for Birth Trinity, © Judy Chicago, 1982. Ink on paper, 42'' x 126''.

"This image reminds me of the land and the countryside I live in: gently rolling hills; fertile, rich farmland; winding, twisting creeks joining broad, placid rivers in a network of lines across the land. The wavy lines are like the plowed furrows of the farm fields that go up and down or around the rolling hills."

Needleworker Martha Waterman
Janesville, Iowa

Friday, December 10, 1982

I feel good about this month's work; we moved forward on exhibition preparation, and I started some new projects. There are now thirty-three completed works and eighty more under way. Who knows? We might still end up with a hundred pieces out of the hundred and fifty we've begun. The staff is really growing into quite a team; our last staff meeting was great.

Friday, January 7, 1983

It's almost 8 a.m. I'm in Houston. I had a very tiring day yesterday. We are getting ready to open our small **Birth Project** *gallery here. The space looks great. Sally's installing the San Diego show today, and we're getting a lot of inquiries about* **Birth Project** *shows. Nonetheless, I think that this period of my life of participatory art-making is coming to a close; I just want to make art alone now.*

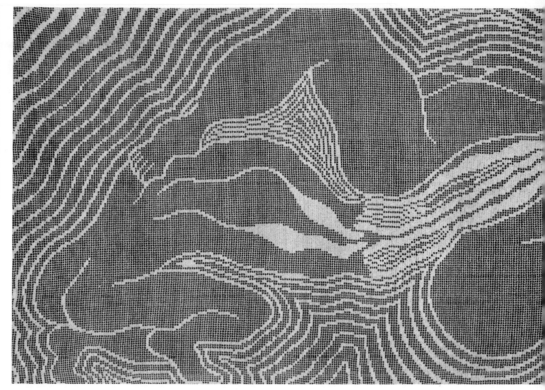

Birth Trinity, © Judy Chicago, 1984. Crocheted by Martha Waterman, Janesville, Iowa. No. 30 cotton crochet thread mounted on linen, 37'' x 106½''.

Another filet-crochet piece, quite different from the one executed by Dolly Kaminski, is this version of *Birth Trinity,* crocheted by Martha Waterman of Janesville, Iowa. In this case, the scale of the crochet and the weight of the thread are much finer, and hence the piece is smaller. The boldness of *Birth* is contrasted with the delicacy of this work, which we mounted on a natural linen, the soft color of which emphasizes the fine detail of the crochet.

"I used an ecru-colored #30 crochet thread for this piece—the finest thread available locally, a three-ply 100-percent cotton. The technique I used is filet crochet. 'Filet' is a French word meaning 'slender thread.' Filet crochet is the making of both the open and the solid areas of a pattern in one step. Filet crochet is worked in horizontal rows, one on top of the other, turning the piece after each row so that there is no right or wrong side of the fabric. The rows may be worked from top to bottom, bottom to top, or side to side.

"I first transferred Judy's pattern to ¼'' graph paper, each square of the grid representing one crocheted square. Most filet crochet is done directly from a graph-paper pattern or printed chart, but this piece was too large and complicated for that. After gridding it, I developed a shorthand method of writing out instructions for each row, which I called 'tablature.' Each row's tablature had to include the direction of the row and the number of open and solid squares in their proper sequence. Once the tablature was done, it was simply a matter of adding one row to another. Judy had already approved the scale of my grid and the color and weight of the thread from the translation samples I had sent. Once I began crocheting, there were not too many changes that could be made.

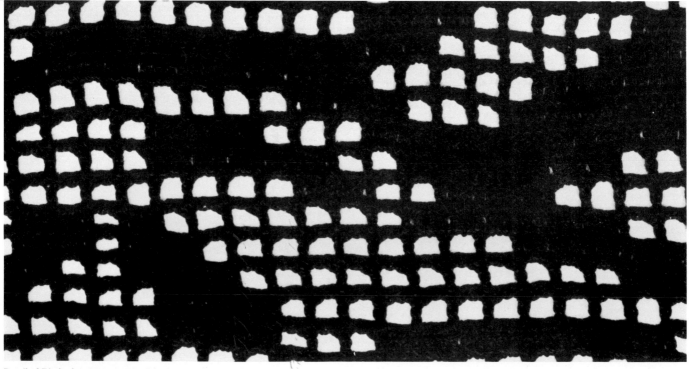

Detail of *Birth*, showing a section of the crochet close up.

Birth (in progress), ©Judy Chicago, 1984. Filet crochet by Dolly Kaminski, Bethlehem, Pennsylvania, in DMC crochet cotton thread, 90'' x 240''.

"I started with a 24'' x 46'' paper pattern, which I mounted on a piece of fiberboard. Gridding was accomplished using seventeen 7'' x 10'' sheets of 16-squares-to-the-inch graph paper, taped together and placed over the entire pattern.

"I began my crochet with a foundation chain stitch. There were 738 squares across the bottom of the graph, each of which translated into three chain stitches of crochet. Therefore, I needed to crochet 3 x 738, or 2214, stitches for the foundation. Four more stitches needed for anchoring and turning the row brought the total to 2218.

"The next row and all subsequent 385 rows consisted of double crochet and chain stitches. The first two rows (after the foundation row) form a border of solid double crochet stitches. Thereafter, each row is a combination of the two stitches, forming either solid or open areas according to the pattern. The solid areas of the image were executed in double crochet stitches, while the open areas are a combination of double crochet and chain stitches.

"Each row took approximately 4 to 5 hours to complete. This included marking out the row on the graph and weaving in the loose ends of thread caused by tying in new balls of thread when needed. As I marked out each section of the row on the graph, I would count the number of stitches needed for each section and write down that number on a separate piece of paper. Then, as I crocheted each section of the row, I would verify that my actual stitches or spaces corresponded to the number I had recorded on the paper, and I would also visually check my work against the graph.

"The thread is of medium weight, a little heavier than that normally used in doilies but much thinner and less resilient than yarn. It is 100-percent cotton, made by DMC and called Brilliant Crochet Cotton. I used a steel crochet hook, size 8. This piece contains 854,993 stitches and will have taken approximately 1800 hours to stitch.''

Dolly Kaminski

208

Detail of *Birth*, showing fetus.

Dolly crocheted this piece from the bottom up, which meant that she started with one 21-foot row of crochet. When I asked her why she hadn't worked the piece from the side (which seemed more logical to me), she replied: "Because I've always crocheted from the bottom up."

Wednesday, November 17, 1982

Well I'm home, it's cold and rainy; my cat, Mully, is on my lap. The staff all had a party for me and baked tons of chocolate-chip cookies, which I ate like mad. I really had a wonderful trip. The building looks great and orderly, and the staff has taken a mighty leap forward while I was gone, which is just what I'd hoped would happen.

Friday, December 3

I have been very, very busy, working more 12-hour days than I'd like. We're finishing up the preparations for our next show and also preparing some new projects. We seem to be getting higher-quality needleworkers, or maybe I'm more willing to take the chance of being perfectly honest with applicants, thereby making it possible to set up projects that are realistic and avoid ego conflicts from the start. We are reworking some of the unfinished projects and giving them out to the new stitchers. We are being very clear with everyone that our goal now is to finish all the work we can, rather than starting any new pieces.

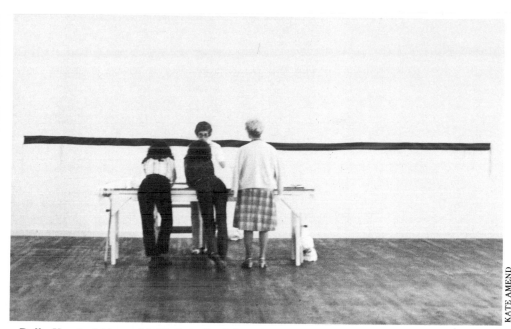

Dolly Kaminski brought *Birth* to Benicia, where Sally and I tried to review a section of the piece when it was only 4 inches high (but 21 feet long!).

Once the gridding was done, there weren't a lot of changes that could be made in the piece, at least not until the end. Dolly and I agreed that some visual adjustment could be done when the crocheting was finished to adjust lines and fill spaces that interrupted the forms. By the time the piece was done, Dolly had spent four hours a day for over three years crocheting *Birth* on a table in her living room.

Marian, Sharon, Jan, and Maria Lo Biondo, Frannie Yablonsky, Barbara Amelia Nace, Carol Davis, and Susan Hill holding *Birth* while Dolly and I discuss it.

By the time this photograph was taken, almost three-fifths of the piece was complete, and it was possible to make out the image. But there was no way to hang it up at the apartment in New York where we were doing reviews. Even with all those bodies behind it, the piece had an amazing presence, and the quality of transparency created by the filet-crochet technique made me eager to see the whole piece done.

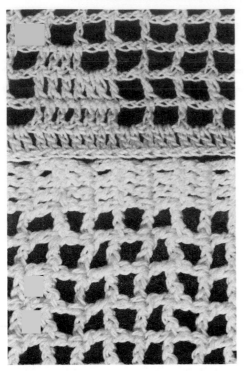

Different translation samples of *Birth*, demonstrating different grid scales and thread weights, colors, and types.

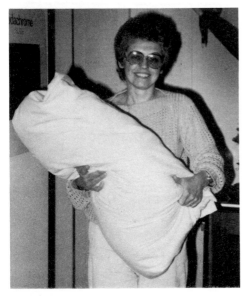

Dolly carrying the crochet like a baby.

"The task that I have now assigned myself (besides faithfully crocheting every day) is introducing, explaining, and educating people I know (neighbors, relatives, friends) to *The Birth Project*—no easy task, because their eyes are not accustomed to seeing the images that Judy has created."
Dolly Kaminski

The first time I saw Dolly with the beautiful crochet project we had begun, I was taken aback by the green plastic trash bag she was carrying it in. Many of the needleworkers brought their pieces to reviews folded and covered with flowered sheets or in garishly colored plastic shopping bags, which drove me wild. I just felt that it was inappropriate to carry art around looking like that. Moreover, a lot of them attached the pieces to frames with colored, and sometimes patterned, fabric. That made it nearly impossible to review, for example, a delicate embroidery on pink silk which had "borders" of bright red and blue stripes.

I don't think Dolly really understood my reaction to the way the piece was wrapped, but, probably just to accommodate me, she made certain that thereafter the piece was carefully rolled on a large tube and wrapped with acid-free tissue (which we sent everyone) and a white sheet.

I was also amazed when I saw where Dolly worked on the crochet. It just seemed incongruous for her to be doing such large-scale work, which was beyond what anyone had ever attempted in crochet, on a modest table at one end of her living room.

Dolly Kaminski working on 21-foot filet-crochet piece, *Birth*, on her dining table in Bethlehem, Pennsylvania.

Dolly Kaminski is avidly interested in feminist theology; her favorite author is Mary Daly.

"My interest in the women's ordination movement in the Catholic Church began around the same time I became acquainted with *The Birth Project*. In the spring of 1981, my youngest sister sent me an article which pointed out why women could not be priests. I, of course, did not agree with the article, and, having quit the Catholic Church some years before, I didn't consider the question relevant in my life any more.

"Soon after that, I happened by chance to come upon a book on the subject of female ordination which sparked my interest, and thereafter I began to look not only for books on the ordination question, but for books on women and religion in general. I became "hooked" and followed through on my new interest, writing letters and, soon after, becoming involved in an organization that is actively working toward the goal of ordaining female priests.

"The relation between my work on *The Birth Project* and my work in support of women's ordination is that they are both expressions of my feminism. Feminism is the only philosophy that has made sense out of the experiences of my life."
Dolly Kaminski

Detail, *Beaded Birth Tear,* ©Judy Chicago, 1984. Beading by Dee Thompson, Honolulu, Hawaii. Size: 34¼'' x 16''.

On Building a Staff

People often comment on my "organizational abilities," and from their remarks, I gather that they must imagine I spend all my time traveling, making speeches, doing interviews, setting up filing systems, and talking to people. This is not at all the case; I spend a great deal of my time making art and—since I stopped generating images for *The Birth Project*—supervising the production of that art and also, whenever I can, leaving Benicia to paint alone. It is true that my journal entries often describe my conflicts about not having enough time to work in the studio, and that's true. I would like to stop having to create systems for exhibiting and caring for my work in addition to making the work. I would like to stop working twelve to fourteen hours a day, seven days a week, in order to have enough time to both work in the studio and attend to whatever administrative and organizational responsibilities I do have. The degree to which I have been free to produce the large amount of art I have created in the last ten years is, in large part, due to the organizational structures which I have built and the people who have taken over the responsibility of administering the projects I started.

In addition to what we call our "core staff"—that is, people who worked full-time for modest wages—we had an array of volunteers, some still with us, some long gone. But while they were with us, they worked as members of our team, and it is that team spirit which has kept us going all these years.

How do you build a team? That is an important question because it has a lot to do with why my structures have worked. (That does not mean that they've worked for everybody, but they've worked for enough people to get the job done.) I used the principles of consciousness-raising to create the organizational structure of both the *Dinner Party* and *Birth Project* teams. One difference between these is that, by the last years of *The Birth Project*, the staff wanted to dispense with the consciousness-raising structure and "get on with the work," which was an overt expression of their personal growth, as they no longer needed the protected space this structure produces.

Our consciousness-raising structure essentially meant that, at all our staff meetings, we went around the table to make sure that everyone had the opportunity to express her own opinion. The consciousness-raising process is basically egalitarian rather than authoritarian in mode, and it encourages people to come forward and say what they think, which is the first step in taking responsibility. This is something women are not often encouraged to do in the world; on the contrary, we are usually punished for expressing our opinions and considered threatening if we either are too assertive or want too much authority. But in my organizations, it was impossible for anyone to be too assertive, to take too much responsibility, or to want too much authority—AS THERE WAS ALWAYS TOO MUCH TO DO AND NOT ENOUGH PEOPLE TO DO IT. The greater the degree to which my colleagues took on responsibility for seeing that my projects succeeded, the freer I was to work in my studio.

Working as a staff member in Through the Flower meant having the opportunity to discover what one could do and, more importantly, what one's limits were. Since women are not generally encouraged to stretch themselves and, in fact, are usually pressured to shrink to fit into the constraints of female role, we do not get much of a chance to discover our real limits. Hence we often live in fantasy about what we are able to achieve.

One day I was trying to explain all this to a friend of mine who himself has several businesses, each of which has a good-sized staff. "But," he asked me, "don't you find that whenever you're not right there, everything goes to hell?" "It did at first," I replied, "but I kept insisting that people accept more of the responsibility this project has required. Finally we got to a point at which everyone had assumed a certain amount of the responsibility, but they kept deferring to me out of habit." "What did you do?" asked my friend. "I left," I replied. "I went off and painted, and it was the right thing to do. As long as I was physically present in Benicia, my staff would keep giving me an amount of authority which I didn't want and which wasn't appropriate. But I had to create a void in order for my staff to realize that they had all grown enough to easily fill it. Now, when I go back, I take my place among my peers."

Although many people worked as staff members through the five years of *The Birth Project*, those who were here the longest and stayed till the end were considered the "core staff."

(Left to right) Marj Moore, Margaret Greer (our first office manager), and Mary Ross working in the small office/apartment we rented before we moved into our building. From the beginning, Mary Ross Taylor has carried a lot of the responsibility for that administration, and it has been primarily as a result of her ongoing commitment that I've been able to generate as much art as I have. But it is important to understand that if I couldn't have worked in my studio, I would have left *The Birth Project*, as the whole point of our structure was to make sure that I could create art and together we could complete it.

Tuesday, October 25

Hazel and I spent all day yesterday working on title pages for the exhibition units—what a drag. In the past year we must have redone them twelve times already, but I think we finally have a format that will work. I want them to reflect the way in which each piece was executed— the number of people involved, what they did, and where they lived. In many cases, the title page will show how one piece was worked by many different people in different parts of the country.

A lot of art is executed by more than one person, but usually, only the "artist's" name is visible. I believe that it is very important to give credit to everyone who participated in **The Birth Project.** *The myth of the individual artist working alone in the studio is oppressive to many women, as they cannot so easily divest themselves of the demands of husbands and children, nor do many of them want to. Demonstrating the way this art has been made will, I hope, suggest that there are other models for art-making than the "heroic" one we've inherited from the Renaissance, when only men were thought to be capable of great art.*

Monday, December 2, 1983

I'm feeling quite frustrated and discouraged; we're getting absolutely nowhere with grants and fund-raising. We're spending $13,000 a month and are going to have to go deeply into debt to finish. We just have to set a cut-off date, or they'll cart us off to the poorhouse. Mary Ross and I figure that if we use up all our resources, take out loans, and drastically cut back, we can make it until the spring of '85, but that's it. This means that all the work must be done by the end of 1984 to give us time to prepare it for exhibition.

We're going to close down our gallery spaces in Benicia and Houston; our exhibition program will continue in 1984, but in a reduced form. Our focus is going to be on finishing all the work and launching a series of exhibitions in 1985.

I have been negotiating for many months now with a major museum in the east. The director wants to do a large exhibition, and this month he is finally presenting the idea to his exhibition committee. It would be a big help to us if our formal exhibition program could begin there. The exhibitions we've had so far have allowed us to work out all our systems. By the spring of 1985 we will be ready to launch The Birth Project *nationwide.*

Mary Ross and Marj worked together on fund-raising, and Marj, who was our bookkeeper (and later, our gallery guide), kept Mary Ross, as well as the rest of us, informed of our continually precarious financial state. Marj acknowledged every donation with a personal note.

Susan Lynn, who worked both in administration and in fund-raising, primarily presented lectures for *The Birth Project* in Benicia and throughout California.

Hazel Kiley at work in the office, which she organized and supervised—an overwhelming task.

Once she arrived, we had an organizational person to attend to the endless details which accumulate in a project like this. In addition to all her *Birth Project* tasks, she "moonlighted" by typing the manuscript of this book, which required an incredible amount of time, patience, and stamina.

(Left to right) Sally, Hazel, Beth Rose (who was replaced as research coordinator by Page Prescott but is considered "core staff" because of her long involvement), and Marj celebrate Hazel's birthday.

Page Prescott took over as research coordinator after Beth left. She put all the research files in order, helped find research material for this book, and obtained all the permissions for quotes and photographs.

Mary Ross shaking hands with our chief volunteer fund-raiser, Clare Skvorc, who was considered part of the "core staff" because of her devoted efforts to generate money. In addition to writing myriad grant applications, they worked with a group of other women to give a series of fund-raising parties.

Deborah Lohrke was our most "invisible" core staff person, as she spent most of her time in the darkroom. In addition to making all the black and white prints for this book, she printed all the photographs for our exhibition units and for our publicity pictures as well.

Michele Maier, the primary photographer for *The Birth Project*, shot most of the black and white pictures, both for this book and for all our exhibition units, as well as all the color photographs included here and most of the slides which document *The Birth Project* art. She traveled all over the country, with me and alone, in order to chronicle the lives of the needleworkers.

Last Monday I did reviews in Houston. There are still seven projects there, but they'll all be done by June, and then The Birth Project *in Texas will be over. I am encouraging the needleworkers to organize a weekend show in Houston before we give up our space there. They've been resistant, but I'm insisting that they have some form of closure. We're already beginning to have trouble with past needleworkers who have become upset when a show is held in their community and the work they executed is not included. I want everyone to have a sense of closure and completion, and I certainly don't want to be badgered to death by unhappy needleworkers for the next ten years.*

The reviews went well, and it was a nice day, but somehow it all got me down. Perhaps it was a sense of loss and imminent separation and the fact that even though I desperately want The Birth Project *to be over, I'm afraid that its end will cut me off from the only community of support I've ever had.*

The *Birth Project* staff, 1980-1985. Top row (l. to r.): Michele Maier, Susan Lynn, Sally Babson, Jon McNally, Ruth Posselt (production), Deborah Lohrke, Marjorie Wolcott Moore. Second row: Linda Moschell (exhibition), Stephen Hamilton, Hazel Hood Kiley. Front: Mary Ross Taylor. Not shown: Margaret Greer (administration), Scott Lewis, Kathleen O'Connor (graphics), Betty Smith (office), Beth Rose, Page Prescott.

Bagged, Crated, and Ready To Go

Thursday, December 15, 1983

The idea of a major Birth Project exhibition was presented to the eastern museum's exhibition committee yesterday, and there was a huge scene. The arguments raged for five hours, during which time several of the committee members (the women, of course) insisted that The Birth Project wasn't art, but politics, and that it was "too controversial." I was stunned. I guess I should be used to these responses by now, but I'm not. I just can't comprehend how anyone can look at these images and think they're "politics." I knew that a lot of people said that about The Dinner Party, but by now I believed that the obvious force of that work would have opened a path for this series.

It's time to bring this story to an end, although its outcome is still unclear. We will probably be able to complete all *Birth Project* work and get it out into the world.

By spring 1985, all the work will be bagged, crated and ready to go.

Will my vision be realized? Will each of the *Birth Project* works travel to a hundred places, where a hundred people will see each work, until a million viewers will have had the opportunity to see art that expresses the power and beauty of the birth process through women's own traditional medium? There is obviously a large and eager audience for this work. Will the systems that operate to exhibit art support and distribute the *Birth Project* art?

The "textile collection" which constitutes *The Birth Project* will have to have ongoing conservation, proper curatorial supervision, and temperature- and humidity-controlled storage facilities. Is it an artist's function to provide this? Who will provide for the work I have created?

I want to move ahead creatively; I have more to say. But who will take care of *The Dinner Party* and, now, *The Birth Project* as well? My dilemma is not simply personal, but rather points up a tragic fact—that women have not yet created a support system which will allow those of us who can express the deepest feelings and dreams of our gender to grow to the height our talent would permit.

This is the explanation for the vast number of aborted careers among women and for the suicides, the "burn-outs," the diminished production of creative women who have had so much to say. The fact that I make art, which involves the production of physical objects, makes this dilemma perfectly clear. Musical compositions go unplayed, books go out of print—but art takes up actual physical space, so it's harder to ignore.

My goal now is to continue making art and trying to make sure that the work I create will endure. I hope that the force of my work will carry it farther and farther into the consciousness of the public and, ultimately, into art history, where my art—like so much other work created by women but still unappreciated—rightfully belongs.

Judy Chicago
Spring, 1984

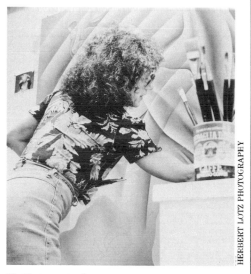

Starting new work.

I keep thinking about what my high-school art teacher, Mr. Jacobson, said to me when he toured The Dinner Party with me in Chicago. We were discussing the controversy surrounding the work, and he said: "Well, you know, Judy, it's just the same old art-historical story." I felt comforted by his words at the time, and of course other people have tried to reassure me that, even though I am encountering continuing resistance to my work now, it will be appropriately recognized later. I try to believe this, but my knowledge of women's history and of how much of it has been obscured makes me quite sure that historical "erasure" could easily happen to my work as well.

It is quite doubtful now that we will have this museum show or any others on as large a scale. If we can't get a Birth Project exhibition into a museum with a supportive director, fat chance we'll make it into those institutions where they hate my work. I feel as though I haven't gotten anywhere—here I am struggling with the museums once again.

Conclusion

I'm glad that I did *The Birth Project* and that it's finished. The review sessions and the home visits to needleworkers in *The Birth Project* allowed me to extend the process I had begun in *The Dinner Party*—to share not only my images, but also my art-making process, knowledge, and experience with hundreds of women, and that was terrific. And it was good to watch the needleworkers realize what they were capable of doing and how the techniques they loved could be expanded and transformed.

In addition, I believe that the subject matter is vitally important, not only because birth has been relatively unexplored—despite the fact that it is a universal life experience—but also because the responsibilities for all those who are born rest primarily on women throughout the world. As long as this is so, women will continue to be limited in what they can achieve. The time, the psychic energy, and the lack of preparation and social support involved in child-rearing make it impossible for us to compete as equals in the world men have made.

In *The Birth Project*, the content—birth, the essential female experience—fused with needlework, a traditional form of women's art. Working with the *Birth Project* stitchers was like being in touch with one aspect of the continuum of women's history: the medieval workshops where women stitched together for the glory of the Church; the all-female Renaissance guilds where women embellished royal robes; the nineteenth-century quilting bees where women coded secrets into their quilts. But this time, we were using needlework to openly express and honor our own experience through this unique form, which has both contained and conveyed women's deepest thoughts and feelings throughout the history of the human race.

It is possible that in some future generation, child-rearing will be seen as the crucial activity of a culture, and the raising of future generations will be the most prized and rewarded profession. It is possible the time will come when both women and men will share the responsibilities of child-rearing equally. But that is not the case now. Exploring the subject of birth brought me face to face with the fundamental cause of women's oppression—as soon as one gives birth to a child, one is no longer free. And, tragically, that lack of freedom is reinforced and institutionalized by the very nature of society.

It may be a high-school girl being deprived of an education because she becomes pregnant; a woman on an airplane desperately trying to quiet a frightened, screaming child while everyone stares at her in disgust; a long-married mother of three whose husband leaves her, her income thereby reduced to poverty level; or a highly gifted artist whose conflicts between self-fulfillment and her child's needs tear her apart with guilt. Whatever her situation, every woman who has a child is punished for having done the very thing which society tells her is her womanly goal.

It has been my privilege and my burden to open the door on a secret reality, one that even most women would like to deny. I have tried to express what I've seen—the glory and horror of the birth experience itself, the joy and pain of pregnancy, the sense of entrapment that goes along with the satisfactions of giving life. I certainly do not feel that I have even begun to convey all of what the birth experience (or, more impor-

---

I have only tried to suggest, through my art, that here is a subject worth confronting, a subject rich in meaning and in significance for women's lives.

tantly, the deep gratification many women say comes with raising a child) is like. I have only tried to suggest, through my art, that this is a subject worth confronting, a subject rich in meaning and in significance for women's lives, and—because women are over half the population, because everyone is born, and because children have to be raised—a subject worthy of the attention of the entire human race.

I have enjoyed the opportunity to extend my art-making into the visual arena of needlework and to participate in the current reevaluation of the nature of "women's crafts." It has meant a lot to me personally and to the development of my art that so many women have offered their needle skills, their time, and a high degree of commitment to enable my image-making capacity to be extended and my images to be made available to so wide a viewing world.

One thing I learned from my experiences with both *The Dinner Party* and *The Birth Project* is that there is a much greater interest in art than most artists realize, if that art can be made to speak clearly about issues relevant to people's real lives. And since not all the hundreds of thousands of artists in America can get into the elite New York galleries, it might behoove us to do some new thinking about who the audience is for our art.

The main problem for me in *The Birth Project* arose from the time lapse between the generation of the images and the completion of the needlework. When I first developed the concept of *The Birth Project,* I had no idea that it would take five years to finish. I imagined that the stitchers would work the way I did—eight to ten hours a day. It was difficult for me to understand that for many women, eight to ten hours of needlework a *week* was hard to find time for.

I gradually adjusted my expectations to be more in line with the reality of most of the stitchers' workpace, and, as long as I was still generating images, I didn't mind how slowly the stitching was going. By the time there were over a hundred works in production, however, it became clear that we at Through the Flower just didn't have the resources to handle any more.

At that point, *The Birth Project* changed dramatically for me. Instead of allowing me to do what I love the most, make images, I had to supervise the production of those images and then be involved in finishing them and preparing them for exhibition—something that only my professional discipline enabled me to do! Moreover, I had to face the fact that I had "given away" the activity I like the best: the day-to-day work in the studio, making the images come alive. If the work had moved at a faster pace, or if Through the Flower had found more financial support, these problems would not have arisen.

I had hoped that the widespread interest in *The Dinner Party* would extend to my next work—not only in the form of participation in the art-making, but by means of financial support as well. During the years when we had our gallery in Benicia, many women in expensive cars drove out to see the work. They were frequently moved to tears by what we were doing but left without writing a check. This drove me wild with frustration. The fact that women still have so much trouble "putting their money where their mouth is" has serious implications for every one of us who is trying to express the feelings of our sex, for, without financial support, our creative work cannot be done and we cannot grow.

For me, the struggle to continue participatory art-making is too much, at least for the present. I suppose that if my new ideas required other people's involvement, I might be willing to do more work in the participatory mode, as difficult as that would be at this time. But fortunately for me, this is not the case. Now I just want to work in my studio, have the joy of painting, and know that after more than twenty years of art-making, the act of creation is still what is most important to me.

Designing for Needlework

I gloried in seeing my designs come alive as a result of the deft manipulations of needle and thread.

Designing for needlework was fascinating, frustrating, and fun. It was totally absorbing to confront and solve the visual problems that arose as a result of using needlework techniques for art-making in a way that has not often been done before. I approached designing for needlework the same way I have approached all my art—from the point of view of what I had to say. I chose a particular needlework technique because it seemed the most appropriate for the expression of my content; or, if I decided to explore an unusual technique, I worked in the other direction, trying to imagine what that technique could express. For example, it seemed to me that the nature of smocking suggested compression. (The fabric is compressed when it is pleated and bound even tighter by decorative stitching.) Therefore, I designed an image which incorporated the very nature of that compression and binding into its meaning.

I have never been interested in grafting a technique onto an already formed image—for example, painting with glazes on a ceramic panel, as one would with watercolor on paper—but rather in having the image arise *through* the technique and become inseparable from it. I certainly didn't want to simply duplicate paintings in thread, though I have referred to strands of thread on fabric as being akin to the strokes of a colored pencil on paper. What I meant by this is that the same visual acuity is possible with the two media, not that the results are the same.

For me, a technique is interesting insofar as I can express something through it that would be impossible to convey in any other way. Because I approached needlework as a medium of personal expression and also brought to it the visual rigor of a trained, professional artist, I was able to utilize techniques that were completely outside the traditional vocabulary of art.

I have already described how I approached smocking. Filet crochet is another ''non-art'' technique I explored. I looked at it in terms of dark and light patterns and tried to choose or develop images with strong positive/negative values. Moreover, by altering the traditional scale of crochet, either by using more delicate thread or by enlarging its size, I was able to push it out of its usual visual associations with tablecloths, doilies, and drapes. My use of batik depended on controlling its color and, more importantly, on the quality of the lines. I told Dianne Barber (the batik artist who worked with me) that if she couldn't batik my patterns without losing the exactness of my forms, then I would do without batik. This stimulated her to push the technique farther, which resulted in fine quality work. This is the same process I employed for all the needlework techniques in *The Birth Project*. If they couldn't be made visually exact, I wouldn't use them.

Sometimes I found it frustrating to encounter needleworkers whose concerns were more closely focused on perfect stitching than on the quality of the art. I was unable to comprehend what difference it made how the back of a piece looked, though this issue came up again and again. As long as the stitching was strong and visually perfect, the back—which we covered anyway—could be a mess as far as I was concerned.

I also found it frustrating to work with people who did not have the visual vocabulary that was second nature to me. And I never understood why so many needleworkers imagined that they could design their own pieces when most of them couldn't even draw. But when a needleworker with highly developed skills was able to imagine how those skills could enliven my image, then a truly creative dialogue took place between us.

I spent a great deal of time in discussions about blending, about the direction of stitches, and—particularly in relation to needlepoint—about the physical levels of the stitching. Almost everyone who worked with me had to struggle with blending, which requires the ability to "see" and to work with color so that hues mingle without visible lines or seams. And almost everyone had trouble with the direction of the stitching. I seemed to be constantly explaining that the direction of the stitches had to follow the outline of the form. I would not allow stitching that resulted in internal shapes or patterns, and every time that happened I insisted that it be taken out. Finally, in all the needlepoint projects, as well as in some of the embroideries, I repeatedly emphasized the fact that the filled areas of stitching had to be lower than the outline, which required everyone to analyze and understand all the sections of the piece in terms of their place in the overall visual scheme. I think that for most of the needleworkers, it was a new idea that stitching had to be a tool in the service of the image rather than an end in itself.

After designing almost fifty fiber and textile works for *The Dinner Party* and more than a hundred and fifty (of which only half were completed) for *The Birth Project*, I feel that I've explored the potential of needlework quite thoroughly. The problem for me lay in the fact that a lot of needleworkers just can't "see." This meant that more than one potentially exquisite embroidery was ended before, in my estimation, it was finished. It was difficult for me to be in the position of knowing that there was something wrong with a piece and yet being unable to fix it with my pencil or my brush. And all the explanations I could offer accomplished nothing if the stitcher couldn't perceive the problem I was describing because her visual powers were not as acute as mine.

On the other hand, the visual potential of needlework is enormous, and I certainly don't feel that I have gone beyond suggesting how many things can be done with it. I do think it's important, however, that the patterns available to most needleworkers be improved. Many stitchers think that the solution is for them to do their own designing, but, as I've pointed out, if they can't draw, this is almost impossible. Additionally, most needleworkers have not been exposed to the contemporary language of art, and their designs are often extremely naive.

Since needlework has historically been an interpretive art, I think it would help matters if new patterns could be produced by trained artists. These patterns might be commissioned by needlework guilds and organizations, and I would hope that the images would reflect the reality of women's lives to some degree. Perhaps kits could be developed to offer guidelines for stitching instead of serving as recipe books. That way, the thirty million needleworkers in America could count on an image framework but would not have to violate the instructions provided them in order to work with their own ideas.

It was my experience that designing for needlework can be great fun. I gloried in seeing my designs come alive as a result of the deft manipulation of needle and thread. And it was marvelous to realize that my images had so much meaning for other women that they were willing to devote countless hours to bringing them to life.

Even though I found many aspects of *The Birth Project* to be frustrating, ultimately all that I learned personally about the reality of women's lives proved enormously meaningful and growth-producing for me, both as a woman and as an artist.

Acknowledgments

The creation of *The Birth Project* involved the efforts of many people. In addition to needleworkers, there were researchers, photographers, designers, administrative people, and numerous other skilled workers. Moreover, there were those who contributed knowledge, advice, support, and financial help. The latter came in a variety of forms—outright donations, bequests, materials, and discounted purchases. And this book itself involved still others, who brought commitment, caring, and excellence to its concept, design, and production.

I would like to thank Loretta Barrett, my editor, for her ongoing support and perspicacity; Stephen Hamilton, my designer and friend; Janet Webb and her staff, especially Mary Folck; Peggy Kimball, whose copy editing transformed a professional task into an act of personal support; Kate Amend, who coordinated the endless details of this book; and my Benicia staff, without whom neither this book nor the overall project could have been accomplished.

I would also like to thank the following organizations and individuals, all of whom extended themselves for the work, for the book, and for me:

Kelly Amen
Jo and Cecil Chester
Creative Arts Printing
Custom Process Lab
Marleen Deane
Rhonda and Paul Gerson
Stanley and Elyse Grinstein
Holly Harp
Trina Harris
Fran Henry and Joyce Freeland
Marilyn Lubetkin and Oshman's Sporting Goods
Ms. Magazine
Judith Meyers
Murray Pepper and Home Silk Shop
Sharon Shore
Manny Silverman and Art Services
Shannon Terry
Ken Wilson and Poly-Investment Western Ltd.
Linda Woolfitt

Who Worked on *The Birth Project*?

The following people were the primary participants in *The Birth Project*. Their contributions were essential to the successful completion of the work.

Sandie Abel, needleworker, Madison, Wisc.
Charlotte Anderson, needleworker, West Hartford, Conn.
Rae Atira-Soncea, needleworker, Ames, Iowa
Sally Babson, technical supervisor/needleworker, Benicia, Calif.
Barbara Baldwin, researcher/writer, Berkeley, Calif.
Dianne Barber, batik artist, Jenner, Calif.
Jean Berens, needleworker, Milwaukee, Wisc.
Susan Bloomenstein, needleworker, Teaneck, N.J.
Rita Borden, needleworker, Glastonbury, Conn.
Geraldine Boruta, needleworker, Benicia, Calif.
Dina Broyde, needleworker, New York, N.Y.
Nora Bullock, needleworker, Kutztown, Pa.
Mary Burke, needleworker, Hyannis, Mass.
Paula Busch, needleworker, Chico, Calif.
Deborah Carlson, needleworker, Whitmore Lake, Mich.
Dorothy Cavanaugh, needleworker, Houston, Tex.
Ginny Weaver Chesley, needleworker, San Anselmo, Calif.
Jo Chester, needleworker, Houston, Tex.
Chrissie Clapp, needleworker, Red Bluff, Calif.
Kate CloudSparks, needleworker, Iowa City, Iowa
Helen Cohen, needleworker, Mountain View, Calif.
Lael Cohen, needleworker, Oakland, Calif.
Elizabeth Colten, needleworker, Teaneck, N.J.
Helen Courvoisie, needleworker, Winston-Salem, N.C.
Jan Cox-Harden, needleworker and researcher, Lawrence, Kans.
Michael Cronan, graphic designer, Oakland, Calif.
Marguerite Crosby, needleworker, Bradenton, Fla.
Jane Dadey, needleworker, Marquette, Neb.
Penelope Davidson, needleworker, Pacheco, Calif.
Pippa Davies, needleworker and researcher, Christchurch, New Zealand
Kom Dixon, needleworker, Chico, Calif.
Joann Russell Duyn, needleworker, Salem, Ore.
Helen Eisenberg, needleworker, Berkeley, Calif.
Maggie Eoyang, needleworker, Berkeley, Calif.
Alicia Erpino, needleworker, Chico, Calif.
Mary Ewanoski, needleworker, Goleta, Calif.
Susan Fisher, needleworker, Kalamazoo, Mich.
Karen Fogel, needleworker, Teaneck, N.J.
Mary Kidd Fogel, needleworker, Austin, Tex.
Laura Lee Fritz, needleworker, Inverness, Calif.
Linda Gaughenbaugh, needleworker, Sacramento, Calif.
Laurie Gelphman, needleworker, Menlo Park, Calif.
Rhonda Gerson, needleworker, Houston, Tex.
Ann Gibson, needleworker, Vancouver, B.C., Can.
Joyce Gilbert, needleworker, Houston, Tex.
Gwen Glesmann, needleworker, Washington, D.C.
Margaret Greer, staff member, San Francisco, Calif.
Davette Gregg, needleworker, Sacramento, Calif.

Kathryn Haas, needleworker, San Antonio, Tex.

Christine Hager, needleworker, Raleigh, N.C.

Betty Hallock, needleworker, Burlingame, Calif.

Etta Hallock, needleworker, San Francisco, Calif.

Stephen Hamilton, exhibition designer, San Francisco, Calif.

Rebecca Hanner, needleworker, Pilot Mountain, N.C.

Joan Hargis, needleworker, Houston, Tex.

Mary Anna Harris, needleworker, Sacramento, Calif.

L. A. Hassing, needleworker, Claremont, Calif.

Leigh Heller, needleworker, Littleton, Colo.

Kathy Herman, needleworker, Cedar Falls, Iowa

Mary Ann Hickey, needleworker, Chicago, Ill.

Carol Hill, needleworker, Chico, Calif.

Susan Hill, needleworker, Julian, N.C.

Helene Hirmes, needleworker, Teaneck, N.J.

Lynn Holyoke, needleworker, Alpine, Calif.

Patricia Hull, researcher/research coordinator, Houston, Tex.

Benita Humble, needleworker, Chico, Calif.

Tere Jensen, needleworker, Cardiff-by-the-Sea, Calif.

Jane Dunbar Johnson, researcher, Lakewood, Calif.

Dolly Kaminski, needleworker, Bethlehem, Pa.

Judy Kendall, needleworker, Mt. Shasta, Calif.

Hazel Hood Kiley, office manager, Benicia, Calif.

Jan Kinney, needleworker, Seattle, Wash.

Joanne Lanciotti, needleworker, Edison, N.J.

Kathy Lenhart, needleworker, Pittsburgh, Pa.

Jan Leone, needleworker, Ft. Lauderdale, Fla.

Scott Lewis, staff, New York, N.Y.

Jan Lo Biondo, needleworker, Vineland, N.J.

Maria Lo Biondo, needleworker, Vineland, N.J.

Marian Lo Biondo, needleworker, Vineland, N.J.

Sharon Lo Biondo-Lesins, needleworker, Vineland, N.J.

Deborah Lohrke, production assistant/staff photographer, Vallejo, Calif.

Mickey Lorber, needleworker, Des Moines, Iowa

Susan Lynn, director of public information and education, Benicia, Calif.

Susan MacMillan, needleworker, Petaluma, Calif.

Jon McNally, photographer, Benicia, Calif.

Beverly McKinzie, needleworker, San Jose, Calif.

Michele Maier, director of photography, San Francisco, Calif.

Gerry Melot, needleworker, Houston, Tex.

Judith Meyers, needleworker, Greeley, Colo.

Franny Minervini-Zick, needleworker, Sebastopol, Calif.

Jacquelyn H. Moore, needleworker, Mendon, Mass.

Marjorie Wolcott Moore, bookkeeper/gallery docent, Martinez, Calif.

Sara Moore, needleworker, Atlanta, Ga.

Patricia Morton, Houston office director, Wilmette, Ill.

Linda Moschell, office assistant, Danville, Calif.

Barbara Amelia Nace, needleworker and researcher, Lansdale, Pa.

Pamella Nesbit, needleworker, Sebastopol, Calif.

Christina Nichols, needleworker, Chico, Calif.

Marcia Nowlan, needleworker, Fairfax, Calif.

Kathleen O'Connor, graphics worker, Tulare, Calif.

Peggy Patton, needleworker, Houston, Tex.

Jennifer Pawlick, needleworker, Webster, N.Y.

Ann Piper, needleworker, Berkeley, Calif.

Candis Duncan Pomykala, needleworker, DeKalb, Ill.

Lorene Pouncey, researcher, Houston, Tex.

Page Prescott, coordinator of research, Petaluma, Calif.

Ann Raschke, needleworker, Lincoln, Neb.

Beth Rose, staff member and coordinator of research, Vallejo, Calif.

Linda Rothenberg, needleworker, Teaneck, N.J.

Rhoda Rothman, needleworker, Mt. Vernon, N.Y.

Pat Rudy-Baese, needleworker, Milwaukee, Wisc.

Jeanette Russell, needleworker, Port Costa, Calif.

Catherine Russo, needleworker, Houston, Tex.

Roxanna Rutter, needleworker, Berkeley, Calif.

Martha Jane Sanford, needleworker, Iowa City, Iowa

S. Lynn Schmidt, needleworker, Chico, Calif.

Rheda Schultz, needleworker, Madison, Wisc.

Phebe Schwartz, needleworker, Bellingham, Wash.

Mary Ann Seamon, needleworker, Houston, Tex.

Elisa Skarveland, needleworker, Pt. Reyes, Calif.

Clare J. Skvorc, staff fund-raiser, Berkeley, Calif.

Margaret Slaney, needleworker, Danville, Calif.

Betty L. Smith, office assistant, San Francisco, Calif.

Marjorie Smith, needleworker, Solon, Ohio

Anne Stafford, needleworker, Orinda, Calif.

Carol Strittmatter, needleworker, Houston, Tex.

Eugenie Taber, needleworker, Kalamazoo, Mich.

Elizabeth Van Horn Taylor, needleworker, Berkeley, Calif.

Mary Ross Taylor, executive director, Houston, Tex.

Karin Telfer, needleworker, Houston, Tex.

Dee Thompson, needleworker, Honolulu, Hawaii

Jane Gaddie Thompson, needleworker, Houston, Tex.

Barbara Velazquez, needleworker, Lockport, N.Y.

Miriam Vogelman, needleworker, Teaneck, N.J.

Judy Wallen, needleworker, Port Alexander, Alaska

Martha Waterman, needleworker, Janesville, Iowa

Kris Wetterlund, needleworker, Minneapolis, Minn.

Merrily Rush Whitaker, needleworker, Clear Lake City, Tex.

Janis Wicks, needleworker, Walnut Creek, Calif.

Hope Wingert, needleworker, Benicia, Calif.

Frannie Yablonsky, needleworker, Somerville, N.J.

A number of people worked on *The Birth Project* in various capacities during the years. Their help was greatly appreciated.

Andrée Abecassis, photographer, Kensington, Calif.
Katherine Ahrens, needleworker, Forest City, Iowa
Annette Alberth, photographer, Allison Park, Pa.
Margie Altergott, researcher, Chicago, Ill.
Gail Anderson, researcher, Cleveland Heights, Ohio
Dyanna Ansang, researcher, Oakland, Calif.
Mikki Baer, office assistant, Danville, Calif.
Anna Beatty, researcher, Seabrook, Tex.
Carol Behun, researcher, Chicago, Ill.
Judy Bennor, needleworker, Cedar Falls, Iowa
Susan Blair, needleworker, San Rafael, Calif.
Chris Blechsmid, needleworker, Sonora, Calif.
Tracey Bowen, researcher, Ontario, Calif.
Nancy Burnett, studio assistant, Corte Madera, Calif.
Donna Butler, needleworker, Walnut Creek, Calif.
Jacqueline Carr, needleworker, Walnut Creek, Calif.
Dianne L. Carty, researcher, Kalamazoo, Mich.
Laura Cavanaugh, studio assistant, Oakland, Calif.
Lili Church, needleworker, Waterloo, Iowa
Robin Cochran, office assistant, Vallejo, Calif.
Diana Coleman, fund-raiser, San Francisco, Calif.
Karin Connelly, researcher, Grinnell, Iowa
Carol Davis, needleworker, Pomona, N.Y.
Robbie E. Davis-Floyd, researcher, Chattanooga, Tenn.
Barbara De Cristofaro, needleworker, Walnut Creek, Calif.
Joann Dinneen, researcher, Chicago, Ill.
Cathy L. Drake, office assistant/researcher, Davis, Calif.
Kirsten Emmott, researcher, Vancouver, B.C., Can.
Dawn Endean, researcher, DeKalb, Ill.
Floralyn Groff Flory, needleworker, Waterloo, Iowa
Elizabeth Fleming, needleworker, Occidental, Calif.
Roberta Fountain, needleworker, Chico, Calif.
Susan Gale, researcher, Philadelphia, Pa.
Nancy Dieball Galloway, needleworker, Cedar Falls, Iowa
Meta Gibbs, researcher, Cheney, Wash.
Diana Gordon, needleworker, Benicia, Calif.
Connie Greany, needleworker, Grundy Center, Iowa
Karen Geeting, Houston office assistant, Stafford, Tex.
Beverly Halm, researcher, Port Washington, N.Y.
Mary Margaret Hansen, photographer, Houston, Tex.
Lynda Healy, studio assistant, Danville, Calif.
Jean Holden, needleworker, Pleasant Hill, Calif.
Lee Jacobs, needleworker, Houston, Tex.
Kathryn Jastrzembski, researcher, Ann Arbor, Mich.
Bethany Johnson, researcher, Houston, Tex.
Daiva Karuza-Gogola, researcher, Chicago, Ill.
Mary Ellen Kelly, needleworker, Waterloo, Iowa
Joan Kennerly, researcher, Houston, Tex.
Susan Klee, fund-raiser, Berkeley, Calif.
Shari Knapp, studio assistant, Oakland, Calif.
Mai Lee, needleworker, Occidental, Calif.
Erika Leeuwenburgh, office assistant, Brooklyn, N.Y.
Bernice Levitt, needleworker, Teaneck, N.J.
Marcia Mannley, office assistant, Vacaville, Calif.
Michele Manning, researcher/writer, Martinez, Calif.
Kathleen Martin, staff, Benicia, Calif.
Julia Wolf Mazow, researcher, Houston, Tex.
Marjorie Wolcott Moore family, Fairfield, Calif.
Jo Murphy, needleworker, Chico, Calif.
Barbara Neff, researcher, South Lima, N.Y.
Eunice O'Hanna, office assistant, Walnut Creek, Calif.
Mark Overmeyer, researcher, Security, Colo.
Bonnie Pasek, Houston office assistant, Houston, Tex.
Ruth Keil Posselt, staff production assistant, Benicia, Calif.
Diane Duncan Rasmussen, needleworker, Tinley Park, Ill.

Sue Ann Schlosser, researcher, Ferguson, Mo.
Audrey Schmitt, needleworker, Waterloo, Iowa
Joy Severin, needleworker, Danville, Calif.
Karen Sexton, needleworker, Pt. Reyes, Calif.
Joan Shretter, researcher, Houston, Tex.
Kathy Schroedel, photographer, Vacaville, Calif.
Kath Ukleja, needlework studio assistant, London, England
Cyndie Van Hook-Drucker, researcher, De Land, Fla.
Gloria Van Lydegraf, needleworker, Chico, Calif.
Alvina Vaughan, needleworker, San Antonio, Tex.
Elizabeth Vincent, needleworker, Houston, Tex.
Lisa Voge, researcher, Sausalito, Calif.
Anne Wardell, needleworker, Janesville, Iowa
Kim West, needleworker, Concord, Calif.
Peggy White, researcher, New York, N.Y.
Debbie Wilson, photographer, Houston, Tex.

Many people wanted to become involved in the project and tried very hard. We appreciated their efforts.

Ita Aber	Bianca Indelicato
Sylvia Aldena	Susan Jaffe
Marcia Bambenec	Sondra Kennedy
Laura Ball	Marcia Lagerwey-Commeret
Marion Beam	Joy Lancaster
Alice Beal	Michele Lester
Susan Pence Beaudry	Kayla Lurie
Meredith Carlson	Beverly Merola
Carol Carrier	Pierrette Montroy
Sara Carter	Theresa Moore
Christine	Susan Mossholder
Kathleen Coleman	Karen Paparelli
Marilyn Cook	Ayn Perry
Sarah Cortez	Joan Phillips
Betty Jo Costanzo	Nancy Randall
Dawsie Craine	Gene Rosenberg
Juanita Crowson	Lani J. Rosenberger
Anne Dana	Mim Golub Saclin
Roberta Daniel	Barney Strucker
Elizabeth De La Hunt	Pam Teague
Cecilia Dobelman	Charlotte H. Teeples
Nancy Edmiston	Joanne Thompson
Rachel Einstandig	Melanie Van Denbos
Linda Ellsworth	Gayle Waring
Marty Frantz	Mary Ellen Wilson
Lisa Gause	M. Van Ouwerkerk
Joyce Gibrick	Florence Whisenant
Dianne Glass	Charlotte Winston
Waynell Gregory	Judy Yokeley
Theresa Halula	Michele Zambory
Susan Hayes	Barbara Znamierowski

And most of all, I would like to thank my friend and colleague, Mary Ross Taylor, for her vision, her efforts, her support, and her belief in me.

The Birth Project was partially funded by a bequest from the late Dr. Nanette Bruckner and by a grant from the California Arts Council.

Sources

1. Jan Butterfield, *Judy Chicago: The Second Decade, 1973-1983*, exhibition catalog (New York: ACA Galleries, 1984).
2. Barbara Sproul, *Primal Myths: Creating the World* (New York: Harper & Row, 1979).
3. Raymond Van Over, *Sun Songs: Creation Myths from Around the World* (New York: New American Library/Mentor Books, 1980).
4. James B. Pritchard, *The Ancient Near East*, Vol. II (Princeton, N.J.: Princeton University Press, 1975), p. 61.
5. Robert Coughlan and the Editors of Time-Life Books, *The World of Michelangelo 1475-1564* (New York: Time, Inc., 1966).
6. Genesis 2:7, 21-22, *Oxford Annotated Bible with the Apocrypha*, Revised Standard Edition (New York: Oxford University Press, 1965).
7. Charles Sheffield, *Man on Earth* (New York: Macmillan Publishing Co., 1983).
8. Lennart Nilsson with Jan Lindberg, *Behold Man: A Photographic Journey of Discovery Inside the Body* (Boston: Little, Brown & Co., 1973; London, George G. Harrap & Co, Ltd.).
9. Photo (Cat. No. 39 NGC 6720) courtesy California Institute of Technology/Palomar Observatory, Pasadena/Mt. Palomar, Calif.
10. Susan Griffin, "Feminism and Motherhood," *From This Earth* (New York: Harper & Row, 1982).
11. Mildred Hamilton, "Giving Birth to a New Art Work," San Francisco *Examiner-Chronicle* (September 28, 1980).
12. Muriel Rukeyser, "Käthe Kollwitz," *The Speed of Darkness* (New York: Random House, 1968).
13. Photo courtesy Dumbarton Oaks, Washington, D.C.
14. Geoffrey Westergaard, "Review and Reaction to the Birth Tear," *The Rice Thresher* magazine, Rice University, Houston, Texas (January 1983).
15. Harold Speert, M.D., *Iconographia Gyniatrica* (Philadelphia: F. A. Davis Co., 1973).
16. Beverly Marshall, *Smocks and Smocking* (New York: Van Nostrand Reinhold Co., 1980).
17. Barbara Karkabi, "Specially Chosen Women Doing Needlework for Artist's Next Project," Houston *Chronicle* (July 9, 1981).
18. Anais Nin, *Under a Glass Bell and Other Stories* (Chicago: Swallow Press, 1948), p. 129.
19. Grace Schulman, "Burn Down the Icons," *A Geography of Poets*, ed. by Edward Field (New York: Bantam Books, 1979), p. 489.
20. Patricia Monaghan *The Book of Goddesses and Heroines* (New York: E. P. Dutton, 1981).
21. *Pictorial Biblical Encyclopedia: A Visual Guide to the Old Testament—2nd Temple Period*, ed. by G. Cornfeld and B. Lurie (New York: Macmillan Publishing Co., 1964).
22. Photo courtesy of the Trustees, The National Gallery, London, England.
23. Ann Hollander, *Seeing Through Clothes* (New York: Avon Books, 1978), pp. 109-110.
24. Otto Nagel, *Käthe Kollwitz* (Greenwich, Conn.: New York Graphic Society, Ltd., 1971), p. 69.
25. Dora Russell, "The Poetry and Prose of Pregnancy," *Women's Coming of Age: A Symposium*, ed. by S. D. Schmalhausen and V. T. Calverton (New York: Horace Liveright, 1931).
26. Jinx Falkenburg and Esther Williams quoted in *Good Housekeeping* magazine (January 1959).
27. *The Random House Dictionary of the English Language*, College Edition (New York: Random House, Inc., 1981).
28. Phyllis Chesler, *With Child: A Diary of Motherhood* (New York: Thomas Y. Crowell Co., 1979), quoted by permission of Harper & Row, Publishers, Inc.
29. Alexander Eliot, *Myths* (New York: McGraw-Hill Book Co., 1976).
30. Geoffrey Parrinder, *African Mythology* (London: Paul Hamlyn, 1967).
31. Judy Chicago, *Embroidering Our Heritage: The Dinner Party Needlework* (New York: Anchor Press/Doubleday, 1980).
32. Susan Brownmiller, *Femininity* (New York: Simon & Schuster/Linde Press, 1984).
33. Katherine Mayo, *Mother India* (New York: Harcourt, Brace & Co., copyright 1927; renewed 1955 by M.N. Inkwell).
34. Juliet Katona-Apte, "The Relevance of Nourishment to the Reproductive Cycle of the Female in India," *Being Female: Reproduction, Power, and Change*, ed. by Dane Raphael (Paris: Morton Publishers, 1975).
35. Emma Hawkridge, *Indian Gods and Kings* (Boston: Houghton Mifflin Co., 1935).
36. Francis Watson, *A Concise History of India* (New York: Thames & Hudson, 1979), p. 117.
37. Census figures for 1971 quoted in *Youth Times* (a Times of India publication, March 7, 1975).
38. Margaret Bourke-White, *Halfway to Freedom* (New York: Simon & Schuster, 1949).
39. Alfred de Souza (editor), *Women in Contemporary India* (Delhi: Manohar Book Service, 1975).
40. Zarina Bhatty, "Muslim Women in Uttar Pradesh," *Women in Contemporary India* ed. by Alfred de Souza (Delhi: Manohar Book Service, 1975).
41. Fran P. Hosken, *The Hosken Report: Genital and Sexual Mutilation of Females*, second enlarged/revised edition (Lexington, Mass.: Women's International Network News, 1979).
42. Mary Daly, *Gyn/Ecology: The Metaethics of Radical Feminism* (Boston: Beacon Press, 1978), p. 156.
43. James Pascal Imperato, *Dogon Cliff Dwellers: The Art of Mali's Mountain People*, exhibition catalog (New York: Kahan Gallery/African Arts, 1978).
44. *Pretty Shield: Medicine Woman of the Crows*, ed. by Frank B. Linderman (Lincoln, Neb.: University of Nebraska Press, 1974), pp. 146-147.
45. Carolyn Niethammer, *Daughters of the Earth: The Lives and Legends of American Indian Women* (London: Collier Macmillan, 1977).
46. Chris Walters-Bugbee, "And None of Them Left-Handed," *Southern Exposure* magazine, Vol. V, No. 1, Institute of Southern Studies, Durham, N.C. (copyright 1977).
47. Richard W. Wertz and Dorothy C. Wertz, *Lying-In: A History of Childbirth in America* (New York: The Free Press, 1977).
48. Barbara Ehrenreich and Deirdre English, *For Her Own Good: 150 Years of Experts' Advice to Women* (New York: Anchor Press/Doubleday, 1978).
49. Marguerite Tracy and Constance Leupp, "Painless Childbirth," *McClure's Magazine* (June 1914).
50. *The Female Experience: An American Documentary*, ed. by Gerda Lerner (Indianapolis: Bobbs-Merrill, 1977), p. 149.
51. George J. Engelmann, *Labor Among Primitive Peoples, 1883* (New York: AMS Press, 1977).
52. Carl N. Degler, *At Odds: Women and the Family in America from the Revolution to the Present* (New York: Oxford University Press, 1981).
53. Grantly Dick-Read, *Childbirth Without Fear: The Principles and Practice of Natural Childbirth* (first American printing, New York: Harper & Row, 1953).
54. Harriet C. Brown, *Grandmother Brown's 100 Years, 1827-1927* (Boston: Little, Brown & Co., 1929), p. 158.
55. Helen Bagshaw, English author and childbirth educator (personal testimony, 1983).
56. Caterine Milinaire, *Birth: Facts and Legends* (New York: Harmony Books, 1971).
57. Photo courtesy of Rare Book Department, Free Library of Philadelphia, Pennsylvania.
58. Isaac Clarence Kulp, Jr., "The Order," *Heckler Plains: A Magazine of Community Living* (Harleysville, Pa.: Blue Print '76, Inc., Spring 1977), p. 43.
59. Photo courtesy of Philadelphia Museum of Art.

The *Birth Project* logo is derived from a traditional birth symbol which has recurred in the needle and textile arts throughout history. These drawings by Judy Chicago are her interpretation of the evolution of this symbol.